MW01264582

The Power of New Covenant Love:

Revealing God's Image by Marriage Union of Man and Woman

By Carl W. Wilson

Andragathia Books

A study of God's purposes and man's perversions of marriage

God created man in his own image, in the image of
God he created them; male and female he created
them. And God blessed them. And God said to them,
"Be fruitful and multiply and fill the earth and subdue
it and have dominion...." (Genesis 1:27, 28a)

All quotations are from the English Standard Version of
Crossway Bibles, a division of Good News Publishers
in conformity to their permissions

Andragathia Books
P.O. Box 621421
Oviedo, FL. 32762-1421
Email address: andragathia@bellsouth.net

ISBN 978-0-9668181-8-5

Table of Contents

Acknowledgements   v

Introduction   vii

Chapter 1   God's Creative
              Design for Marriage   1-16

Chapter 2   God's Good Marriage Perverted
              to Death by Self-Righteousness   17-38

Chapter 3   Christ's New Covenant
              Union by Suffering Love   39-56

Chapter 4   Important Application of
              New Covenant Love in Marriage   57-72

Chapter 5   Marriage Unity and Children   73-92

Chapter 6   Conflict of Our Old Nature
              and Love in the Spirit   93-112

Chapter 7   Communication by New
              Covenant Love   113-124

Chapter 8   Covenant Love Uniting
              Male and Female in One Flesh   125-146

Chapter 9   New Covenant Love as Mission   147-162

Chapter 10   Good Sexual Roles for Marriage
              Union Destroyed by Change
              From God's to Man's Wisdom   163-178

Chapter 11   Insanity of Sameness of Equality:
              History of Sexual Perversion   179-204

Chapter 12   The World's Last Night
              of Adultery And The Day
              of Glorious Wedding   205-230

Chapter 13   From Rejected Wife
              to Eternal Bride   231-250

Chapter 14   Epilogue: Practical Ways to
              Experience the Power of
              Covenant Love in Marriage   251-262

Addendum A   Devotion with God Together   263-264

Addendum B   The Power of Sexual Surrender   265-276

Selective Index   277-286

Acknowledgments

This is a book that has grown with the help of many people God has given to assist me. I have learned from my own successes and failures, and I have gained meaning from the word of God through the years. My wife Sara Jo, children, grandchildren, and now great grandchildren have helped me most. I was strongly motivated to write this book because I believe Christ has led me to see the mystery of true union in marriage, and I am thankful that I am learning to submit to this miraculous working by his word through his Spirit.

For most of my books, including this one, I am indebted to my faithful and efficient secretary of many years, Linda Koval. I am not a great writer, and her patience has helped me in writing and rewriting to make things clear and fun. She has done miracles in setting the type and getting things ready for publishing. Lindy Gordon has been a very efficient and pleasant editor whose help has been indispensable. Judy Hagey did some editing before taking fulltime work. Gary Wilson, an experienced technical artist has helped revise the cover, and fit it for use for this book.

The board of directors of Andragathia, Inc. a non profit organization has been more than faithful and supportive in the work. Also, this book would not have been possible without the support by prayer and gifts to the organization from a small group of friends and churches.

While God has morning by morning taught me these truths, without the support of all these wonderful people, this book would not exist. Our glorified Christ in heaven works through his people as his body using our gifts from him to communicate his word. May he receive all the glory forever for what is done by us in any way he may use this book. I am thankful to him and all who have helped, especially to my wonderful lady and wife, Sara Jo for being my partner and friend all these years.

Carl

Introduction

In each country every normal man and woman has an interest in the story of romance, and best-selling fictional books and magazine articles often feature this as a major theme. Marriage and sexual union ranks with high importance for almost every relationship. It is, and has been, central in every civilization known in history. Yet marriage is being forsaken for selfish individualism, and because of this, churches, governments, and businesses are studying how population changes – resulting from declining marriages – will affect them. Sexual roles in marriage are important human responsibilities for all life and peace.

The heroism of our military on the battlefields, and the boldness of our leading sports figures in the arena, still exalt the idea of individual supermen, even though many of these men are moral failures. The fact that more women are the leaders in church marketplace and government has caused a proclamation of "the end of men." Yet best-selling novels, *Newsweek (4/12)*, report the fact that many top women have dreams and fantasies of sexual surrender to men. And leaders seek to explain the growing mass shootings by young men, but they fail to mention that almost all of these young criminal men have a hatred for women and are from dysfunctional homes. Somehow it seems that many psychoanalysts and Christian counselors fail in understanding the secrets of sexual union and the meaningful happiness in marriage focused on here.

This book is a serious study of the biblical meaning of marriage, why and how loneliness instead of love prevails in a growing majority of relationships worldwide, and how truth is needed and can be attained about God's plan. It reports facts of a possible world crisis because of change in sexual roles. It does not offer an easy high emotional jag, but if followed through to full understanding, it will lead to joyful, purposeful change. Instead of joining the crowd in joking about Adam and Eve and their naked shame in Genesis, you will appreciate and can find the fullness of God's love, and see real help in love and marriage union.

The created purpose of sexual differences and their union is shown in the Bible to reveal different aspects of God's image, and in union, to show his character. Because we are all sinful, our selfishness makes our sexual differences a ***basis for competing instead of accepting*** each other. Selfishness can change the culture, destroying civilization. Our selfish individualism causes us to always focus on what will help us and how to help others, when the answer is the mystery of how the design of male and female is to glorify God. His covenant love can restore union that gives it great meaning, joy, and pleasure Only by God's love can we be changed supernaturally by Christ and the Holy Spirit. The Bible teaches how to have the powerful love of God between a man and wife to be a witness of his love to the world.

The world acts on the information that seems logically correct in the culture. Our selfish perversions then hinder what is good. I show that in prosperity by nature men by their wisdom want to exalt themselves as supermen. That leads to abuse, first by men, and then by women, as they react and seek to become superwomen. Sinful men and women reject and change civilizations that God has enabled them to construct together by common grace, and in doing so, they destroy the goodness of marriage as well as the civilization. The most tragic loss and the resulting loneliness and anger go beyond men and women; sadly, children are also greatly affected. By pride we are blinded to truth.

Columbus said he was called by the Spirit of God to sail west to find the Indies, believing the world was round. But men believed the world was flat, and they laughed at this truth that changed modern thought. Jesus brought a holy, heavenly, supernatural perspective of truth into a sinful, demonically deceived, selfish world, and men put him to death. But Jesus changed history so that it is dated B. C. and A. D. God's designed purpose of the differences of male and female has been changed in our culture, and his truth is being rejected. Our world is demonically led into a tragic crisis of tribulation by a disbelieving elite. I pray that God's Spirit will lead you to see more clearly from his own word and the facts as reviewed here.
Carl W. Wilson, 2013 A. D.

Chapter 1
God's Creative Design for Marriage

A Heart Search for God's Designed Good

Deep in the heart of every man and woman is the desire to find and relate to the other sex. On one of my first days of organic chemistry experiments, I saw a lovely lady with beautiful reddish blond hair, a wonderful smile and attractive in every way struggling to set up an organic chemistry apparatus in our laboratory. As a male champion I immediately volunteered to help. This initiated a friendship that led to a courtship, and later to a marriage that has, by God's grace for two strong-minded people, resulted in 65 years of marriage.

Interest in the opposite sex for both men and women is a major universal focus for us all, at least in all the 25 countries, in rural, city and even slum areas of all the races among which I have worked. Each of us wants to find that one person who is a complement to our own personality for an intimate relationship that will remove the feeling of being alone. While this desire is confused and even distorted by cultures of lust and selfishness, even this natural interest prevails, but in a degraded way. The women's magazines on the store racks show the desire of women to dress, find cosmetics, perfumes, et al., to attract a man. The magazines for men broadcast our male aggressive sporting or business ability to be strong, able to provide for, and protect a woman in order to attract her.

While God created Eve to be the companion of Adam as his partner to bear God's image for them to conquer or "have dominion over" the world, there were striking differences to provide mutual help, and to accomplish his kingdom on earth, beginning in the garden. Those differences were not only to give complementary help for each other, but to show differences of God's image for his glory.

But even while they were both innocent, they needed to learn to obey in order to carry out God's plan. After sin, all required education as God's children. It is said even of God's Son, as a man "he learned obedience by the things that he suffered" to reveal God's image of perfection (Hebrews 5:8, 9; cf. Philippians 2:5-10, et al.). Our test and growth as God's adopted children involves education/discipline in our faith to fulfill the specific purpose he has for each of us (Hebrews 12:1-7). Growth may involve difficulties, requiring prayerful study, patient communication, and the need for counsel with others. This is the way to experience his love, joy, peace and fulfillment together.

Jesus said, "Take my yoke upon you and learn of me, for I am gentle and lowly of heart and you will find rest for your souls. For my yoke is easy, and my burden/service is light" (Matthew 11:29). The illustration of a yoke is that of working under a sovereign ruler who has power for control (1 Kings 12, et al.). The service of those under demonic world powers is extremely heavy and painful, leading to eternal death. God designed marriage for our good, and also to have help to serve together for his glory. Marriage was the last act of God's creation to reveal his image to the world before he could call all of it "good."

The devil's work in every civilization has led sinful men to change the culture to make love and union more difficult, and to destroy God's divine purpose for sex. In the New Covenant Christ gives the power of his love by his Spirit, and access to his throne for help in marriage as his disciples. This book will put a new perspective with greater meaning to God's plan for your marriage. It will show how your marriage is important for you to have and enjoy your spouse, your children, and for your children to fulfill their purposes, and for God to be glorified.

This book will also reveal the painful great tribulations of the devil's perversion. It will show that man's sinful nature is demonically used to lead man into perversions of truth, and destroy God's good. As sinners men and women think they are wise as God, that they can own and control the world themselves, and that they know what is good and what is evil. They try to change all inequalities that offend our individual selfishness (Genesis 3). Sexual differences for marriage are the most basic differences.

The wonderful understanding of God's original plan in the Garden of Eden, which now seems lost, can only be understood by grasping the love of God in Jesus Christ that passes knowledge. It is achieved only by trusting in Christ's sovereign love at work in you. In short, help only comes by accepting the heavenly perspective of the Creator's purposes for his own glory. Security in the wisdom of heaven alone gives meaning on earth. Accepting God's heavenly plan gives answers to the world's troubles. Until we grasp that divine anchor, our life's ship will slip back into the storm.

The Design and Purpose of Marriage of Christ by Creation

The Right Source of Understanding

Jesus Christ, the Son of God, frequently used the reference to God's creative work, "in the beginning," regarding marriage. This confirms the importance of the sexual identities of man and woman in marriage for fulfilling God's purpose for the world. Jesus criticized humans' perversions of God's design, noting their sin and "the hardness of their hearts." He said, "*in the beginning, it was not so,*" but since the fall, human desires have been diverted to idolatry and divorce (Matthew 19:4, 8 and Mark 10:6; 13:19). Moreover, Jesus referred back to the perversion of the devil "*from the beginning*" and his deception in the lie that destroyed love for God, truth, harmony in marriage and brought death to mankind (John 8:25, 44). If, as Christians, we trust Christ as our Creator, Redeemer and Lord, it is important that we understand and comply with Christ's will of sexual identities in marriage as taught in Genesis, the book of beginnings. It will seem strange that Jesus and Paul, who make this matter most clear, were both single, but they had achieved the objective of God's utmost purpose of marriage and therefore did not need it. Hold your hats and sit tight as we go through this amazing revealed truth.

That wonderful initial relationship of sexual identities in marriage, to be fruitful and multiply and to have dominion for him, was what God pronounced "very good" (Genesis 1:28). Genesis 2

3

explained the vision of how the man and woman related to each other, and were to reveal God's image through their dominion over all the plants and animals and all the created order. As we see the created design and purpose for marriage, we can then see how the other Scriptures uphold and explain the wonderful picture of God's intended relationships for us. It sheds light on how we can find fulfillment in our marriages.

These visions of man and woman in marriage in Genesis 1 and 2 are the foundation for our proper understanding of male and female human sexuality. This chapter will consider the original design for marriage, then in Chapter 2 the story of the devil's deceptive efforts to ruin and destroy it, and later, the way of human redemption, and how this redemption should affect marriage renewal and fully achieve the designed purpose.

Original Visions of Complementary Divine Design

Complementation has long been a central concept in much of Christian teaching. But it is frequently misunderstood because the idea is viewed from a human perspective, which casts a shadow over the sunlight of the center of divine meaning.

Genesis reveals God's original design for marriage. In Genesis 1:25-28, God shows the sequence and progressive priorities for humans—male and female and the harmony in creation.

> And God made the beasts of the earth according to their kinds and the livestock according to their kinds, and everything that creeps on the ground according to its kind. And God saw that it was good. Then God said, "Let us make man in our image, after our likeness. And let them have dominion over the fish of the sea and over the birds of the heavens and over the livestock and over all the earth and over every creeping thing that creeps on the earth." So God created man in his own image, in the image of God he created him; male and female he created them. And God blessed them. And God said to them, "Be fruitful and multiply and fill the earth and subdue it and have dominion over the fish of the sea and over the birds of the heavens and over every living thing that moves on the earth."

4

In Genesis 2:7-9 and 15-25 the human relationship with God, and each other—especially male and female—and their relationships in promoting God's purposes over all creation are further explained.

> Then the Lord God formed the man of dust from the ground and breathed into his nostrils the breath of life, and the man became a living creature. And the Lord God planted a garden in Eden, in the east, and there he put the man whom he had formed. And out of the ground the Lord God made to spring up every tree that is pleasant to the sight and good for food. The tree of life was in the midst of the garden, and the tree of the knowledge of good and evil. The Lord God took the man and put him in the garden of Eden to work it and keep it. And the Lord God commanded the man, saying, "You may surely eat of every tree of the garden, but of the tree of the knowledge of good and evil you shall not eat, for in the day that you eat of it you shall surely die." Then the Lord God said, "It is not good that the man should be alone; I will make him a helper fit for him." Now out of the ground the Lord God had formed every beast of the field and every bird of the heavens and brought them to the man to see what he would call them. And whatever the man called every living creature, that was its name. The man gave names to all livestock and to the birds of the heavens and to every beast of the field. But for Adam there was not found a helper fit for him. So the Lord God caused a deep sleep to fall upon the man, and while he slept took one of his ribs and closed up its place with flesh. And the rib that the Lord God had taken from the man he made into a woman and brought her to the man. Then the man said, "This at last is bone of my bones and flesh of my flesh; she shall be called Woman, because she was taken out of Man." Therefore a man shall leave his father and his mother and hold fast to his wife, and they shall become one flesh. And the man and his wife were both naked and were not ashamed.

The Meaning of Marriage by Christ in Creation

God gave two visions to his people through Moses.[1] The creation of mankind, after the rest of creation, showed that the earth and universe *were fit for humans,* and that Adam was

---

[1]For more understanding of this creative work by Christ and its tremendous importance for Christian faith, see my book, *True Enlightenment, From Natural Chance to Personal Creator,* Chapter 34.

superior to the rest of creation and designed to rule over all creation in a way to show he was made in God's image. The climax of it all was making the sexual differences. The first vision was from the perspective of man on the earth observing the process of creation for which he was to be responsible to govern. The creation of the human as the final act of creation also points to his superiority. Unlike any other elements of creation, either inanimate or animate, God *decreed* to make male and female with a likeness to himself. "And God said, 'Let us make man in our own image.' " Being in God's image, man had, as his son, the ability to understand the relationships of all nature and its creatures and had the *divine* potential to *exercise dominion over creation.*

Moreover, the extension of that power over the earth was to come through the physical union of their sexual differences to multiply offspring. Their children would continue to reflect God's image as they spread and controlled all the earth. The union of one man and one woman in marriage was God's plan for expanding his kingdom from the beginning. The second vision reveals how this would occur. The end of this revelation decrees that successive offspring of male and female were to leave father and mother to form a new union to continue the process (Genesis 2:24, 24).

In the first vision God establishes his purposes for humanity: both male and female exercising authority over creation. This implies equal intellectual ability to understand and distinguish the thoughts of God involved in the created order, including all the plants, trees and animals. The progression in creation—beginning with lower forms of life and culminating in human life—is evidence of the value God places on living creatures. Only the man and woman were given the ability to understand the unity and harmony of God's creation. This vision shows the sovereign good power of God, but also the awesome importance, power, and glory of humans over and in the world.

Psalm 10, among other passages, expresses man's glory as an image bearer of God. It is important to understand that God gives the first vision (Genesis 1) **as the foundation for understanding the second** vision. The Genesis 2 vision reveals the manner in which the man and woman were to relate to each other, to the animals, the lower life forms beneath them and how they were to control the world with responsibility for "keeping" it for God.

God's Goodness is Magnified Most in Union in Marriage

The most important and awesome issue, and the subject of this book is that ***the differences of male and female were critical*** to revealing God's image, and for spreading the glory of the goodness of his image to the whole world. The male was to reflect one aspect of God's image and the female another. Only by submission to their differences is God's person fully revealed, and then expanded, through their offspring, to the entire world.

God reveals his love and honor of man in this. Repeatedly, after each day, and finally after God's work was finished, the quality of that work was said to be very "good." It is awesome to understand that every detailed aspect throughout the whole was a design made for mankind ***for good***, and that God gave this to man to enjoy for ultimate pleasure and fulfillment. The love of the Godhead designed it, performed it by his eternal Word, and implemented it through the power of his Holy Spirit. God lovingly and deliberately created everything good for man, who was made to be his son, in his likeness. He gave all for male and female. The second vision in Genesis 2 presents marriage as the crowning "good" of all creation.

Again, God's love and purpose for man made everything *good*. The Hebrew for good means pleasant, beautiful, beneficial, pure, right, valued, and kindly.[2] The word used in the translation to Greek in the Septuagint is *kalos*. This word expresses the appearance to man of what is beautiful, fair, of good purpose, right, and noble, as equivalent to the Hebrew. There is another Greek word for good which has an important different connotation that will be discussed later that is not used here.

Modern science has explored the universe and found it is precisely designed for man's good, a phenomenon scientists cannot

---

[2] The Hebrew word for good that is used in the two visions is *tob*. In the lexicons (*Gesenius' Hebrew and Chaldee Lexicon*, 319).

explain. Rees, the Royal Astronomer of England, showed that if the universe varied even slightly in any of six different quantities neither the cosmos, or life, and especially human life, could exist.[3] Likewise, without the union of marriage the whole design of nature will cease and fall apart. The union of male and female is absolutely *essential* for the *meaningful purpose of the entire created universe to continue.*

We see the significance of the male/female distinctions revealing God's goodness in the fact that following the fall these differences become the central focus. This is the subject of the next chapter. God's plan of redemption hinges on these differences, for it is the woman's offspring who crushes the serpent's head (Genesis 3:15). This book will demonstrate that Scripture shows the differences have been a central and important point of temptation and attack by Satan in an effort to prevent the fulfillment of God's redemption. A later chapter will show that the demonic destruction of every civilization has occurred by minimizing, changing and distorting sexual roles.

Second Vision Defines How Relationships Would Work
The *most important factor* in the first vision for understanding the second is that all God's design of creation was a general revelation of *his goodness in character and power.* In the second vision, God explains that the trees in the garden were all good for man's enjoyment. Even the forbidden tree of knowledge was good, but not to be eaten. It was good for man *if he observed its designed purpose.* The fruit of the forbidden tree was *in the midst* of the garden. It was central to divine authority, and was there with the Tree of Life (actually Hebrew is "tree of *lives*"). The Tree of the Knowledge of Good and Evil represented all the knowledge of God's information that was involved in creation, both visible and *invisible.* Its place in the garden reveals God's sovereign plan in creation. All creation was for man's good, to enjoy *under God's*

---

[3] Martin Rees, *Six Numbers.* Cf. Carl Wilson, *True Enlightenment*, 562.

sovereign control. Denying God's sovereignty proved to be catastrophic for man.

The first vision indicates both male and female were made in the image of God, but that the two were not the same. God did not make two male associates to rule his world, but *two humans with differences to reveal his whole image* or character to all creation. Those differences gave them the power to reproduce. Then by reproducing they would *extend the knowledge of his power and goodness* throughout the entire world.

The second vision reinforces the *essential sameness* (she was flesh of his flesh) and equality of the first vision, but *defines their differences* and their relationship. Thus, based on the first vision, the second reveals *how the male and female were to relate to each other under God,* and how their sexuality was designed *to extend his rule* over the whole world. Therefore, the second vision is basic and highly important to interpreting the first. The second vision shows that under God's blessing and control the man and woman in marriage would together, as partners, keep the garden. In sexual reproduction they would multiply the work of "keeping" it and extend the garden. Genesis 1 does not tell the extent of the plants and animals in the world, only that they were created, but Genesis 2 indicates that at the time of creation they were limited to the garden and later multiplied and expanded.

While both man and woman contained the image of God equally, their minds perceived differently; they communicated differently for different purposes, and had different physical abilities. All these differences complemented each other and made union possible and important. Thus, together they would understand the garden and in their pure expressions of unity, expand it. Under the care of the man and woman, as God's gardeners, the plants of the field would provide food for the animals. There were no predators or carnivorous animals. In the garden, nature was in perfect and complete harmony. Isaiah envisioned a return to Paradise after the second coming of Christ, the judgment of evil and the renewal of righteousness:

The wolf shall dwell with the lamb, and the leopard shall lie down with the young goat, and the calf and the lion and the fattened calf together; and a little child shall lead them. The cow and the bear shall graze; their young shall lie down together; and the lion shall eat straw like the ox. The nursing child shall play over the hole of the cobra, and the weaned child shall put his hand on the adder's den. They shall not hurt or destroy in all my holy mountain; for the earth shall be full of the knowledge of the LORD as the waters cover the sea (Isaiah 11:6-9; cf. 65:25).

The wonderful good fruit of the trees were all for man's sustenance and all that was necessary for health. The control of, and extension of the natural grasses, fruit trees and animals were of pure genetic origin with no degenerative mutations.

The garden was the source of a mighty river that divided into four branches and flowed throughout the whole earth, called Pangaea. Its water evaporated under a canopy so that "a mist was going up from the land and was watering the whole face of the ground" (Genesis 2:5, 6). There is now evidence that all the world once had a tropical climate. Thus the earth was without storms and violent climate/weather fluctuations. Continuous regulation of the water supported plant and animal life. The man and woman's unity in marriage, with their complementary minds, easily kept the garden. The painless reproduction of children was vital to this expansion and peaceful operation of nature and harmonious life.

Important Male and Female Differences For Revealing God

Thirdly, and most importantly, their differences, both mentally and physically, manifested two different aspects of the image of God to make known his glory. This does not mean God is anthropomorphic, or has human form, but that man's male and female forms are *the vehicle of revealing the various aspects of the character of God*. This was important for portraying God in their dominion, and for upholding and expanding the natural order in peace and unity. The creation account is really evidence of God's goodness. Marriage as good is the crown.

10

God's goodness is a prominent idea in creating the sexual differences of man and woman. After creating Adam, God again communicated within the Godhead, "it is **not good** that man should be **alone**" (Genesis 2:18). God's image in man alone was incomplete; it failed to express the love and oneness of God's character and extend the knowledge of his **goodness** for all his creation. The essential importance of sexual differences for all creation is God's desire to show his **goodness** in the unity of his image in marriage of man and woman. The goodness in all the rest of creation had no meaning apart from man and woman enjoying and ruling over it, keeping it good for God's glory.

It is important to recognize the difference between **aloneness** and **independence**. The feeling of aloneness implies a desire to be with and joined to another meaningfully. Independence implies the desire to be self-sufficient and drives one to greater and greater aloneness, preventing the completion of the desire to complement and end the aloneness. Independence paints one into a corner of the deepest kind of aloneness and incompleteness. It is a destruction of the whole meaning of God in creation. It also must lead to the rejection of the union of God in the Trinitarian union of the Godhead and a rejection of the goodness of God. It ultimately leads to atheism.

Knowing someone intimately, as in the marriage relationship, is the basis of genuine love and joy. The experience of union in the fleshly relationship was expressed as "Adam **knew** Eve, his wife, and she conceived" (Genesis 4:1). To say that Adam had physical relations with his wife would have been inadequate to express what occurred. There is a deeper meaning of this word *"knew"* that is not only fleshly but spiritual. It implies completing the desire to be one in heart and mind that *allows*, not *makes* the union possible. God's knowledge that united the Father and Son in the Spirit shows his love. Adam and Eve's experience of the presence of the goodness of God in their differences reflected that goodness to all creation. The differences were fully accepted as good, with no shame or conflict, creating joy in marriage. "They were naked and not ashamed." Their knowledge of each other gave deep meaning.

The main point of this book is to emphasize that the union of sexual differences in marriage is an acceptance of, and also a demonstration of the goodness of God. Again, the ***marriage union is for the main purpose of manifesting the love or goodness of God in all his created work!*** This is an awesome—almost overwhelming—fact to comprehend. That is why the desire to find the right one and to unite with that person is such a strong feeling. An even more important fact is that the deep desire to have union with God for eternity is the ultimate union that each heart desires, and to which marriage points. The relationship of man and woman in marriage is symbolic of our union as the bride of Christ. I will expand on this symbolism, a Scriptural symbolism, more fully in this book.

Adequacy of Complementary Equal Companionship

The context of the woman's creation in Genesis 2 is important. First, Adam examined and named all the animals, which was an activity that required evaluation. As such, it showed Adam's ability to understand the nature and abilities of all the particular animals, including the serpent. None of them were found equal to Adam for communication and suitability as a companion. This ***reveals a distinct gap*** between man and animal life and the need for another creature who would be adequate for and like Adam. A rib was taken from Adam's own side and from this his wife was generated.

This idea used to be laughed at, but in the modern understanding of genetics and DNA the use of certain cells to clone an organism or like animal is occurring. Moreover, it is believed that early in fetal development certain human cells may be of either gender. The creation of Eve was a miracle of God, designed and directed by him, to make a perfect companion and helper. Adam recognized his wife as of his essence and equal to him. He observed, "This at last is bone of my bone and flesh of my flesh. She shall be called Woman, because she was taken out of Man." The words of Adam, "this at *last*..." is the Hebrew word *paam* which the blacksmith used to describe the completion of a tool, or of a desired step now taken. Adam recognized that his wife was adequate in a way that no other creature could be. Adam's "at last," shows Adam's acknowledgement that the final goodness of God in creation was complete.

Relationship of Submission for Supplementary Actions

Eve's creation as "a helper fit" for Adam (2:18, 20) does not imply inferiority, for the word "helper" is even used of God helping his people. More importantly, **submission** to another person does not involve less authority and value, but a willingness to unite with the above authority in order to share authority (or influence or dominion). The clearest example of this kind of submission is seen in the relationship of the Trinitarian God. The Son of God was and is "one with the Father" and is at the same time submissive to His father (cf. John 14:9-11). Their equality and unity makes the submission of the Son to the Father and the Spirit to both a beautiful and pleasant relationship. Jesus said,

> Truly, truly, I say to you, the Son can do nothing of his own accord, but only what he sees the Father doing. For whatever the Father does, that the Son does likewise. For the Father loves the Son and shows him all that he himself is doing, and greater works than these will he show him, so that you may marvel (John 5:19-20).

The submission of the Son grants him the power of the Father to do great things which he would not otherwise do. This is the same kind of relationship God envisioned for man and woman in marriage, enabling them to accomplish his purposes in the world. The husband should communicate intimately with his wife and she with him, so that as he leads the family to accomplish great things together; they can see greater things accomplished by their joint efforts. In this, both man and woman were to get the benefits and glory. This was the relationship in Eden, as the second Genesis vision portrays.

It is important to note that God had placed Adam in the garden and given him *instructions* ***before*** *creating his wife*. God presented the animals to Adam for him to name and control; he showed

Adam the many wonderful fruits he was permitted to eat, and he directed Adam to keep the garden. Adam was not to eat of the tree of knowledge and warned that if he did, he would die. All of this, even the warning, was from the goodness of God. Adam, therefore, was apparently the teacher and guide for his wife about their relationship with the animals, including the serpent. He also instructed her about the privileges of all the fruits in the garden and their responsibility to tend the garden—as equal partners. God's sovereignty over Adam and his wife was indicated in the tree of knowledge. God communicated *his message* to Eve ***through her husband***. Adam's teaching to her was God's word, not his. Neither the man nor woman was to seek a kingdom of their own but rule together for God. This relationship established leadership and unity. In Eve's response to the serpent, it is evident that she had been taught by Adam, and knew about the privilege of most of the permitted desirable fruits from most trees, and also the prohibition of the Tree of Knowledge (Genesis 3:2, 3). Eve's disobedience was to God's word, which she knew from her husband.

The original eternal decree to create man as male and female shows the design of both to be submissive and obedient-- Adam directly to God and Eve to God in submitting to him. The male was to be the leader, to see the issues of the will of God, and to instruct the woman. She was to communicate equally with him, to help him evaluate and apply knowledge. Working together, they were to keep the garden and exercise dominion together.

As the garden was to grow, they would need new workers. Their offspring, the result of their union, would supply these workers. Their reproductive organs and powers were good and holy, designed to join two aspects of God's image to reflect the character of God to, and in their children. Adam was not only to know and give God's word, but to give the seed for new life to the woman. She was to be the submissive receiver and God thereby created a child (Genesis 4:1a) to multiply and expand the divine image in the offspring (cf. Genesis 5:1-3) and thereby expand his work worldwide. All this is explicit in the record and implicit in the natural form at creation. This design of male and female sexuality was a holy work, and accomplished God's purposes for his glory and for their joyful pleasure and the good of the world.

But the children were then to separate from parents as a new unit to freely extend the garden in their own way, and to continue to multiply. The relationship of parents to each other was *always to be priority* over that with their children (Genesis 2:24). The children in a new marriage formed another unit for work and reproduction as separate but related teams. Such submission of male and female in God gave maximum freedom to unite in perfect accepting love and to enjoy the satisfaction of fulfilling their purpose and reflect God's glory. Such was the realized dream world of Eden.

Being one in marriage offered the most pleasure and joy in united love of Adam for Eve and Eve for Adam. The children would be born with ease. The children would thrill Adam and Eve when they saw God's image in them and the promise of their ability to extend the work. The whole reflected the goodness of God, but the maximum goodness for all creation was to be seen in the goodness of the union of the persons of male and female in marriage. The purpose of the sexes in marriage was showing God's goodness by their union in love. As these conditions and relationships existed there was rest in creation on the Sabbath day.

Conclusions

The creation of man as male and female for complementary union in marriage revealed God's goodness, and by reproduction would extend this revelation in their dominion for God by filling the earth. While both sexes equally bore his full image and worth as man, their created differences of expressions when united allowed the revelation of his goodness in the world. Each could know and understand God and his information in creation, and could communicate with him (or pray), and with each other. God spoke to each as individuals as accountable to him. The succession of creation gave Adam/the male *priority in knowing and leading* Eve/the female in God's will. Her created nature gave complementation to supply *the relational information* to receive her help for him in their union and work. The male's submission to God in leading for both required his recognition of her created equal worth, and the necessity of her communication for his responsibility to decide and perform God's will. The female's trust and submission to her husband's leadership allowed their union, and revealed God's goodness which set an example of submission and trust for their future children through successive generations. Their dominion for God required male and female. Union by differences of expressions of his image revealed God's goodness as the growing work of creation and resulted in rest in completion on the Sabbath.

Chapter 2
God's Good Marriage Perverted
to Death by Self-Righteousness

Introduction: Deceptive Choice of Fruit to Individuals

This chapter on marriage failure and its pain is hard to read, but it is essential to understanding the way to joyful union and the importance of Christian marriage today. Our world has lost the ideal of marriage as designed in creation. Jesus identified the problem as "the hardness of men's hearts." Selfish individualism motivates one to justify seeking his/her own happiness no matter what it does to others. Jesus was addressing the religious liberals or Sadducees, who accepted the Greek philosophy of Aristotle who allowed whatever makes one happy, and the Pharisees, the self-righteous legalistic conservatives, who found a loophole in the Mosaic civil law to allow for divorce.

Our hardness of heart continues. Studies show that today in America the lower and middle classes are abandoning marriage as a cultural institution. While this trend is less pronounced among the upper educated classes, many of them also have multiple marriages and affairs and do not maintain monogamy. Most of the world's men and women still seek the one and only for them, but it would appear that the dream of finding the perfect person and holding to them for life is occurring less frequently. The breakdown of marriage affects everyone in the family, as well as the rest of society. What has happened to the "good" marriage designed by the Creator?

Transformation of Sexuality by Seduction to Disobedience

God's ideal for marriage, as established in Eden, did not last. While many are familiar with the biblical account of the fall, few understand or fully appreciate the magnitude of what changed in that one act of disobedience. It is crucial to understand what changed in human nature and how that change affected God's plan for marriage and the potential for godly marriages to influence the world for God. The account of the highly significant change is as follows.

> Now the serpent was more crafty than any other beast of the field that the LORD God had made. He said to the woman, "Did God actually say, 'You shall not eat of any tree in the garden'?" And the woman said to the serpent, "We may eat of the fruit of the trees in the garden, but God said, 'You shall not eat of the fruit of the tree that is in the midst of the garden, neither shall you touch it, lest you die.' " But the serpent said to the woman, "You will not surely die. For God knows that when you eat of it your eyes will be opened, and you will be like God, knowing good and evil." So when the woman saw that the tree was good for food, and that it was a delight to the eyes, and that the tree was to be desired to make one wise, she took of its fruit and ate, and she also gave some to her husband who was with her, and he ate. Then the eyes of both were opened, and they knew that they were naked. And they sewed fig leaves together and made themselves loincloths (Genesis 3:1-7).

The Conditions and Reality of the Temptation
The details of the fall are different than the generally accepted view that *"Eve* ate the apple and got us into this mess." The Genesis account relates that Eve and Adam were both walking *together* in the garden and encountered the serpent. According to Genesis 3:8, "She gave to her husband, *who was with her.*" Moreover, in Hebrew, the term of address the serpent directed to the woman is the plural for "you." The serpent's statements included her husband. "Did God actually say, 'you (both) shall not eat…'" The English translation of you does not indicate the plural. Adam and Eve were both working as normal, tending the animals and keeping the garden—exercising dominion—when they encountered the serpent. From Eve's response, it's clear that Adam had passed on to Eve the instructions regarding the trees in the garden from which they were allowed and not allowed to eat. She was a secondary recipient of the message about the tree of the knowledge of good and evil (cf. 3:2).

The *devil's influence on the serpent is intentionally omitted* so the reader sees the event precisely as Adam and Eve saw it. They were ignorant of demonic influence in the world. If the devil had been mentioned, it would not have adequately portrayed why the temptation was so real to man. After the fall, Adam and Eve came to understand the influence of the devil and passed this knowledge on to their descendants.

World's Common Knowledge of Devil using the Serpent

Throughout Scripture, the devil is described as a ruling angel or *messenger of God* who led a group of angels in heaven to rebel, precisely to wrest dominion from Adam and Eve. The devil is called "the god of this world" who uses the desires of the world to seductively control man. He has successfully gotten most of the world to doubt that he even exists. Following Adam's fall, every man who sought to be the world leader, is identified with the devil's aspirations. Nimrod of Babel and also the later king of Babylon, and of Tyre, et al. are described with the characteristics of the devil. His temporary gaining of world leadership over all men was everywhere asserted and assumed.[4] The whole of the biblical record identifies the devil with the serpent in Adam and Eve's deception. Through the first parents, all of humanity is deceived and in conflict with the Devil. Jesus specifically identified the devil with the initial lie in the garden that brought death on man (John 8:44). The Devil still deceives all men (Ephesians 2:1-3) and after the fall used the fear of death to keep man in bondage to the world (Hebrews 2:14). The Devil is also identified in later Jewish writings.[5]

Further evidence of the Devil deceiving all the world is in the fact that all known historical records of ancient civilizations reveal that everywhere *people believed in one supreme evil spirit* using other evil spirits that motivated mankind to commit evil acts.
The Devil was called by different names in each culture, which must have come from one earlier primordial event.[6] After Adam

---

[4] This subject requires a book in itself so check *Westminster Dictionary of the Bible*, Devil 138, Satan, 534, and kings of Babylon, Tyre etc., or topical books.

[5] "The books of Adam and Eve," The Psuedopigrapha, R. H. Charles, editor, 123, and in "The Wisdom of Solomon," 2:24, et al.

[6] I have researched this and the evidence is given in my new book, Carl W. Wilson, *True Enlightenment*, Chapter 1, p. 8, 9.

and Eve and before the flood, humans lived nearly 1,000 years and history was orally passed on until about 3,000 B. C.[7] when writing began. This story about Eve tempted by the serpent was repeated and spread orally, and revealed in symbolic statues of art in all cultures with much fidelity and credibility as seen here.

The University Museum, University of Pennsylvania

Fertility or mother-goddess figurines with heads of serpents and high bitumen crowns date from the fourth millennium B.C. of Ur.

Early cultures often portrayed Eve in association with the serpent. This statue from Ur of the Chaldeans depicts Eve with the head of

---

[7]John Heim of Oxford with Stephen Olson confirmed this. Cf. Matt Crenson of AP, "Human's Common Link Not so far Back," in *Orlando Sentinel*, July 2, 2006. See my discussion of this, *True Enlightenment*, 302.

serpent.[8] It is a woman presented as having the head of the serpent now crowned, symbolizing the serpent's victory through her. In Babylon the woman was seductively presented in statuettes with a serpent coiled around her; the Canaanites also portrayed a serpent goddess.

Demonic Use of Serpent Revealed in the Biblical Account

But to understand man's sin and fall, it must be recognized that at the time Adam and Eve knew nothing about the devil as an evil spirit, and his heavenly rebellion. Naming the devil as an evil spirit in the form of a serpent in the biblical account would falsely depict the temptation as it came to Adam and Eve. They had no apprehension of evil and believed this most crafty serpent, who had been created by God, was offering advice for their good. The devil's evil intent was hidden from them.

The event brought to light and later established the idea of the devil and how he works, presenting himself as an angel of light, and using the wisest of teachers to deceive other men (2 Corinthians 11:3, 13-15). This information about the devil being involved, and using the serpent was known only after the event. Apparently, God revealed this later, and the knowledge of the devil's revolt and influence was spread throughout the world

Adam had previously evaluated all the animals, including the serpent, and none of them was found adequate as a companion. Adam knew the serpent as the craftiest of all the higher animals (Genesis 1:24, 25; 2:19, cf. 3:1). He would certainly have explained to Eve about the highest animals, including the serpent, since he had considered them as companions. He would have told her she was superior to them all and was the only one adequate to be his companion.

Thus, Adam and Eve knew the serpent's craftiness exceeded all others. The Hebrew word *arum* for "crafty" or "subtle" seems first to have the idea of "uncovering the naked truth," to know the facts. Later, the same root came to mean "prudent." The Greek

---

[8] Henry Snyder Gehman, editor, *The New Westminster Dictionary of the Bible*, (Philadelphia: The Westminster Press, 1974), 852.

translation of the Septuagint (of *phronimutatos*) emphasizes "understanding" so as to be "highly prudent." Later in the biblical record, the serpent's form is changed from being "more crafty than," or above "all the beasts of the field," to one lower than "all of the beasts of the field," and he is consigned to crawl on his belly in the dust (cf. Genesis 3:1, 14). Although the serpent's original form is not described, it is only said he was cursed. He was no longer one of the highest creatures, but became the lowest. At the time of the temptation, the serpent must have been a very attractive creature.

The serpent's ability to communicate may have seemed to them as a new evidence of craftiness or an anomaly. This would have attracted the attention of Adam and Eve. Moreover, the serpent's statement of apparent knowledge and ability to evaluate what God had told Adam about the garden suggested a new level of knowledge.

Most cultures have stories of animals speaking, and it is known that animals can be trained to understand some human communications, to respond to commands, and to a certain extent, to communicate among themselves.[9] In the Garden of Eden the serpent apparently was superior to other animals in ability to communicate. But the serpent's communication with Adam and Eve was beyond the usual—a phenomenon—which would have captured their attention.

Paul warns that the devil continues to deceive those who seem highly intellectual in order to exert his control over men and women (2 Corinthians 11:3, 14, 15). It is important to see this principle of the devil's working. He gains control while humans are unaware that they are being deceived. No man will knowingly succumb to deception, so the devil works without them seeing their deception.

---

[9] Modern science highly believes that through animal communication man evolved to talk and studies animal communication. Cf. Robert Gange, *Origins and Destiny*, (Waco, TX: Word Publishing, 1986), 125-127, 130; such study is known as Zoosemiotics. See *Animal Communication, Wikipedia free Encyclopedia* with references of recent studies.

Nearly every civilization has been destroyed by this tactic—deceiving the intellectual elite. But what the devil achieved with Adam, through the serpent, he attempted, but could not, with Jesus and his followers (Revelation 12:9, cf. Matthew 4:9; Matthew 13:38, 39; etc.).

Devil's Temptation Was to Control through Serpent's Word

The temptation was a test of trust in the serpent's word over God's word. While both Adam and Eve were present, the devil specifically directed the conversation to the woman to teach her. Since she was created after Adam, and learned God's instructions from him, she was therefore, by nature, open to being taught through another. Paul refers to Eve being created second and the one deceived (1 Timothy 2:13, 14).

The serpent did not directly attack God's prohibition, but suggested God was a legalist, controlling her in everything. "Did God actually say, 'You shall *not eat of any* tree in the garden'?" This denied the freedom and pleasures God intended, and thereby created doubt about God's goodness and the liberty and responsibility God had given man in creating him in his image.

Eve had understood from Adam and responded correctly by saying, "We *may* eat of the fruit of the trees in the garden, but God said, 'You shall *not* eat of the fruit that is in the midst of the garden (the center of control), neither shall you touch it, lest you die'." Eve did not mention it as the fruit of "the tree of the knowledge *of good and evil*," as God's exclusive right, which would have brought to mind that God's limitations were designed for their good and to protect them from evil.

At this point, the serpent directly accused God of lying to them in order to keep them under divine control, and of denying them the freedom to be like God himself. Now the serpent addressed the woman exclusively: "But the serpent said *to the woman* 'You will not surely die. For God knows that when you eat of it your eyes will be opened, and you will be like God, knowing good and evil'. " This seductive lie appealed to her as an individual, "it is *evil to be in submission*."

Eve's attention was now drawn to the tree and its benefits for her—and away from God and his command. She considered its threefold potential, and was led to eat.

> When the woman saw that the tree was good for food, and that it was a delight to the eyes, and the tree was to be desired to make one wise/give insight, she took of the fruit and ate, and gave some to her husband who was with her and he ate. (Genesis 3:6)

The three appeals were physical pleasures, material treasure (Jesus warned of the evil eye of desiring material wealth, Matthew 5: 21-24), and the pride of being right or knowing what is good or evil.

The Bible repeatedly warns that the devil's worldly appeal is through idolatry. The Canaanite god, Baal, in Hebrew means "to possess" and his female consort, "Ashtoreth," means "to be rich." The Canaanites, and later Israel, rejected the Creator, and they turned to worship the material creation. Worship of the god and goddess is revealed in Scriptures as worshiping demons (1 Corinthians 10:19-21; Deuteronomy 32:17; Psalm 106:36, 37). These replaced Jehovah in the temple as their national God. Jesus identified trusting truth in nature as not worshiping God but mammon (Aramaic word for god of wealth). John the apostle identified these temptations as "the desires of the flesh, the desires of the eyes, and the pride of life" (1 John 2:16). Idolatry is a breach of union with God, and was considered spiritual adultery by God's bride. This spiritual meaning will be examined in a later chapter.

Lie of Life Apart from the Creator Is Bondage and Death

Adam followed his wife's action, likely believing it would result in the same unity, love and pleasure they had enjoyed before. In believing that the word of God was a lie, and rejecting God's word for the devil's lie, they disobeyed. Mankind then became a slave to sin and lost his freedom. Jesus accused the disbelieving Jews of having the sinful nature from the devil, and having this event in view, offered them freedom by obedience, "If you *continue in my word*, you shall know the truth, and the truth shall make you free" (John 8:31-44). Human nature changed as a result of Adam's unbelief. Jesus warned men that the devil was the murderer, and if they continued in their spiritual death, they would die in their sins. He told them freedom only comes by trust in the Father's love that produces obedience.

Adam and Eve's Sin Natures Made Differences Offensive

The radical change in Adam and Eve's marital union was immediate. They saw themselves as individuals: "Their eyes were opened." They saw their naked differences and were ashamed or offended with fear. They used fig leaves to try to cover their offense. Moreover, their change derived from their guilt and spiritual death.

> And they heard the sound of the Lord God walking in the garden in the cool breeze of the day, and the man and his wife hid themselves from the presence of the Lord God among the trees of the garden. But the Lord God called to the man and said to him, "Where are you?" And he said, "I heard the sound of you in the garden, and I was afraid, because I was naked, and I hid myself." He said, "Who told you that you were naked? Have you eaten of the tree of which I commanded you not to eat?" The man said, "The woman whom you gave to be with me, she gave me fruit of the tree, and I ate." Then the Lord God said to the woman, "What is this that you have done?" The woman said, "The serpent deceived me, and I ate" (Genesis 3:8-13).

Their immediate spiritual death was evidenced by their fear. At creation, God breathed his spirit into humans, so they were able to know God. Now, aware that they are fleshly mortals, they hide in fear. Their *selfish individualism,* or each seeing himself as wise as God and being like a god, resulted in spiritual death. Spiritual death confirmed their pursuit of self-control and therefore a lost relationship to God, and progressively, with others. Adam and Eve's personal face-to-face relationship to God is threatened. Adam saw himself individually as good and questioned the goodness in the woman, who was different from him. Likewise, Eve saw Adam from the selfish individual perspective of her self-wisdom and was also threatened by his differences.

Therefore, individual self-governance or autonomy replaced unity and love for each other and for God. As individuals they saw, not from the perspective of the Spirit who had created them, but from a physical perspective, or *as an individual fleshly natural male or female* (1 Corinthians 2:14). This new condition and perspective was passed to all their descendants. The apostle Paul reminded the elect:

> Therefore, just as sin came into the world through one man, and death through sin, and so death spread to all men because all sinned (Romans 5:12).

> You once walked following the course of this world, following the prince of the power of the air, the spirit that is now at work in the sons of disobedience – among whom we all once lived in the passions of our flesh, carrying out the desires of the body and the mind, and were by nature the children of wrath, like the rest of mankind (Ephesians 2:2, 3).

Spiritual death and a fleshly perspective produce the following results.

Fleshly Selfish Individualism was Revealed in Three Results

As individuals, Adam and Eve were now *in competition* with each other and with God as to what was good and evil. Their sexual differences, which they formerly welcomed as they complemented each other in caring for the garden, now became a threat. Their selfish autonomy had several immediate consequences for sexual relationships. Their differences threatened their *self-confidence* (they were afraid) and challenged their *unity in marriage* (ashamed, or who was better?). The differences were an offense to unity that drove them to *minimize their differences and make them alike* (they covered themselves with fig leaves). Individual selfishness inevitably threatens self-confidence, unity with others, and creates the desire to eliminate differences and a desire to make others be like us. The selfish sinful individual must attack differences as a threat.

The only difference then existing was their sexuality. The offense of these differences would later extend to race, language, ability, class, and nation. This is the source of the desire to make each sex the same that leads ultimately to homosexuality, and makes homosexuals so hostile to heterosexuals. The selfish individualism from sin is the modern motive for promoting "politically correct" sameness—sexually, economically, racially, socially, and politically. It is the source of the desire of a one-world dictatorial government that would equalize everything.

Secondly, because Adam and Eve now saw themselves as individuals who were as wise as God, *God's sovereignty as their Creator was an offense to their self-righteousness*. Now each believed they knew what was good and what was evil, or right and wrong. In their sin nature, every person is self-righteous and must establish his/her own self-esteem. Under the influence of Satan's lies and seeking to be wise in their own eyes, men and women change all things, calling "evil good, and good evil, putting darkness for light, and light for darkness, and bitter for sweet and sweet for bitter" (Isaiah 5:18-21). Every man is right in his own eyes (Proverbs 16:2; 21:2). When men and women reject their worth as God's good creation and exchange it for the world's self-esteem, it leads to division and discord. This division begins in rejecting God, extends to the family, and from there to business, to the community, and to the nation.

As day cooled and night approached, the person of the Word of God came and spoke, calling to Adam. Both Adam and Eve ran and hid, not wanting to hear what he had to say. Thus they reacted to God's presence in fear and sought to distance themselves from him. They no longer wanted to hear his word. A bias against God and his word was now evident.

Thirdly, the man and the woman began to *judge and blame others.* Self-righteous self-esteem must put blame elsewhere. Adam, who had received the word from God directly and knew it was from God himself, did not interrupt and correct his wife, but joined her. Afterwards, Adam's reaction was to judge her and blame her for the sin. She also did not confess to committing a deliberate wrong, but gave the excuse she was deceived and it was the serpent's fault. Worst of all, they implied *God was at fault* by the creatures he gave—the wife you gave me … the crafty serpent you created. Since man's fall all men in self-righteous pride naturally refuse to admit guilt, but turn to judge and blame others (Romans 1:32-2:3).

Even though Adam and Eve now saw things as right in their own eyes, it did not mean that they or their offspring were as bad as they could be in every way. It did mean every thought and act was for selfish reasons. They worshiped and did good to others in order to be accepted by God and other people. But this meant and means that their standards deteriorated from what was good in God's eyes and included a personal motive for self.

God's Resultant Acts of Justice and Grace for Man

The LORD God said to the serpent, "Because you have done this, cursed are you above all livestock and above all beasts of the field; on your belly you shall go, and dust you shall eat all the days of your life. I will put enmity between you and the woman, and between your offspring and her offspring; he shall bruise your head, and you shall bruise his heel." To the woman he (God) said, "I will surely multiply your pain in childbearing, in pain you shall bring forth children. Your desire shall be for your husband, and he shall rule over you." And to Adam he (God) said, "Because you have listened to the voice of your wife, and have eaten of the tree of which I commanded you, 'You shall not eat of it,' cursed is the ground because of you; in pain you shall eat of it all the days of your life; thorns and thistles it shall bring forth for you; and you shall eat the plants of the field. By the sweat of your face you shall eat bread, till you return to the ground, for out of it you were taken; for you are dust, and to dust you shall return." The man called his wife's name Eve, because she was the mother of all living. And the LORD God made for Adam and for his wife garments of skins and clothed them. Then the LORD God said, "Behold, the man has become like one of us in knowing good and evil. Now, lest he reach out his hand and take also of the tree of life and eat, and live forever—" therefore the LORD God sent him out from the garden of Eden to work the ground from which he was taken. He drove out the man, and at the east of the garden of Eden he placed the cherubim and a flaming sword that turned every way to guard the way to the tree of life (Genesis 3:14-24).

God's Curse to Serpent as Representative of Evil

Because Adam and Eve knew the serpent as the only source of evil, God addressed the serpent as the symbol of evil. But God knew the bigger spiritual picture. God pronounced humiliation on the serpent; but offered mankind hope in symbolically predicting a victory by the seed of the woman over the serpent. The woman's seed, or her son chosen by God, would crush the serpent's head in victory. But in achieving victory, the son of Eve would suffer a wound.

This prophecy is the first mention of the Good News of a messianic victory over evil. The promise of a Messiah given through the women's offspring established the prophetic principle of a miraculous gift of a child who would save. In God's plan, the woman who sinned would, by faith in God's promise, through her female nature and image of God, produce the male who would win the fight over evil. In bearing children, she would contribute to mankind's redemption. After this promise to Eve, the Bible continues to follow the history of the conflict of good and evil, of God's elect children in conflict with men under the devil's influence, to the end of Revelation. The principal laid out in Genesis 3, that the seed of the woman would conquer evil, was revealed in a series of miraculous births, culminating in the virgin birth of Jesus. Christ "appeared to destroy the works of the devil" (1 John 3:8).

But demonic leaders would consistently seek to kill the offspring of God's elect. This began with Cain's murder of Abel and continued with Pharaoh ordering the drowning of the Israelite boys, and Herod the Great killing Bethlehem's babies at the birth of Jesus. The conflict between good and evil, God's elect and the Devil will continue until the return and reign of Christ. This conflict will be consummated at the end times when the devil and his angels will be cast out of heaven and seek to attack the Son of the woman who was exalted to reign in heaven. At that event, the heavenly hosts will sing, "Now the salvation and the power and the kingdom of our God and the authority of his Christ have come," (Revelation 12:10).

Mutual Sexual Suffering Given to Create Unity in Differences

Woman's Pain in Childbirth and Dependence on Husband

As a result of their disobedience and new found autonomy, God imposed suffering and dependency upon the man and woman, male and female to forcing them rely on each other in marriage— the woman in the area of her unique feminine power and the man in his unique area of muscular strength and courage.

> To the woman he (God) said, I will greatly multiply your pain and conception/ pregnancy (Hebrew is *harah),* and in pain you shall bring forth children (Hebrew is *ben,* sons). Your desire shall be for your husband, and he shall rule over you (Genesis 3:16).

In contrast to Eden, where childbirth may have been easy and painless, sin resulted in increased pregnancies and painful childbirth. The woman would by nature want the physical relationship more often to feel her self-worth; she would need help and care in having children. This would create the longing or desire for a husband. The word "desire" has the idea of *running after* (Hebrew is *shug*), or yearning for a husband in a long-term relationship. The word for "rule over" *(mashal)* has the connotation of forming a decisive opinion or giving a judgment of control. The word is used about the sun "ruling over the day," asserting God's word will definitely, naturally work in that manner. The woman's condition in her suffering would cause her to let her husband assume the role of the decision maker. In other Scriptures, childbirth is an analogy for God giving birth to his redeemed people in a New Jerusalem (Isaiah 66: 7 ff.). The pain of childbirth gives way to joy in the victory over death and the redemption of God's people.

Exactly how this changed childbirth, making it more painful and the woman more dependent on God and her husband, is not explained. However, the Dutch zoologist, Jan Lever, has made an interesting comparison of other animals, especially the anthropoids, and humans.[10] Some of his comparisons offer suggestions which I offer as speculation.

Lever points out that at four to five months the baby passes through a period like cats and dogs when they are born, but the human fetus continues to grow in the womb for another four or five months. Unlike cats and dogs, at full birth the human baby's sense organs are fully useful, but a newborn human's head is proportionately much larger than other animals, making for a more difficult delivery. Also, based on the helplessness of the baby, we might expect the birth weight of a human to be lower than the anthropoids. But the newborn infant, on average, weighs much more than the young of anthropoids—almost twice as much. If the children were originally born several months earlier like cats and dogs, it would have been easy for the woman and she would not need help with the child as an infant. God's change for the woman might have been, among other things, to extend the gestation period.

Man's Physical Strength Tested by Corruption of Nature

God's word to Adam meant his superior physical strength would be tested. God said to Adam, "You have listened to the voice of your wife and have eaten of the tree of which I commanded you, 'You shall not eat' " (Genesis 3:17). Adam obeyed Eve's word instead of God's and was not the leader that God had made him at creation. His punishment was to be pain and suffering, testing his strength to produce food and to survive under the curse, for he no longer would have access to the fruit trees of the garden.

---

[10] Jan Lever, trans. Peter G. Berkhout, *Creation and Evolution*, (Grand Rapids: distributed by Kregel, 1958). See Chapter 5, The Origin of Man, esp. 178-191.

Cursed is the ground because of you; in pain you shall eat of it all the days of your life. ...You shall eat the plants of the field (not just fruit). By the sweat of your face you shall eat bread, till you return to the ground, for out of it you were taken; for you are dust and to dust you shall return (Genesis 3:17). (Addition mine)

Hard work, along with the threat of sickness leading to physical death, was his test. This was a threat to man's self-worth that is found in success in his work. Man needed a partner to help him work and survive.

This meant that Adam would have to prayerfully look to God to bless his efforts to provide for him, his wife, and children. Often in Scripture a man's faith and blessings from God were linked to his work for and treatment of his family. If the man trusts God with a tithe and treats his wife and children well, God will bless his work to provide (e.g. Malachi 2:14-16; 3:10-12; other prophets, 1 Timothy 5:8). Thus, the man's curse required trust in God and help from his spouse, in the same way that Eve's curse, required trust in God and help from Adam.

The change, resulting in pain for Adam, was a result of the curse of the ground or earth's soil. The source of this pain was the change of the earth, "thorns and thistles it shall bring forth." The Hebrew word for "thorns" is not one of the usual ones, but *gots* which means, "that which cuts or wounds." The word for thistles is *dardar* meaning, "that which uselessly proliferates" or gets out of control.

Paul, seemingly referring to this curse, said, "creation was subject to futility [or bondage to decay], not willingly, but because of him who subjected it in hope" (Romans 8:20). The condition of the earth since the curse offers a sense of futility of mind because it is locked into a process of decaying.[11] The wounds and proliferation of thorns that man must contend with would seem to portray the broader curse of nature, which inflicts pain and spreads

---

[11] The scientific discoveries showing corruption of nature are in my book *True Enlightenment*, chapter 14 the New Generalized second law shows nature runs down in energy and information and in chapter 23 I give the evidence that the forces of nature are declining.

beyond man's control, *e.g.* weeds, diseases, earthquakes, storms, etc. God inflicts natural calamity to cause man to seek his help, and especially hope in him for final rest in a new heaven and earth with the resurrection (Romans 8:18-25).

God's curses compel the man and woman to trust God and to rely on each other as a family. By grace, Adam's faith in God's help is seen in his proclamation of Eve as the mother of future generations and in the fact that God clothed their nakedness with skins (3:20, 21). Their pain and struggle *limited their wisdom.*

Conscience Selfishness Required Exclusion from Garden

Selfish Sin Nature with Destructive Consequences
The *critical issue* resulting from man's sin was his nature to see himself as *equal with God in knowledge* of good and evil. Self-autonomy produced self-righteousness and selfishness which destroyed unity with God and each other. God could not allow man to continue to perpetrate evil for self-gratification. Therefore, lest Adam and Eve eat of the Tree of Life and live forever, they had to be excluded from the garden. God's justice must not allow them to continue in earth's knowledge, to increasingly do harm to others, to nature, and most of all, to use their God-given image of intelligence to dishonor God himself. God's presence in the midst of the garden with the Tree of Life was symbolic of his footstool of control. Man's expulsion from the garden had eternal implications and is the reason for eternal hell. Sinful man in paradise would dishonor God and be destructive of peace and blessing.

Hell reveals God's justice to honor his glorious image and protection for man's good. But with the expulsion, there was revealed a way of hope in redemption whereby God's purposes for man would be achieved in a liberated earth and an eternal righteous city like the Garden of Eden.

Man's Two Approaches to God: Sacrificial Death, Works
The only gate to the garden was to the east where cherubim and a flaming sword were on guard to prevent reentry. It was at

this gate where Adam and his sons, Cain (meaning "strong") and Abel (signifying "nothingness" or "weakness") had to come to meet with God. Both Cain and Abel had grown into working men who knew the consequences of sin. At this east gate to Eden Abel brought to God the sacrifice of the blood of a lamb, acknowledging his guilt. His offer was accepted. Cain offered produce from tilling the ground, and it apparently was given in pride. God told Cain his grain offering would have been acceptable if given in the right spirit, but warned Cain that temptation to sin was close ("sin lies at your door"). Their offerings symbolized two ways for Adam and Eve's descendants to gain God's forgiveness and alleviate their suffering in life.

Instead of repenting at God's warning that the sin of hate was at his door, Cain responded in prideful jealous anger and killed his brother Abel. The apostle John, referring to the commandant to love in the New Covenant, also refers to the contrasting love for the world that produces antichrist. John linked this to Cain's hatred of Abel and his righteous sacrifice (cf. 1 John 2:7-3:8-15). As a result of Abel's murder, Cain's work of the ground was cursed. But in spite of this curse, because of his appealing cry to God, Cain was marked by God's grace, and allowed to continue to dwell in the land of Nod as a nomad. Nod was a wilderness *east of the gate* of the Garden of Eden (Genesis 4), a constant reminder to Cain that the gate was still there. The Garden of Eden was never mentioned after the curse and Cain was marked for protection. The east gate was likely destroyed by the worldwide flood.

Men with Evil Sin Natures Spread and Dominated World

Continuing in Cain's self-righteousness nature, his descendants used their intelligence to develop a culture of abuse. Their evil culture expanded throughout the world. Cain's descendants glorified entertainment, married multiple wives, and continued his murderous ways.

God gave Eve another believing son, Seth, and from his son Enosh or Enos (meaning "mortal") elect men "began to call on the name of the Lord." The witness continued about 800 years to

Enoch (meaning "teacher") who warned evil men of God's coming judgment on their continuing evil (Jude 14-16). The death of the father of the race, Adam, would be shocking. His death occurred near that time was a warning to the world that had grown in its evil. Soon afterwards, God translated Enoch out of their midst to heaven. Cain's demonic descendants continued to proliferate.

The conflict of evil men with the witness of God's elect, reached a crisis of sexual sin and rebellion at the time of Noah. Men who were heroes were exalted, taking all they chose from the daughters of men. "Every thought and intent of their heart was only evil continually," causing God to regret that he had ever created man. In judgment, God destroyed the whole world, delivering the only one righteous man, Noah, and his family. Through their unity in marriage, they again were commanded to fill the earth. Noah's righteousness derived from the understanding that sacrificial death was the access for grace, and when delivered from the flood, he appealed to God by the sacrifice of clean animals. Through Noah's animal sacrifices, God covenanted with Noah and mankind to withhold any future judgment by a worldwide flood (Genesis 6-9).

But all men again rebelled under the powerful leader Nimrod to unite in knowledge against God at the tower of Babel[12], and God divided the earth from one continent into many and thereby confused the languages and made many nations. Several hundred years after the continents were divided, God initiated his redemption plan through the marriage of a man and woman of faith. Together Abraham and Sarah would produce the seed and the nation through whom the serpent would be crushed, the god of this world defeated, and people of all nations be blessed.

---

[12] Nimrod is by firm tradition linked to Babel, and in unclear tradition back as far as Chaldean history to early feminism that is traced to the dove goddess, Semiramis, Ashtarte, Hera of Greece, Juno of Rome and the Queen of Heaven with the "nimble serpent, "suggesting demonic sexual perversion of marriage.

Conclusions

Demonic deception had *apparently* derailed God's plan for marriage. The crowning revelation of God's goodness—the union of male and female—and by this union, the power to reproduce and fill the earth, was seemingly ended. In leading the heavenly rebellion, the Devil attempted to capitalize on humans' sinful desires for control and to become their own gods. He used what appeared to be the wisest creature, the serpent, to plant the desire for freedom from God. He succeeded in getting Adam and Eve to believe a lie and eat of the tree that they thought would make them like God. With this false enlightenment, the man and woman died to God and forfeited the power of God's Spirit submitting to the devil, the liar and murderer. Man's free access to God and to the Tree of Life ended. Now their desires turned toward the gods of this world and their own ability to prosper, to gain the world for self, and to seek fulfillment of fleshly desires by their own efforts.

When sin entered the world, evil became the dominant force. The great loss was the revelation of God's goodness as represented in the union of male and female. With their eyes opened, the sexual differences that they had once found good now became an offense. Their differences threatened their individual autonomy to be as God. They covered these differences with fig leaves. Their new realized individualism made them fear and reject God's word when he called. The demonic drive to produce equality in the same way for any kind of difference began with efforts to make women like men and men like women. The complementary good that united them into one partnership of his image for meaningful shared rule of all creation was changed into competition for selfish individualism.

As individuals, men's strength to work has been used to selfishly accumulate and control their wives and others. With women deemed equal as men, sex became an act of pleasure without responsibility or caring. For men the satisfaction was also the domination in the act. Instead of wanting help from the man with children, in childbirth and in nurturing, women must be like men on their own and any children would be minimized and turned over to conscripted surrogates paid for by women's own efforts. The devil's attack that got the man and woman to promote the individual self, divided and destroyed union and witness to a good God. This was the demonic tool to gain power in the world to destroy as the enemy of God

But in all this, God's mysterious power and goodness was at work to reveal his justice and loving kindness. God chose men and women like Abel, Noah and his wife, and others, who, by his Spirit, witnessed God's righteousness. Also they were shown that he would accept a substitute sin offering, through which they could find forgiveness and acceptance. They were given hope for entrance to his throne and the Tree of Life through the east gate and beyond the cherubim. The love of future men for their wives would bring union and witness to God's goodness.

God's Mysterious Plan of Grace for a New Covenant

Paradoxically, as man was allowed to do evil, God was planning good. After dividing man into many nations, God chose one man to build one nation of his own with a covenant plan to show his justice and mercy to all other nations. Through this one man, he would give a seed that would bless all nations. This seed of the woman would crush the serpent's head. These workings of God were a mystery to men until the victory of that seed over the devil and death. In a mysterious way, men of all nations would be shown God's mercy, and would be included among his elect with eternal life.

Chapter 3
Christ's New Covenant
Union by Suffering Love

Introduction

The crowning piece of creation, the union of male and female in a complementary relationship, ended with man's sin. This union was no longer good. Adam and Eve's naked differences were a shameful offense. By appealing to human fleshly desires the devil gained control. His deception continued, spawning successive cultures of perversion, moral corruption, destruction and death that destroyed marriage as well as the entire civilization. Despite God's judgments—designed to end human misery and reveal his justice—the sons of Cain continued to reject God's witness as faithfully lived out by the sons of Seth.

As this chapter will reveal, man's ***individual belief that he is wise as God was the central problem*** that kept man in bondage to sin and demonic seduction. Sin distorted man's understanding of good and evil. God instituted a new covenant with Abraham to restore the relationship between man and woman and with God.

A Nation of People to Reveal God's Savior through a Marriage

About 150 years after the tower of Babel and God's dispersing people into different nations and tongues, God called a man and woman of faith, Abram and Sarai, to be the source of a nation as his covenant people. God said their seed would witness to and bless all the nations. Through their seed, God would send the Savior to crush the head of the serpent and lead the way to the tree of eternal life in a New Covenant. God's New Covenant would deliver from sin and death and fulfill his original purpose that men reign and reveal God's glory.

The central theme of this book is that the New Covenant of Christ offers God's most wonderful meaning and purpose for union in marriage. Christians who read this chapter probably understand the basic idea about the New Covenant. But most do not see that it is fundamental to God's plan for Christ's mission and for man in the world. Also, a person who has not yet become a Christian may have his eyes opened to the blessing marriage can be to his or her life and give glory to God.

Allowing man to sin was not an accident, but was part of God's hidden eternal plan, which also included his New Covenant of grace. Mankind's sin required that God reveal his holy character of righteousness and justice. It also provided the opportunity for God to express his sacrificial love and grace that justifies, sanctifies and glorifies his elect believers. The unbelieving world struggles with suffering, wondering how a sovereign God who allows sin and suffering, could also be one of love. But the paradoxical question is how would God's righteous justice be seen if God did not deal with sin? If the world was not dominated by man's sin, God's mercy and grace of sacrificial love would not be needed or seen in Christ as the only Savior.

God's Old Covenant, Foundational to New Covenant Meaning

God's plan was to reverse man's trust in himself as a god, knowing good and evil, and bring many to trust instead in his Son. This reversal would fulfill God's original design that man would rule over creation, and be free from demonic forces. The covenant with Abraham and his believing descendants calls for them to trust God and in obedience prepare the foundation for the New Covenant in Christ.

These evidences of God's character progressively unfold in the Bible until they are fulfilled in Christ's life, death, resurrection, ascension, sending of the Holy Spirit to the believing church, and will be fully consummated in his return in glory and power. This chapter reveals how the New Covenant believer in Christ discovers the meaning and joy of marriage, and walks in freedom with Christ to witness to his love. The objective of the New Covenant is to call men and women back to trust in God and no longer be dead to God and controlled by their individualistic demonic fleshly desires.

The foundation through Abraham's covenant was clearly based on God's working in the male and female union in marriage.

This chapter shows how the fulfillment of the old covenant in the New Covenant changes man and woman back to trust in Christ and makes possible the renewal of union by love in marriage spreading the meaning of God's love. It focuses on how this amazing change by the New Covenant occurs for any individual, male or female.

Initiation of God's Founding of National People

Around 1900 BC, at the time the Sumerian culture was invaded by Elamite armies, God called Abram out of Ur and out of Haran. God chose Abram and his descendants to carry out his plan for the nations.

> Now the LORD said to Abram, "Go from your country and your kindred and your father's house to the land that I will show you. And I will make of you a great nation, and I will bless you and make your name great, so that you will be a blessing. I will bless those who bless you, and him who dishonors you I will curse, and *in you all the families of the earth shall be blessed*" (Genesis 12:1-3).

After Abram sojourned 25 years in Canaan, both his and Sarai's faith faltered. God met with him and formed an everlasting covenant with Abram. The sign of the covenant was circumcision. This indicated that Abram's heirs would be the result of faith in God's working and not just by sexual reproduction. The marriage would be a union of faith producing a miraculous child when Abraham was 100 and his wife 90 years old. The promise to Abram to have a seed that would bless the world centered squarely through their faith in the Holy Spirit working through their marriage union and not just a physical relationship. His name was changed from Abram (exalted father), to Abraham, (father of many or all) and hers to Sarah, a higher meaning of princess. He was told that the nation he found would occupy the land of Palestine, but the promise would not be fully realized for 400 years when his descendants would then conquer and destroy the Amoritic people who dwelled there. Israel's destruction and occupation of the land would come as a just judgment against the Canaanite peoples who had become extremely sinful.

Abraham understood the Promised Land in Palestine would be a foreign land for him. His descendants would occupy the land centuries later. The name Hebrew probably means "sojourner," indicating Abraham and his wife hoped for future resting place. "For he was looking forward to the city that has foundations, whose designer and builder is God" (Hebrews 11:8-13, cf. 10). As a nation under God, the Israelites were the vehicle God chose to reveal his oracles (the Bible) through his law and the prophets. These Scriptures were truth for the world (Romans 3:2), to show the sinfulness of all and God's provision of saving righteousness through Abraham's seed—God's own incarnate Son, Jesus Christ (Romans 3:21-26; cf. Galatians 3:7-9).

The usefulness of the nation as a revelation was based entirely on the man and woman having children and transferring the Scriptures from one generation to the next. Some illustrations of God's plan though marriage and children follow:

> Hear, O Israel: The LORD our God, the LORD is one. You shall love the LORD your God with all your heart and with all your soul and with all your might. And these words that I command you today shall be on your heart. You shall teach them diligently to your children, and shall talk of them when you sit in your house, and when you walk by the way, and when you lie down, and when you rise. You shall bind them as a sign on your hand, and they shall be as frontlets between your eyes. You shall write them on the doorposts of your house and on your gates (Deuteronomy 6:4-9).

> He established a testimony in Jacob and appointed a law in Israel, which he commanded our fathers to teach to their children, that the next generation might know them, the children yet unborn, and arise and tell them to their children, so that they should set their hope in God and not forget the works of God, but keep his commandments. (Psalm 78:5-7).

Israel's Passover Included Implications for the World

Many Christians do not appreciate the importance of the Exodus event for the whole world. The Egyptian Pharaoh, Thutmose III, who had suppressed the Hebrews and killed their children, was competing with Moses for the throne. When Moses slew an Egyptian, he fled from the Pharaoh into the Sinai Peninsula.

Thutmose III had built the most powerful empire in all the Mediterranean Sea area. In seventeen successful campaigns he had conquered all of Palestine and influenced Asia Minor. At this time, the early Greek Minoan Empire was the other major power in the Mediterranean with its capital at Kenosis in Crete.[13] These two powers joined with one another, and together shared the corrupt culture of the time of materialistic greed, and extreme sexual lust. The capital at Kenosis was almost completely destroyed by a massive earthquake in the fifteenth century B.C., about the time of Israel's amazing exodus from Egypt. The Egyptian Pharaoh Amenhotep II was Thutmose III's grandson. He was a transvestite and a sexual anarchist. He and his army were all destroyed in the sea at the exodus.

Eating of the Passover sacrificial lamb was *the significant event* for the formation of God's people. The deliverance of the Hebrews from Egypt was *the turning point of political history for the Mediterranean world*. The exodus established the renown of the power of Jehovah, the sovereign God of creation, and revealed that Israel was his elect people. The destruction of the Egyptian's army and great power displayed in the exodus brought fear of the Hebrews throughout that area of the world for generations (Exodus 23:27; Deuteronomy 2:25, Joshua 2:8-11; 9:9, 24). Later, at the time of the conquest, the Tell el-Amarna Tablets from Egyptian vassals in Palestine reveal the fear in the Canaanite tribes when later under Joshua, Israel attacked and conquered them.[14] The weakening of the Egyptian military power that followed the exodus probably caused Pharaoh Akhenaton to renounce all the Egyptian gods in fear and to turn back to worshiping Re, the son of the supreme spirit god Horus, who was initially worshiped as the only god by the Egyptians.

---

[13] See Arthur Evans' record of Crete and Egypt, "Crete," *Encyclopedia Britannica*, 679,680.
[14] Jack Finnegan, *Light From The Ancient Past*, (Princeton: Princeton University Press, 1959), 108-111.

Christ's New Covenant Passover Fulfilled God's Plan

Christ's last Passover meal is central to the meaning of the New Covenant. *Israel's original Passover meal contained the basic concepts of God's redemption plan—a plan which would be revealed in all its fullness in Jesus' death and resurrection.* God's plan to bless all the nations of the world was initiated in the covenant with Abraham and Sarah and fulfilled in Christ

The Passover meal was *family centered*. Each large or several small Hebrew families killed a lamb, roasted it and ate together. To protect them from God's judgment of death, they sprinkled the blood over their doorposts. The sign of the sacrificial blood caused the judgment of the death angel to "pass over" the home, sparing the elder son—the heir-apparent in each family. But in the houses of the Egyptians that were not protected with blood, the death angel killed the firstborn sons. The death of the Egyptian sons was the last of the plagues sent by God to disparage their idols and render justice to the Egyptians for killing the Hebrew male babies (Exodus 1:16). God instituted this Old Testament Passover to later give meaning to his New Covenant people who would be blessed by Abraham's seed.

Christ's Passover New Covenant Meaning for All Nations.

A millennium and a half after Israel's deliverance from Egypt and Joshua's conquest of Canaan, Jesus held the Passover meal as a symbol of the New Covenant, extending Abraham's blessing in its real meaning for all people. Jesus understood his final Passover feast was a fulfillment of the promise to Abraham—the New Covenant blessing for the whole world.

Only the day before Jesus celebrated this feast, the Gentiles/nations had sought Jesus—a sign, he understood, that the family of God includes people of all nations. He said that it was time for him to die as a grain of wheat that would fall into the ground and bring forth the harvest of the world. This was the sign that it was time for him to die and be raised to glory and draw men from all the world to himself (cf. John 12:20-32). Jesus' disciples and others in the upper room at the time did not see the worldwide significance. Only after the resurrection, the Great Commission, Christ's ascension to glory and the coming of the Holy Spirit at Pentecost did they understand the larger implication.

Jesus followed the usual order of the Passover but gave its fulfilled meaning in God's plan. Jesus, as the elder brother of his spiritual family of believers (Luke 8:20, 21), began the feast with the first of three cups of wine by *predicting* that he would not eat this feast again until after *his future coming in kingdom power to celebrate the marriage supper of the Lamb* with God and his people. (cf. Hebrews 2:7-17) That event would consummate the offer of his salvation to the world.

Participation in Christ's Cross Ends Dominant Sin

The dominant self-centered sin nature was still evident in the apostles and was the primary purpose for the New Covenant. As Jesus' Passover supper began, the competition over who was greatest and would receive the highest place of reward in the kingdom was in hot debate. This debate had been going on since the middle of his ministry and came up again shortly before the triumphal entry. As Jesus ate the meal and drank the second cup of wine with his disciples, he promised them, "You may eat and drink with me at my table in my kingdom and sit on thrones judging the twelve tribes of Israel" (Luke 22:30). Their reward was assured.

But Jesus then rose, wrapped himself with a towel, and washed the disciples' feet. In this act, he taught his disciples that, although the Father had made this decision and given him all authority to appoint and exalt them in his kingdom, the exaltation to greatness depended on the greatest humility in the lowest service, which he had demonstrated. Jesus' humility formed the context of serving the elements and the New Covenant.

When he completed his work as a lowly servant, he said that they were all clean, except one. During the meal, Jesus told the group that one of them who would betray him and gave the sop to Judas. Jesus then dismissed Judas, who went out, motivated by the devil, to betray him. Jesus also warned that all the other disciples would fall away. Pridefully, Peter responded that even if all the others did, he would not. Jesus then predicted that Peter would deny him three times before the cock crowed the next morning. All the disciples' ambition and Judas's greed were motivated by demonic influences (James 2:14, 15). Such an effort by the devil almost always precedes a mighty working of God.

At this point, the New Covenant was instituted, using the Passover elements reserved for the covenant remembrance. A portion of the unleavened bread, known as the Aphigomeon or 'after dish,' was broken off and reserved, along with the third cup of wine. These were set aside to be eaten later, symbolizing the power of the covenant with God. Jesus then served the bread and wine saying they signified his broken body and shed blood—a sacrifice and suffering he would bear for all mankind for their sinful failure to obey God's commands. These elements linked the meal to the Passover in Egypt where the blood of the lamb saved the Israelites from death and symbolized a type of sacrifice for man's sin.

Alfred Edersheim, the Jewish scholar, has shown that all the tabernacle and temple sacrifices symbolize aspects of atonement that reflected the Passover lamb and meal. The tabernacle was patterned after the meeting with God at Mount Sinai which was like the entrance to meet with God in the Garden of Eden.

New Covenant Suffering Love in New Commandment

Using these elements of the broken bread and wine, Jesus instituted the new eternal covenant foretold by the prophets (Jeremiah 31:33; Ezekiel 36:25-27; Isaiah 54:88; 55:3) that was planned before the foundation of the world (cf. 1 Peter 1:10-21). This would be a covenant sacrifice for all people worldwide who would come to know him. His redemptive love in his death would be the basis of forgiveness for all sin; and would thereby write the law on their hearts. This law is summarized as love for God with all our hearts and then for our neighbor as ourselves

The redeemed are to teach these commands to their children and in this way continue the covenant from generation to generation. Jesus had affirmed these commands as the first and second commandments (Mark 12:29-31), but in the Sermon on the Mount he declared his disciples should go beyond this to be like the Son of God by loving even their enemies (Matthew 5:43-48). Adam and Eve disobeyed this law of love when they ate from the Tree of Knowledge. In this act, they moved toward independence, seeking to be wise as God and to self-righteously know what was good and evil. Their sinful nature placed them in opposition to God and accentuated their sexual differences.

The regular practice of the early church was to have a fellowship meal and then serve the elements as the symbol of Christ's sacrificial death at the end. The gospels of Matthew, Mark, and Luke made these central in the supper. John wrote his gospel much later and the richer Christians were selfishly discriminating against the poorer believers. Both Paul and James acknowledge that in some of the early churches the discrimination cancelled the true meaning of the sacrificial death of Christ in the elements served at the end of the feast. There was a need to clarify the purpose and proper use of the meal. The whole idea of the New Covenant needed clarifying.

Tradition says the apostle John was asked to write his gospel after the other three because he was more informed than any apostle.[15] He was one of the initial apostles, was one of the three of Jesus inner circle, and he had taken in Jesus' mother Mary who had all the family secrets about Jesus, and was "the apostle whom Jesus loved." John omitted even the mention of the elements of the Passover meal that were central in the other three gospels, and widely and commonly used. In contrast, John focused on and emphasized the basic meaning of the covenant.

John recorded the Lord's humble foot washing then stated the new commandment and the meaning in the elements. Jesus said to his disciples,

---

[15] Cf. Carl W. Wilson, *The Fulfillment*, in commentary on writing of Gospels.

A new commandment I give to you, that you love one another just *as I have loved you*, you also are to love one another. By this all people will know that you are my disciples, if you have love for one another (John 13:34, 35).

After John indicated a New Covenant disciple is one who keeps the first commandment, he showed the importance of this to the New Covenant in that immediately afterwards Jesus referred to the law of love at least five or six times. While God's love and its implication for Christians was displayed by the eating of the elements as stated in the first three gospels, the new commandment was not fully emphasized. Also later, in his first epistle, John explained that the new command was not really new but was a fulfillment of the old in Christ (1 John 2:7-9). John emphasized that Christ came to destroy the works of the devil in our lives (1 John 3:4-10), and this dying to sin and living to Christ was possible because we are born of the Spirit. The foot washing incident in John's gospel is not for instituting a new ritual, but an example of a disciple humbling himself to serve us in love.

John's epistles and the other apostolic writings repeatedly refer to this commandment of Christ's sacrificial love as the basis of Christianity and as the fulfillment of the old covenant law. Paul and Peter both repeatedly emphasize love as central. Christ's terrible suffering and death for our sins is recorded in all the gospel records following this teaching.[16] James, the Lord's brother, refers to loving the poor and unlovely as the royal law of liberty (James 2:8).

Discipleship by Death Taught by Jesus and the Apostles

This teaching of the relationship of the old covenant to the new agrees with Jesus' own previous teaching. After he had appointed the twelve apostles, Jesus used the Sermon on the Mount to teach the real meaning of discipleship (Matthew 5-7). He said he was the light of the world and that his disciples would also become the light of the world. He then said that he did not come to destroy

---

[16] Carl W. Wilson, *The Fulfillment*, pages 349-386.

the law and the prophets, but to fulfill them. He went on to explain that in fulfilling the law, his disciples would be empowered to keep the law in their hearts. As a result, they would even be able to love their enemies, demonstrating that they were sons of God (Matthew 5:17-48). A pure transformed mind for Christ's sake as a light to the world was the way of obedient love.

Elsewhere, Jesus had repeatedly emphasized that *only by accepting his cross and dying to self would they be his disciples*. Indeed, after clearly predicting his own death, he said,

> If *anyone would come after me*, let him deny himself and take up his cross and follow me. For whoever would save his life will lose it, but whoever loses his life for my sake will find it. For what will it profit a man if he gains the whole world and forfeits his soul? Or what shall a man give in return for his soul? For the Son of Man is going to come with his angels in the glory of his Father, and then he will repay each person according to what he has done. Truly, I say to you, there are some standing here who will not taste death until they see the Son of Man coming in his kingdom (Matthew 16:24-28; cf. Luke 9:23-27).

A week later, with Moses and Elijah present, Jesus revealed *his future glorification and the fulfillment of God's redemptive purpose to reward the disciples* to his three closest apostles, Peter, James and John, In Luke's account of the transfiguration, Jesus "appeared in glory and spoke of his *exodus* which he was about to accomplish in Jerusalem" (Luke 9:31). That exodus would be his resurrection and ascension. The three disciples heard the Father then say that Jesus was his Son whose authority exceeded that of Moses and Elijah. The real exodus for God's elect people is in the resurrection with Christ.

In the New Covenant, a true disciple is clearly identified as one who responds to God's love as manifested in the death of Christ, and is willing to die to self and his earthly, fleshly life to show God's love to the world. The true disciple finds his real life in eternity with Christ. This is the heart of God's New Covenant with the elect: only those who are willing to lose their lives and die with Christ as their sin offering are truly disciples. Knowing and trusting God's love is the only way for any man to die to self.

The Good News Is Christ Risen and Glorified to Save

The New Covenant *centers in the greatness of Christ* who died, was raised to power and glory with all authority to justify and forgive, to give life and power by his Holy Spirit to sanctify, and to raise the believer from the dead to share his glory in a new heaven and earth. The gospel is the good news of his personal sacrifice to save us from the demonic evil of sin and reconcile us to God. Christ, the head of the church, is now the glorified Lord, reigning over all in heaven and on earth and under the earth. (Ephesians 1:16-23). Paul said,

> And even if our gospel is veiled, it is veiled only to those who are perishing. In their case the god of this world has blinded the minds of the unbelievers, to keep them from seeing the light of *the gospel of the glory of Christ,* who is the image of God. For what we proclaim is not ourselves, but Jesus Christ *as Lord*, with ourselves as *your servants* for Jesus' sake. For God, who said, "Let light shine out of darkness," has shone in our hearts to give the light of the knowledge of the glory of God in the face of Jesus Christ (2 Corinthians 4:3-6).

The only way we are able to die to self and lose our life is to believe that Christ paid the price for our sin and that we live now in the power of the Spirit and will receive our eternal reward when Christ returns. Only when this is real can the New Covenant be realized in the life of a believer. The religions of the flesh that are dressed as Christianity will fail. Paul said,

> They are of no value in stopping the indulgence of the flesh. If then you have been raised with Christ seek the things that are above where Christ is, seated at the right hand of God. Set your minds on things that are above, not on things that are on earth. For *you have died and your life is hidden with Christ* in God. When Christ who is your life appears then you also will appear with him in glory (Colossians 2:23b- 3:6; cf. also John's teaching 1 John 2:15-17; 3:1-3).

Manner of Dying to Self to Become a New Covenant Disciple

Disciples Are Men Elected and Called of God

Disciples are elect, known by the sovereign God before the foundation of the world. Through the Spirit, the elect are led to respond and are given to Jesus from the Father (John 17:6-11). Jesus taught that no man could come to him unless they are taught of the Father by the Spirit, and he is drawn to come to him as a gift from the Father (John 6:37, 44, 45; 17:6). Paul and other apostles teach that sovereign election is a gift of God's grace to those who believe. They then receive the heavenly blessings of salvation through the blood of Christ (Ephesians 1:3-6, etc.). This sovereign working is known only by God whose thoughts and mind are above man's. But **God invites sinners** to respond and lets them know he is near (Isaiah 55:6-8). While the sinner's response occurs in a logical sequence, it is a simultaneous work of the Spirit through the word of God.

Process of Change to Faith from Individualism to Union

Repentance is the beginning. The process of change begins with a change of mind. First, the sinner must *repent*. This involves humbling himself and confessing his disobedience and dishonor to God and harmful actions to others. He then must confess his sin by publicly being baptized. Everyone must accept the word of God that reveals and declares he/she is a sinner and repent of their unbelief and the ways they have selfishly offended the Creator.

John the Baptist came calling men to repentance and baptism for cleansing. Jesus himself said that his purpose was "not to call the righteous, but *to call the sinners to repentance*." His disciples baptized those who repented. (John 3:23, 4:2; Luke 5:31; Matthew 28:19). Jesus told Nicodemus, who was "the master rabbi of Israel," that he had to be born of water and the Spirit to see or enter the kingdom of God and understand heavenly things (John 3:3-15). On the day of Pentecost, Peter demanded that all repent and be baptized (Acts 2:38). Wherever Paul preached, he repeatedly called men to repent first, and then have faith in Christ (Acts 20:20, 21).

Repentance is the humble beginning of a mental state of submission to God that believers need to repeat continuously.

Water baptism was an outward symbol indicating the inward cleansing by the Spirit of the heart attitude. This act is not the physical agent of cleansing, but the public vocal expression of the Spirit's work within. Water is the essential cleansing agent; it is vital for life and growth. The repentant sinner is baptized to show he has died with Christ and received new life. Water has natural powers that make it *a symbol of the cleansing* work of God's word, giving life by the Holy Spirit (Priests used water in the temple to cleanse and heal, cf. Leviticus). Jesus said, "It is the Spirit who gives life; *the flesh is of no avail.* The words that I have spoken unto you, they are spirit and they are life" (John 6:63). Jesus' work of forming the church was "by the *washing of water with the Word*" (Ephesians 5:26, 27, Colossians 2:11-15).[17] Confession of sin and baptism indicates publicly a change of mind or heart in response to God's word. This is a spiritual heart cleansing and not a magic physical or fleshly influence to make a man acceptable to God. The thief on the cross who confessed Christ was told he would be in paradise with Christ, and he confessed, but he was never baptized. Baptism is a public confession of heart repentance and dying to self.

It is precisely by the act of repentance, demonstrated by public baptism that a person confesses the wrong of his selfish autonomy. This act of humbling is critical and offers the only possibility of (or hope for) change. Baptism is an indication of the dying of the old Adamic nature and beginning of new life in Christ. Paul explains this in Romans 5:12-6:8. Only when one dies with Christ can one be made alive by the Spirit and have faith in Christ as the Lord of glory.

---

[17] Discussions of modes of baptism and of infant and adult baptism are important, but diversionary from the issue of spiritual change and are not given here. See my discussion in Carl W. Wilson, *The Fulfillment,* 47 and 62-65 on circumcision baptism. The meaning of water baptism is to be avoided in dividing Christians (cf. 1 Corinthians 1:7).

Faith in the risen Christ is the next step. Faith is both granted by God's grace and a response of the repentant. On the one hand, sinners are commanded to repent and believe, and on the other, they are told God grants repentance and faith by his Spirit (Acts 11:28; 17:30; Ephesians 2:8, 9). Repentance from our old will to trust Christ, gives humility for obedience of New Covenant love in Christ. This *begins with the mind of Christ to humbly obey* so that we begin to love (Philippians 2:1-11). The Spirit imparts faith in the resurrection so that we are willing to lose our lives as a result of Christ's love. Paul then said, "Therefore, my beloved ...work out your own salvation with fear and trembling, for *it is God who works in you* (by his Spirit), to will and to work for his good pleasure." In this way "in the midst of a crooked and twisted generation...you shine as lights in the world, holding fast to the word of life...." (Philippians 3:12-16). God desires that repentant sinners humbly submit to his judgment of what is good and evil and not ours.

When a person comes to faith in Christ, the Holy Spirit comes into their heart. *The indwelling of the Spirit enables the believer to experience the miraculous* reality of the risen glorified Christ and to know with certainty that he/she is a child of God with the hope of glory (Philippians 1:27). Following his resurrection, Christ showed the apostles his wounds, pronounced peace as the priest after the peace offering, and then "breathed on them and said, 'Receive the Holy Spirit' " (John 20:19-22). The breath was a symbol of renewal of Christ's presence at the creation of Adam (Genesis 2:7). At the Passover New Covenant ceremony, Jesus had promised to send the Holy Spirit to those who believe (John 14:15-17). He commanded the disciples to not preach until they had received the Holy Spirit, which occurred after his resurrection and ascension to the throne of heaven. That Spirit would give them the power to witness to his substitutionary death (Luke 24:46-49; Acts 1:8).

The power of the Christian life and ministry is not from self effort, but only from the Spirit of Christ. Jesus taught the disciples "without me, you can *do nothing*" (John 15:5). Paul also insisted

53

on experiencing the Holy Spirit and continuing to trust the Spirit and not the flesh (cf. Acts 19:2; Galatians 3:1-9, 14; Ephesians 3:14 ff.). Paul said "we are the true circumcision/covenant people who *trust God in the Spirit and have no confidence in the flesh*" (Philippians 3:3). When we humble ourselves, repent from trusting in self and submit to Christ's love through the power of the Holy Spirit, we are released from the bondage of the flesh to love God and serve others. Paul stated this clearly saying,

> For the *love of Christ controls us*, because we have concluded this: that one has died for all, therefore *all have died*; and he died for all, that those who live might *no longer live for themselves but for him* who for their sake died and was raised.
>
> From now on (through the Spirit), therefore, we *regard no one according to the flesh.* Even though we once regarded Christ according to the flesh, we regard him thus no longer. Therefore, if anyone is in Christ, he is a new creation. The old has passed away; behold, the new has come. All this is from God, who through Christ reconciled us to himself and gave us the ministry of reconciliation; that is, in Christ God was reconciling the world to himself, not counting their trespasses against them, and entrusting to us the message of reconciliation. Therefore, we are ambassadors for Christ, God making his appeal through us. We implore you on behalf of Christ, be reconciled to God. For our sake he made him to be sin who knew no sin, so that in him we might become the righteousness of God. Working together with him, then, we appeal to you not to receive the grace of God in vain (2 Corinthians 5:14-6:1).

The apostles repeated this many times in various ways (cf. Romans 7 and 8:2-8; Galatians 2:15-3:14; Colossians 2:9-13; 3:1-4). Peter taught the same (1 Peter 4:1-4), as did the author of Hebrews (Hebrews 10:5-25). The old life of the flesh is replaced by the life of Christ in the Spirit.

The *motive of a true disciple is to please Christ*, knowing that we will be judged at the judgment seat of Christ. This judgment is not for punishment as the world would judge, but to receive an eternal reward (2 Corinthians 5: 9, 10; 1 Corinthians 11:32). His love motivates us to love as he loves and show his sacrificial love.

We will not be perfect, but *our aim will be to be like Christ* (Philippians 3:8-16). *Humility or submission to Christ's suffering love are the key words that reflect death* with Christ as he demonstrated at the Passover.

Submission in Marriage Witness as New Covenant Love

How does the humility of submission change our self-centered self-knowing control, to be a disciple who witnesses to the world of Christ's suffering love? All of the apostles see marriage and the home churches as the starting point to demonstrate this New Covenant love to the world. That was symbolized by "love feasts." How this occurs will be explained in chapter 4.

In Ephesians and Colossians, Paul explains that our transformation begins with election in which Christ frees us from the dominion of darkness. He then proceeds to marriage, the family and social relationships. In Ephesians 5, he calls us to unity and to walk in love as Christ loved us. This requires putting off the old man and being filled with the Spirit, rejoicing together, seeking the will of God. He then speaks "of *submitting to one another* out of reverence for Christ" (5:18-21). He then tells how the wife submits *to Christ* under her husband and the husband submits to Christ in sacrificial love. This proceeds to the submission of children to parents (6:1-4), of the employee to the employer (worst kind— slave to master and master to slave 6:5-9). He concludes saying this is a battle with the devil that we are fighting and we should be armed for battle (6:10-20). Peter traces the same pattern (1 Peter 1 ff.) with different words. He refers to the new birth by the Spirit in hope through Christ. He says we are called to a holy life because we are ransomed from our futile ways by the eternal Passover lamb. We are a chosen race, sojourners in a foreign land. He then says, "Be subject for the Lord's sake to every human institution." He says we should by free from evil, "living as servants of God" (2:13, 16). He calls us to submission to government, to employers and to be willing to suffer as Christ. He then deals more extensively with marriage, calling wives to submit to their husbands in the same way Christ submitted to the Father. To husbands he writes, "Likewise, husbands, live with your wives in an understanding way" recognizing she is equally an heir to the grace of life" (2:21-3:7). He concludes by saying, "Have unity of mind, sympathy, brotherly love, a tender heart and a humble mind. Do not repay evil for evil or reviling for reviling, but on the contrary, bless, for this you were called that you may obtain a blessing" (3:8, 9). He then tells us that we should be prepared to "make a defense to anyone who asks you for a reason for the hope that is in you" (3:15) and be armed for battle.

Conclusions

The unity in marriage of Adam and Eve that God created was the consummation for making creation good. This was all changed to individual self-righteousness by sin, which demonically led male and female to see their differences as evil instead of good. They were driven by the fear of death to pursue the worship of the material creation to show themselves as gods who are equal with God. The New Covenant objective was to break this power of the devil, forgive and reconcile men to God and to each other. God's sovereign elective suffering love in Christ's death and resurrection is the source of the power to turn male and female to trust Christ, and to be free to find that reconciliation by the power of the Holy Spirit. The faith that nothing can separate from the love of God is the key for the Spirit to overcome individual commitment to the flesh. Under the power of God's love, believing men and women can accept and forgive each other and unite in love. The love of Christ is the only answer to end the rebellion of man and his isolation in loneliness.

Paul and all the apostles have a focus on the church as a body that has gifts from Christ to humbly serve and grow in sacrificial love (Ephesians 4:1-16; Romans 12:1-10; 1 Peter 2:4-10; 5). The next chapter discusses how humility in the New Covenant transforms marriage so it can be a loving union that gives joy and witnesses to God's love. This is often misunderstood and wrongly practiced, making it ineffective.

Chapter 4
Important Application of
New Covenant Love in Marriage

New Covenant Love Begins With Man and Wife in Marriage

God's whole revelation in the Bible unfolded to his designed point of the New Covenant. The fundamental beginning point for application is marriage, which is the foundation of all social relationships. From the creation of Adam and Eve, God's command to Noah after the flood, and the purpose of Abraham and Sarah's children, the marriage love produced offspring. This was central to the covenant calling, all designed and leading to the New Covenant in Christ to bless the world.

Only New Covenant love can enable a male and female to be joyfully and continually joined together in marriage, and reflect God's image in the most profound way, extending the kingdom of Christ. Dying to self in marriage brings the Spirit's power and the fruit of the Spirit. If suffering love for Christ does not begin with our closest neighbor or our marriage partner, it will not continue anywhere else. Union with Christ in his love for us that gives us the Spirit's power will be shown in this and the next chapters as the only way we can transcend our selfish fleshly differences, and truly join in bearing the sufferings of this world together. This suffering love alone will show the love of God to the world that is in demonic bondage and trials.

As described at the end of the previous chapter, Paul and other apostles proceeded with the *application* of the Christ's New Covenant love *to marriage* and other human relationships. Only as we are gripped by Christ's love can we love. Christ based the New Commandment of the New Covenant on *his love in us*. Having the servant humility from faith in Christ's love to obey unto death is the only way to be free to unite in love together. This is what gives us joy, hope, and peace through God's love as well as power for our ultimate protection, exaltation, and power. This humility to trust God to love through us is what allows *God to work in us* by the Spirit, and only then can we cease grumbling and complaining against each other (Philippians 2:5-3:12). Such faith in Christ *enables endurance* for the discipline for suffering, pointing to the joy of victory (cf. Hebrews 12:1-7). The sin natures of all men demand God's wrath, and marriage is the most vital place for manifesting New Covenant love of discipleship for Christ's kingdom.

After man and woman's sin and the offense of their differences, their need for each other was enhanced by the curses. These needs, along with their desires from creation motivated by God's general revelation of his law and grace, enabled the race to continue to maintain civilization as well as life to lead to the New Covenant. New Covenant love in marriage was God's planned way to reveal his good love to the world.

Apostolic Application of N. C. Discipleship to Marriage

Paul's Presentation of Humility of Cross in Marriage

The apostle Paul showed that the right perspective for the Christian life is that the Christian should put off the old fleshly man that has died with Christ. As Christ's disciple, the Christian should now live unto the new man by the risen reigning Christ, exercising suffering love through the Spirit, Christ's love and power in us (Ephesians 4:20-24). The key is humble obedience to die with Christ so he can show his suffering love through us. In the following chapter of Ephesians Paul's application of the New Covenant in marriage is explained.

Paul introduced the application of New Covenant by exhorting Christians to *be wise* in the world, *being filled with the Spirit,* to rejoice and not follow the world's escape from the suffering by drinking wine. He began his application by reminding *every person,* male or female, to *"be subject to one another,"* rather than exercising the natural selfish autonomy of the sin nature (cf. Ephesians 5:15-21).

He then defined how this submission works specifically for both husband and wife in marriage. The context is that of Christ's example and submission to die for them on the cross as exhibited to his church in the upper room when he served the bread and wine and initiated the New Covenant with the New Commandment in the upper room. Paul said,

> Wives, *submit* to your own husbands, *as to the Lord*. For the husband is the head of the wife even as Christ is the head of *the church*, his body, and is himself its Savior. Now as the church submits to Christ, so also wives should submit in everything to their husbands.
>
> Husbands, love your wives, *as Christ loved the church* and *gave himself up* for her, that he might sanctify her, having cleansed her by the washing of water with the word, so that he might present the church to himself in splendor, without spot or wrinkle or any such thing, that she might be holy and without blemish.
>
> In the same way (as Christ loves his body, the church) husbands should love their wives as their own bodies. He who loves his wife loves himself. For no one ever hated his own flesh, but nourishes and cherishes it, just as Christ does the church, because we are members of his body.
>
> "Therefore a man shall leave his father and mother and hold fast to his wife, and the two shall become one flesh." This mystery is profound, and I am saying that it refers to Christ and the church. However, let each one of you love his wife as himself, and let the wife see that she respects her husband (Ephesians 5:22-33).

These instructions are the same teaching of submission of men and women maintained throughout the New Testament. Paul repeats the same instructions in Colossians. He said, "And above all these put on love, which binds everything together (gives unity) in perfect harmony." Then in obeying the word of Christ sing and be thankful. He then tells how the wife is to submit to her husband and how husbands are to love their wives as is pleasing to the Lord (Colossians 3:14-28). He repeats these roles in other contexts to be discussed.

Peter's Call to Christ-like Death in Marriage

The apostle Peter taught this same view of submission to show Christ's suffering love as Paul did. In writing to Jewish exiles throughout the Roman Mediterranean world about sanctification by the Holy Spirit of Christ's death (1 Peter 1:1, 2), Peter calls the elect to "*be subject* for the Lord's sake to every human institution" show suffering love, first to all governing powers, and even to abusive slave owners as Christ did in suffering for our sins (1 Peter 2:13-25). He concludes with the application of this New Covenant love to marriage.

For what credit is it if, when you sin and are beaten for it, you endure? But if when you do good and suffer for it you endure, this is a **gracious thing in the sight of God**. For to this you have been called, because *Christ also suffered for you, leaving you an example*, so that you might follow in his steps. He committed no sin, neither was deceit found in his mouth. When he was reviled, he did not revile in return; when he suffered, he did not threaten, but continued entrusting himself to him who judges justly. He himself bore our sins in his body on the tree, that we might die to sin and live to righteousness. By his wounds you have been healed. For you were straying like sheep, but have now returned to the Shepherd and Overseer of your souls.

Likewise, wives, be subject to your own husbands, so that even if some do not obey the word, they may be won without a word by the conduct of their wives, when they see your respectful and pure conduct. Do not let your adorning be external—the braiding of hair and the putting on of gold jewelry, or the clothing you wear— but let your adorning be the hidden person of the heart with the imperishable beauty of a gentle and quiet spirit, which in God's sight is very precious. For this is how the holy women who hoped in God used to adorn themselves, *by submitting to their own husbands*, as Sarah obeyed Abraham, calling him lord. And you are her children, if you *do good* and do not fear anything that is frightening.

Likewise, husbands, live with your wives in an understanding way, showing honor to the woman as the weaker vessel, since they are heirs with you of the grace of life, so that your prayers may not be hindered. Finally, all of you, have unity of mind, sympathy, brotherly love, a tender heart, and a humble mind. Do not repay evil for evil or reviling for reviling, but on the contrary, bless, for to this you were called, that you may obtain a blessing (cf. 1 Peter 2:20-3:9).

Thus Peter shows that the way of sanctification by the Spirit is through submission in suffering love. As the elect of the Old Covenant displayed such love, it is now fulfilled in the New Covenant. This suffering love of wives proceeds from the suffering love of Christ for us and of the husband as under Christ. Peter ends by extending the call to all Christians to be humble showing suffering love as Paul began.

Explanation of Woman's and Man's Roles as N.C. Disciples

Explanation of Wife's Humble Dying Love by Paul
Paul presents the subjection of the wife *"as to the Lord/Christ" through her husband*. As Christ submitted to the Father in suffering love for sinners, a wife demonstrates submission in suffering love to Christ through her husband. This follows the plan of creating Adam first in the Garden of Eden and instructing him in regard to God's will for his work and privileges. Then Eve was created and Adam instructed Eve about God's will, and she was to follow him. This means that the New Covenant husband is to lead her by *seeking to know Christ's will* and not his own. This role of conveying God's will continued from Adam.

The church should teach that the husband's right to leadership puts the responsibility on him to seek and know God's will by prayerful study of God's word. He is held responsible, and is accountable if he does not lead his wife and family to follow Christ's word. Discovering God's will obviously should involve communicating with his wife to know her thoughts and desires.

The wife may think the husband is making a mistake or being selfish because it causes her and the children suffering, when he is actually being led of God. The best illustration is that of Joseph, the husband of Mary, the mother of Jesus. He took her on a long difficult journey to Bethlehem when she was heavy with child and near birth of baby Jesus. There they had to live in a manger under difficult circumstances. When the baby Jesus was under two years old, Joseph took Mary and the baby from Bethlehem to the hostile foreign country of Egypt where he had no job, and where the people of Israel had been enslaved. Then when he went back to Palestine after the death of Herod, Joseph decided not to go to Bethlehem, but to Nazareth to start all over again. All these decisions that were a hardship and threat to Mary and the child were done out of God's direct leading of Joseph by an angel. So a husband's leading may be genuinely of the Spirit yet still be difficult.

Peter says suffering love should be given to a husband who is *not obedient*. When a wife submits with a witness to the suffering love of Christ, *she points the husband to his responsibility to know and lead by the loving will of Christ*. This is especially true if she does not agree with him and thinks he is wrong. Because she understands that she is following Christ's will in submission to her husband, she can be *free knowing God will guide and protect her* through her husband's decisions, good or bad. She is dying to self and losing her life under the control of Christ's Spirit so that in the end she will be rewarded and exalted.

Also this trust in God and respect for him will influence her husband who wants to please her, and to have her intimacy, help, and pleasure. Moreover, her submission will release power in her for maximum pleasure from her husband in their physical union. Her complete surrender will usually be manifest in her obvious deep pleasure, which will gain her husband's trust and desire to please her more in every way.

Most importantly, her aspect of the image of God in the love of their marriage union will be communicated to the world through the gospel by her life of faith. Through their uniting love, they will expand the work of Christ through their children. Her submission to her husband "as to the Lord" shows that the objective is to give God glory in their union. The power to her by submission in these ways will be explained further in other chapters.

Conflict with her husband will only cause a reaction and her loss of influence, while submission and trust can make him want her help and influence, and gives him the desire to help her. Her role in submission in suffering love motivates unity of the two different aspects of God's image before the community and through the children, and extends the witness to God's love to the world. *Showing the image of God's love is the main purpose* of suffering love by the woman and the man.

Husband's Submission as Head under Christ by Paul

The New Covenant love of the husband and his submission to Christ is connected to *the powerful idea of Christ's loving authority over the church,* which is his bride. Jesus is the head of his body the church and his suffering love has been shown through union to his people in the church as the Savior. The cross and death of Christ is the main and only source of seeing suffering love. This is integral to the concept of the New Covenant command to "love one another *as I have loved you."* It is in this context of the husband's faith in Christ's power and love that the wife is to be submissive to her husband, and he as the head "in everything."

Paul prayed that the Christians might have knowledge of Christ's authority to fulfill the blessing for his people,

> [I am praying] that you may know what is the hope to which he has called you, what are the riches of his glorious inheritance in the saints, and what is the immeasurable greatness of his power toward us who believe, according to the working of his great might that he worked in Christ when he raised him from the dead and seated him at his right hand in the heavenly places, far above all rule and authority and power and dominion, and above every name that is named, not only in this age but also in the one to come. *And he put all things under his feet and gave him as head over all things to the church, which is his body,* the fullness of him who fills all in all (Ephesians 1:18-23).

This emphasis of Christ as the head of the church is extended through Ephesians into chapter 2, where Christ is shown as the authority over every believer, including the Gentiles. In chapters 3 and 4, Paul talks about the Holy Spirit and his work to produce the love of Christ in his church. In chapters 4 and 5, Paul further shows the application of Christ's New Covenant love through the individuals in the church.

The ***husband's authority is from his submission to Christ as head*** to show sovereign love. The husband dies to self to the leadership of Christ. The effort of the demonic influence in the world is to obscure and sever Christ's headship over the husband from the idea of his headship over the wife. This reduces the wife's relationship with her husband to a purely humanistic relationship. It also makes it very easy to appear that the woman's submission is one of a slave. Indeed, any abuse of the wife comes from a disobedient husband.

To understand the removal of authority, take the following example from the military. Removing the authority of the commanding general from over the lieutenant (who is to instruct the privates in carrying out his orders for the nation's benefit) would let the lieutenant arbitrarily do anything he desires. That would allow personal abuse of the army's privates and destroy the army's objective for the people. Removing the husband's relationship from Christ is much worse than this illustration, because it removes not only the controlling authority, but ***the caring love required for the wife to respond to him,*** which is stated fully here for the husband in his submission in the marriage. If the husband is not held and motivated by the sovereign love of Christ, he will not and cannot suffer in love for his wife. Knowing Christ's love will prevail against all evil conditions or abusive words or acts of his wife, this enables him to suffer for Christ and for her sake.

Paul spells out the husband's submission in leading his wife, saying that the husband should love his wife "***as Christ loved*** the church and ***gave himself up*** for her." This is a clear application of the New Commandment of the New Covenant (cf. John 13:34, 35). The husband as Christ's disciple is to die to self so that he may minister to his wife. She is to be loved even when she is selfish and when she fails. Christ also accepts his bride the church in her many failures and sins.

Christ's objective of suffering love for the church sets forth the objectives of the husband's for his wife. The objective of Christ's love for the church is to enable her to fulfill her abilities, or be "holy and without blemish" when she is presented to the Father. This is the purpose Christ has for every chosen individual in his church (Ephesians 1:4, Colossians 1:22). The husband is to guide and furnish blessings of grace from God's word for her to please God. Jesus ***does not compel but lovingly motivates,*** guides, accepts and forgives when she fails. The husband is not, therefore, called to find fault and dictate legalistic improvement. He shows his wife what is right prayerfully in love from Christ's word.

A husband also should enable his wife to develop in her abilities and opportunities, as Christ seeks to improve the church. Further education and use of equipment, if she has the ability and desire, will help her husband and the family. He therefore is to help her in all she does to manage the family, and to assist her in assisting him to provide. To this Paul adds Christ's creation of Eve as Adam's partner ***from his own flesh*** to be equal and like him. She is a part of him by nature, and loving her is logical because he loves himself.

Loving and caring for your wife is a fulfillment of loving your neighbor as yourself or loving yourself. The link to the idea of the second commandment (Lev. 19:18) is seen in that in the Song of Solomon where the feminine form of neighbor is repeatedly used (1:9, 15; 2:2, 10, 13; 4:1, 7; 5:2; 6:4). The words used for "caring for" the fleshly body are "nourishes and cherishes." The Greek word (*ektrephō*) for "nourish" is applied to feeding children to help them grow as in Ephesians 6:4, but here for the wife, is used with the strengthened form, showing progressive development, no doubt spiritually and physically. The husband who argues to get his wife to change and improve is acting from his sin nature, and will receive a reaction. But by sacrificial, and caring love, his wife will want to respond positively with his help to improve.

There are many ways a man should show suffering love. The curse of nature gave the man the calling to work hard to provide for his wife and their children. Therefore, it is the man's calling and demonstration of New Covenant love to work hard to provide for his wife and all his family. Paul said, "If anyone does not provide for his relatives and especially for the members of his household, he has denied the faith and is worse than an unbeliever" (1 Timothy 5:8). If the man's work is prosperous and he has wealth, he is enjoined to share with those in need with a view of treasures in heaven (cf. 1 Timothy 6:17-19). Paul saw idle men as not showing the tradition of Christian love (cf. 2 Thessalonians 3:6-9).

I have had several women complain to me and end up divorcing their husbands because they neglected providing, leaving the burden of family provision to their wives. This failing in the call for sacrificial unselfish provision for the wife increasingly grows in degrading societies, as in America and the whole Western world today.

The word "cherish" gives a sense of warm gentleness of care, both physically and especially spiritually (cf. Septuagint 1 King 1:1, 2; 1 Thessalonians 2:7). The implication of this may be seen in English with men being gentle (gentlemen).

Man was made to be the leader to communicate God's message with authority. That is why the male nature is more decisive, and he normally has a stronger, lower voice. His physical design was to be the aggressor to woo and attract a wife; to acquire her love; and find and give pleasure to deliver the seed for new offspring in extending Christ's dominion to the world. He finds satisfaction in his submission to her attraction, which allows him to have headship over her in her loving submission to him. His nature of strength for headship should often be conveyed in warmth of concern as expressed in Paul's words to "nourish and cherish." This modifies the man's calling to be the head in the union of marriage. These aspects of godly maleness show God's image in union in love with that of the woman's in marriage.

Paul Concludes Linking One Man and Wife to Creation

Paul concluded the application of New Covenant discipleship love in marriage by two important relationships to Christ—Christ's beginning plan at *Creation* and marriage of Christ to his *church.*

He referred back to the Genesis 2:24 statement that Jesus had summarized as God's intent in the beginning. "Therefore a man shall leave his father and mother and hold fast to his wife, and the two shall become one flesh." This plan for marriage revealed that all future marriages should be separate units so that the union of two aspects of God's image would, in successive marriages, also reflect his sacrificial love. Also, this statement makes it plain that the love of man and woman for each other is of primary importance and supersedes love of parents for children and children for parents. Therefore all subsequent marriages by offspring should be uniquely separate and require leaving parents.

Paul ended his call to submission in New Covenant obedience by claiming Christ's suffering for his church is a *mystery*. He then reaffirmed the man should love his wife as himself, and the woman should *respect* her husband. The Greek word used for respect is the same he used to introduce the subject in which he said, "submit to one another out of *reverence* for Christ" (Ephesians 5:21). It is the word for "fear," not in the sense of "terror" but of "awe," by the power of Christ's authority given to her husband to speak for him. The mystery is that the church (of which the husband and wife are a part) is already spiritually united to him as his bride by the Holy Spirit. His bride the church will be united openly to him at the marriage supper of the Lamb at Christ's return when he will drink the wedding cup (Luke 22:16; Matthew 22:2ff; Revelation 21:2, 3).

Paul continued to extend application of submission in love to one another begun in Ephesians 5:21 to children and parents, and to work relationships, such as slave and master, and showing how the union of love in marriage influences all other tangent relationships (Ephesians 6:1-9).

Peter's Explanation for Application of New Covenant Love
Peter also presents the submission of Christ in the context of submission to all governing authorities and slaves to their abusive authorities. He links these to Christ's submission in which he

suffered unjustly when giving his life in atonement (1 Peter 2:18-25). Peter then follows this act by presenting the roles of submission of man and woman. He begins by encouraging the woman to use the power of her trust in Christ's suffering that led God to give him victory. Peter ended with a reminder to the man of God's power to reinforce his accountability to him in his leadership of his wife, and then gave this idea of submission in suffering love an application to all relationships (1 Peter 3:1-9).

Christ, who committed no sin but suffered for our sin, is the wife's guiding shepherd in the suffering as she, like Christ, subjectively obeys her husband (1 Peter 2:21; 3:1-6). She is to show suffering love to her disobedient husband,[18] and to point him to Christ to whom he is responsible. Peter teaches that the wife's beautiful, quiet love for Christ in her heart may cause the disobedient husband "to be won without a word by the conduct...." The wife, who suffers unafraid by heart obedience and with respect and pure conduct, is reminded that this suffering brings God's support and power, when outward adornment for beauty cannot. The wife is reminded that Sarah was obedient to Abraham without fear, and became the mother of the nation of Israel.

Peter then reminds husbands to be **understanding** of their wives. This certainly involves hearing their views, and **showing honor** to them for who they are, and in their roles being not as strong as they are (weaker vessels). Peter then reminds the husband that the believing wife is *an heir with you of the grace of life* (1 Peter 3:7). She will be equal in eternity after the resurrection. Paul also warns that in eternity the complementary aspects of male and female will not apply, and also race and economic status will be abolished (Galatians 3:28, 29). Jesus had previously declared equality and no marriage, with no gender or racial discrimination after the resurrection (cf. Mark 12:24, 25; Matthew 8:5-11; Luke 13:29).

---

[18] Extreme, irrational, meaningless, life-threatening danger in Scripture calls for escape so extreme wife abuse is not the issue here (cf. 1 Samuel 19:10ff; John 10:39; 2 Corinthians 11:33).

Moreover, Peter warned the husband that the living Christ will deal with such a husband if he does not repent, and God will not answer his prayers, and will cause him frustration in work, resulting in scarcity and anxiety (1 Peter 3:7). This is in agreement with the Old Testament (cf. Malachi 2:13-16). Peter reminded the husband and wife and all, that God sees all our acts and calls us to return good for evil (1 Peter 3:8-12).

Peter concluded with the way Paul began his application of husband and wife: by saying Christian love by submission applies to all Christians. And he said that "God resists the proud but gives grace to the humble" (1 Peter 5:5; cf. James 4:6).

Examples of God's Working in Suffering Love

One illustration of influence by suffering love was told to me by a young woman who came to Christ through our ministry, and later went to France to work for Christ. A woman in her church told of how her husband drank excessively, cursed her, and was harsh. The Christian worker found that the wife was arguing and seeking to make her husband change. She turned with her to Peter's instruction and instructed the wife to show such suffering love. The wife asked, "How?" The missionary made a suggestion to her, saying "Fix your husband's favorite meal, dress in your most beautify negligee, and welcome him home with a grateful attitude." The shocked woman did as instructed to show Christ's love to the husband by showing good for evil. She returned a few days later to the missionary telling how her husband had been converted and radically changed.

To a group of women, I once taught Peter's words of the importance of a wife suffering when her husband is disobedient, and I told the aforementioned story. One woman in the group responded angrily, saying, "Been there, done that, it didn't work." Her words revealed she was not dead to self and suffering *for Christ's sake*, but only sought to be nice to her husband to manipulate him for herself. Therefore she did not have New Covenant submissive obedience to Christ to suffer *for his glory*. As a counselor, I have seen many instances when women want men to change for their benefit, or for "Christian improvement." This is another method of getting what they want.

I recently counseled with a couple who was separated. The husband had tried to serve the Lord, but had been accused wrongly by those involved. He became angry with God for not vindicating him. The husband took an honorable, secular job where for a time he tried to witness. But eventually he joined his worldly customers in drinking and carousing. God stopped answering his prayers for his work. He lost his good job, one of his children became very ill, and he became miserable and even had demonic thoughts of suicide. Repenting and dying to himself renewed his love for Christ. Christ gave him forgiveness and faith with suffering love, and turned his life around.

Why New Covenant Suffering Love Manifested in Marriage

Christ's New Covenant suffering love ends the wrongs of Adam and Eve's sin nature. By faith in Christ's love, a husband and wife humble themselves, no longer seeing themselves as wise as God and being the ones who know good and evil. They become obedient to death as Christ, showing love for God and for each other.

The suffering love of man and woman in marriage gives them blessing in unity, but the main purpose of marriage is to show God's goodness and love to their children and the world. In the place Christ is preparing for his bride in the New Jerusalem, there will no longer be marriage. In refuting the unbelieving Sadducees about their views of marriage, Jesus said, "You are wrong, because you know neither the Scriptures nor the power of God. For in the resurrection they neither marry nor are given in marriage, but are like the angels in heaven" (Matthew 22:29, 30). Male and female will be individuals with their own separate rewards. This teaching had in view the call of the great commandment to love God and to love our neighbor (Matthew 2:34-40).

In Christ's covenant male and female are equally heirs to eternity. Peter and Paul taught that while their roles of husband and wife now reflected God's love, in eternity that witness of love will no longer be needed.(1 Peter 3:9; Galatians 3:28, 29). The reason is that his disciples who have taken up the cross to die with him will enjoy perfect love in heaven such as Christ and the Father had enjoyed. That love is what they are heir to. Jesus prayed that they may be with him in heaven and be one as he and the Father are one (John 17:20-24). He said, "I made known to them your name and I will continue to make it known, that the love with which you have loved me may be in them, and I in them" (17:26). Therefore, the witness of his suffering love, and the extension of the kingdom through their children will no longer be needed. All men and women in heaven will enjoy the complete perfect love of God.

Single Men and Women Uniquely Show God's Image of Love

God's great love is sufficient in this world for certain people who have this gift, and they, as singles, witness to God's love in devotion to Christ. The world always tries to distort the image of Christ, and falsely claim he was sexually involved with Mary Magdalene or someone else. Jesus did not marry or need to marry because he experienced the perfect love of the Father in his earthly sojourn. Jesus spoke of some who had this special gift of serving singly (Matthew 19:10-12). The apostle Paul continued as a single man, having experienced the vision of God's love in heaven, witnessing to the love of Christ (2 Corinthians 12:1-10). While marriage was God's normal calling, Paul saw his own gift as a single serving out of love for Christ as desirable for others (1 Corinthians 7:6-17).

Conclusions

New Covenant love is the only way to unite individual men and women who each see themselves as best, and who compete to change and exceed the other. Only New Covenant disciples who believe in God's sovereign love to accept and give eternal life can humble themselves and let Christ love through them. Then the wife can die to self to trust God to lead and care for her and the children by her husband. Only by Christ's love can she feel free to communicates her ideas, but quietly humbly submit in everything to him. The man is to let Christ love his wife through him as his own body, and as Christ loved us, die to self in sacrificing for her. Both husband and wife surrender and transfer the power of their whole sexual identity and control to each other in loving unity. The love of Christ frees from self to fulfill union in marriage.

Chapter 5
Marriage Unity and Children

Importance and Purpose of Children to God

In a world where there is sickness, weakness, and mortality, having children is an intuitive essential for the continuation of the race. Children that inherit and reflect our features and look to us for care, give us a sense of pride and significance. A man's power to give a woman the ability to conceive and have a child is awesome. For a woman to conceive and produce a child is very wonderful and exceedingly important. Watching our baby develop and grow to reason, speak, walk, and do creative things, is of great interest, gives joyful entertainment, and is an accomplishment for mankind. Having a child mature, learn, work, and take responsibilities is deeply satisfying as a contribution to civilization. Experiencing a child's love stirs deep emotion. Experiencing their suffering, pain, and sorrow touches the depth of our souls and motivates us to respond with help. When our children react and rebel we are deeply hurt. Sharing the worship of God with a child gives a sense of maximum heavenly fulfillment.

When a civilization declines in desire to have and care for children, its selfish interest is nearing its destructive end. Having children was not our idea and not in our power to produce, but comes from God. Mankind, male and female, accomplish most by extending his culture from God-given intelligence through his children. This chapter will help us see the importance, delight, proper relationship, and eternal praiseworthiness of having children. This will include something about how each parent can influence and best help train children to be mature responsible adults and glorify God. This will also be basic for understanding Trinitarian theology, and will be appreciated and give understanding in and from later chapters.

Parenthood is Revealed in God Himself and Very Important

An integral aspect of the person of God is the parent/child relationship. To love a child is *integral to who God is*. God chose Abraham and the nation of Israel to be his inherited family through which to save all men. But all nations of people at the beginning of their civilizations have believed in one Great Spirit or High God who rules and works through His Son (Romans 1:20-25). [19] Paul claimed all men knew God and then rejected him for worship of natural creation. This fact about all peoples was discovered by the greatest scientific ethnologist in objective comparative religion, J. Schmidt, and the science of archaeology has confirmed this of all nations.[20] The quality of God's power and deity is known by all men through general revelation of creation. By this knowledge they create a culture and expand and continue it through their children.

However, the Bible declared that God the Father has *manifested himself* in his *only begotten Son*, and nowhere else. The unity of one God is manifested in the Trinity which includes his perfect and complete revelation of his character in his Son. "No man has seen God at any time; the *only begotten* of the Father, he has revealed him" (John 1:18). Jesus Christ is the unique Son and therefore made God known as no other, because Jesus was God who came in the flesh as his Son. No other religion rightly has claimed God incarnate.

Jesus said, "If you had known me, you would have known my Father also. From now on you do know him and have seen him" (John 14:7, 9; cf. Col 1:19).While mankind previously had the understanding that the One Sky God of the universe had a son, *the only Son who was begotten* into the world was Jesus. He is the only clear revelation of God the Father. The true test of Christian belief is the belief that God the Father came as his Son in the flesh (1 John 4:2, 3). To deny that God has a Son who came into the world is the pivot point of heresy. True worship of God

---

[19] Carl Wilson, *Man Is Not Enough*, Chapter Two.
[20] Wilson, *True Enlightenment*, 511-513. E.g. Sumerians worshiped An and son Enlil, Egyptians worshiped Horus and son Re, Uranus and his son Zeus, et al.

understands and is based on the familial nature of God and that the perfect revelation of the Father came only though his Son. God's final revelation confirms the importance of the paternal relationship in his eternal nature. Parental relationship does not originate from nature, but from God himself and the essence of God. The model for parenthood is God as Father and is shown to us in Jesus' dependence and communication with him. Jesus taught us to depend on, trust God as father, and to come to God as Father.

God's Creation of Man Shows His Desire for Children

God created Adam from the dust of the ground, and by His breath or Spirit entering him in personal confrontation. In the Garden, God's face was toward Adam as his child. Eve was made by a creative act from Adam. There was no sensuous or fleshly involvement by God in creating either. Adam and all of mankind, both male and female, were made as children of God with his likeness and image. He (man and woman) are called sons of God (Luke 3:38; Genesis 5:1-3). These acts of creation show God's desire to reveal his likeness in the world. God had a perfect love between him and his eternal Son throughout eternity, and other children of men were *not needed* by him, but were a free desire of his creation, as was his desire to redeem men (John 10:17, 18). God's eternal Son became incarnate because the first man failed to continue to reveal God's image as a son because of sin. Jesus Christ is therefore the second Adam that came to give and renew life lost by sin (1 Corinthians 15:45-47).

Disciples of Christ who live for him have his Spirit to show his glory in the world (John 17:10; 2 Corinthians 3:18). Those who accept Jesus as God's Son in the flesh are born of God's Spirit and now are accepted and adopted into the family of God as his children. The world does not now recognize Christians as God's sons, but at the return of Christ and the resurrection, the believer will be changed into his glory to be like Christ. Having humans as sons eternally is God's plan in Christ. Those humans who become eternal sons through Christ are born by human generation into the world. In the act of union, God's love is shown as the main purpose of marriage.

To exemplify the importance of his love in the union of marriage, God calls some couples to be infertile, which shows marriage alone is valuable to reveal God's love. If no children are born, a husband and wife may still *know* each other and reach a deep expression of marriage love for union. Many childless marriages may witness to God's sacrificial love between a man and woman according to God's purposes in that marriage. This reveals that the oneness of marriage love has a designed *purpose in itself.* That does not diminish the responsibility to produce children when we can, nor does the priority of man and woman becoming one to demonstrate God's love reduce the importance of valuing any child that is born.

God at times calls individuals as special instruments to serve as singles who have the commitment to show his sacrificial love as an individual. Paul and others were amazing examples of God's love for him and others. He commends men and women to this calling, especially in times of world tribulation, while saying that marriage is God's normal plan (1 Corinthians 7:6, cf. whole chapter). A single person so committed and serving Christ shows the value of the individual with God's image as God's child, as does the lack of marriage for men and women in heaven to which both men and women are heirs. This will be further explained.

God's Purposes for Men and Women to Have Children

Revelation of God's Continued Presence as Creator

Scripture reveals several occasions that show that God wanted men to have children in his image and created them to bear them. As husband and wife grow to know each other, they unite the two aspects of God's image into one by union in the flesh. That act of union may or may not result in producing a new child. As mentioned, the birth of a child involves not only the fleshly mechanics of God's working in nature, but of *God's creative working* in the process of sperm and egg uniting. Eve said, "I have gotten a man *by the help of the Lord*' (Genesis 4:1). That means that every new child is a product of God's special working and design as mentioned in Chapter 1. The fact that God creates the child in the womb shows he desires us to have children for his purposes.

Multiplication of Children to Extend His Kingdom

Another indication that God wants marriages to produce children is that **he commanded** Adam and Eve to *"multiply and fill the earth."* This is the third indication of God's purpose for children. *Man's dominion over all the earth is made possible by begetting children* in his likeness and extending their control throughout the whole world. Adam and Eve were finite and local. Their dominion began in a local garden and they and their children were to extend it to the whole earth. A progressive Adamic dynasty was a necessary part of God's plan to extend his rule through Adam and Eve. This ended with the abuse of marriage and God's judgment in the worldwide flood. In beginning over again after the flood, Noah and his wife and sons were again also commanded **to multiply and fill the earth** (Genesis 9:1).

God's Plan of Redemption Involved Children

The whole picture was changed when Adam and Eve sinned and died to God spiritually and were excluded from God's presence in the Garden of Eden. The devil working through the wise serpent had deceived Eve and Adam, and led them into a condition of rebellion and spiritual death for all men. "By one man Adam, sin entered into the world and death by sin, and so death passed to all men, because all sinned" (Romans 5:12). The first child that God enabled Eve to conceive from Adam was Cain, who was a disbeliever and a murderer. The sinfulness of the first child confirmed the *need for redemption of all successive children.* Abel, the second child, recognized this need by offering the bloody sacrifice of a lamb. This symbol of death for sin as the way of righteousness was hated by Cain.

This revealed another important purpose of God in wanting his people to have children in marriage, which was that God's plan for the *coming of the Messiah to save man* from his sin and its consequences are *linked in his plan by childbirth*. God promised Eve that "her *seed (child)* would crush the head of the serpent, and the serpent would bruise his heel" (Genesis 3:15). Abraham's call to form a family for God was for him to have *a seed* that would bless all nations (Genesis 12:1-3). That depended on Sarah having a child by a miracle in old age. The birth of a child who might be the Messiah was the desire of every Hebrew woman, and the birth of this special man who would save the people was constantly in the thought of the nation. The birth of *a child who would be Immanuel, God with us,* who would save his people, was prevalent in the prophetic period (Micah 5:2; Isaiah 9:7 and elsewhere). Mary's divine conception was the fulfillment of that plan to give a woman a child to redeem lost men (Luke 1:26-38). The Shekinah glory of God's presence that overshadowed the tabernacle and temple, and over Christ and the three apostles on the mount, "overshadowed" Mary, making possible the divine conception (Exodus 13:21;19:9; Luke 1:35;9:34; Matthew 17:5)

Knowledge of God's Saving Love is Extended to Children

God's people were told that they should *teach God's will to their children* in various conditions at all times of day and night. They should do this to perpetuate the faith in God to love him and their neighbor (Deuteronomy 6:6, 7). The Psalmist reminded the people of Israel that they were to teach the law to their children, who would teach it to their children in successive generations (Psalm 78:4). Parents having children before whom they lived and taught the law of God was central to the nation's fulfillment of its covenant with God. Through believing children the love of God was to be extended and perpetrated.

In the New Testament, children of believers were important to Christ and his church. Jesus said, "Let the children come to me, do not hinder them for *to such belongs the kingdom of God*" (Mark 10:14). He took a little child and said to His disciples, "Unless you turn and become like children you will never enter the kingdom of heaven" (Matthew 18:3). Jesus is saying that a new disciple should be childlike but he is also saying that we should include children. Peter said the gift of the Holy Spirit and salvation was promised to "you and *your children* and for all who are far off whom the Lord your God calls to himself" (Acts 2:39). Our mission of witness for Christ should first begin with our children. Having and including children to expand Christ's kingdom is part of the Great Commission. (cf. chapter 9).

Having and Managing Children Gives Victory over Devil

Paul taught that the ability to manage his children was a father's and husband's responsibility in order to be a leader (1 Timothy 3:4; Titus 1:6). He also taught that women should have children, and thereby they would "be saved" from the temptations of the devil in the world (1 Timothy 2:15). Paul found that young women without husbands and children tended to be gossips and busybodies caught up in sensual desires and turning aside to follow Satan (1 Timothy 5:13-15). Only when the church faced a crisis of persecution that required extreme dedication in service were Christians encouraged to refrain from marriage (1 Corinthians 7:5, 25-33). Jesus also had warned of being pregnant in tribulation time (Matthew 24:19).

Building Cultures Reveal Man's Divine Origin to World

Mankind cannot build a cultural civilization without successive generations of children. The differing gifts of each individual must work together to build a culture, and this requires successive generations that can continue what has been learned to continue to build. Culture of civilization is the product of God's creative working mind through successive generations. Brilliance of culture reflects God. When God is rejected, the people deconstruct the culture and remove social relationships that are meaningful. The sinful nature of anti-Christ people will seek to cease having children to be free from responsibility.

Each child is different by God's plan and purpose, but all children are made in his image (cf. Psalm 139:13, 14; Jeremiah 1:4, 5). The different abilities of each person are critical for building each successive culture through the children. When Stephen Hawking produced the history of modern physics and astronomy he entitled it, *On the Shoulders of Giants*. All but about 100 of the 1264 pages are about Christian scientists, but this was not mentioned.[21] David P. Goldman has commented on the facts that culture reveals man's divine origin.

> Why do people raise children? Human beings are the only animals whose continuity depends on culture as much as it does on DNA. We cannot make a future for ourselves without our past. All cultures exist to ward off the presentiment of death. Breaking continuity with the past implies that our lives have no meaning past our own existence.

Goldman then refers to a statement by Harvard Professor Daniel Bell,

> In this sense, ***religion is the awareness of a moment of transcendence***, the passage out of the past, from which one has to come (and to which one is bound), to a new concept of the self as moral agent, freely accepting the past (rather than being shaped by it).[22] (Emphasis mine)

Man's Pride and Lust to be Wise as God Rejects Culture

The culture shows divine intelligence and therefore reminds the sinner of God. When a culture reaches a point of brilliance, and man knows much about nature, he begins to think he created it on his own from nature. When man denies God to assert his individual freedom, he must therefore deconstruct culture. He also seeks to make all people equal materially, sexually, and economically.

---

[21] Stephen Hawing, editor, *On the Shoulders of Giants*, (Philadelphia: Running Press, 2002), cf. pages 1-1160 and Einstein, 1161-1164.
[22] David P. Goldman, *How Civilizations Die*, (Washington D. C.: Regnery Publishing Company: 2001), 19, 20.

When secular minds try to remove differences, they will hinder and destroy the civilizations that God enabled them to build through the successive generations.

Moreover, these secularly minded people then have a propensity toward death as did Nietzsche, Freud, Kierkegaard, Derrida, and others. Man and women who reject God for material prosperity want fewer children. This results in moving toward ending humanity, which changes culture. The unbelieving mind then moves toward urbanity and unity through new means of communication and transportation. This appears progressive, but is deceptively ending civilization that was built by faith in God. The rejection of God in culture promotes infertility.

By man's sin, the natural process of producing children may have been genetically damaged, and on occasion the child may be imperfect. While the imperfections are demonic, God enables the child to be born, and it is a product of God's sovereign will. God's attendance in the oneness of man and woman in their union to produce a child shows God's purpose for each child and children in general. Some "defective" children have amazing gifts. Some of these gifts include intuitive musical or artistic abilities, which reveal God's working even through something that seems defective. These gifts and the children that possess them build character and patience in parents and add to the culture.

Avoiding Responsibility for Children in Various Ways

For marriage to fulfill God's plan, and for a happy marriage and family it is *highly important to correctly evaluate the question of "family planning,"* contraception, abortion, and infanticide. By 1910, some form of contraception had been used by 98% of women in America, and since the 1970's the use of contraceptives have been spreading to most developing countries. Whole societies such as China have legalized limits to children. The extreme of selfish individualism that avoids the responsibility of producing children is homosexuality. In a later chapter the threat of declining fertility for world civilization and growth of homosexuality will be considered.

Birth control is not something new. It is historically known as far back as the time of the earliest civilizations, and is in written documents back to the early times of Abraham and the patriarchs. The Egyptian papyrus Kahun Gynaecological Papyrus, dealing with issues of women's health including contraceptives, is dated 1850 B. C. Very early silver coins from Cyrene (modern Libya) indicate birth control. Greeks such as Hippocrates, Theophrastus, and others discussed birth control back in the seventh century B. C. The Romans also had various kinds of contraceptives, such as condoms produced from animal skins. China reported birth control also in the seventh century B. C. The use of chemicals in plants, sponges, and condoms are not new, but modern means are the most sophisticated.

This is of great interest, especially for women of child-bearing age, and also to men who want freedom from responsibility. There are various reasons for birth control usage. There are hundreds of thousands of women whose health is involved and many who die from gynecological problems. But the main reason is individualistic greed by reducing the number of children for which to be responsible. After a civilization loses faith in God, and reaches a highly productive materialistic stage, usually about after 250 years, it becomes urbanized, and more advanced in communication and distribution of goods. Then, the increased number of children becomes a hindrance to wealth. The turning point is when the educated elite shift from the worship of God to nature worship of Baal or mammon and their goddesses. At that point women want to have fewer children so they can compete with men and be independently free. Then various ways of reducing children are used.

The Hebrew people became a threat to the Egyptians in the fifteenth century B.C. because they had a high birth rate, and numerically were becoming a threat to gain authority. At that time the Pharaohs passed laws to kill or prevent Hebrew births. God's death angel killing the first born Egyptians and passing over the Hebrews was the cause of the Exodus. One of the reasons the Christian church spread to dominance in the Roman Empire was the birth control of the Romans, and the high birth rate of the Christians. Christians had great affection for each other, practicing loving monogamy, and not destroying their children. This is reflected in the writings of the post-apostolic fathers that contrast the differences of Christians with the world (cf. the very early *Epistle to Diognetus*, chapter v).

Birth Control can be in God's Will

The Bible does reveal practicing birth control can be in God's will. God's own plan at times put birth control as a higher priority than having children. Sarai and Abram were restrained from having children until she was 90 years old and Abram was 100. There are many other such incidences in Scripture. Even at the time of the birth of Christ, Elizabeth and Zacharias were kept from having children until they were old. This was God's way of showing those children were for special redemptive purposes. These times of birth control by God showed his power and control in history over whom and why these children were born.

God has given man the intelligence to know how to find methods of birth control, and that intelligence has been used throughout history. It is reasonable that God can simply lead Christian believers to practiced birth control without it being wrong. But since birth control and elimination of children is most often used when civilizations have turned to trusting wealth or mammon instead of God, and man and women want freedom for sexual pleasure without responsibility, the choice to use birth control should be based on a clear conscience for faith that any man or woman is being lead of God for his purpose and will. "So, whether you eat or drink, or whatever you do, do all to the glory of God" (1 Corinthians 10:31). "But whoever has doubts is condemned if he eats, because the eating is not from faith. For whatever does not proceed from faith is sin." (Romans 14:23).

Every couple must be convinced by the Holy Spirit that they are being led for divine purposes in these matters. Some reasons for prayerful considerations may be: for a critical ministry purpose, in times of war and great danger, for a woman's health or when a man's health severely limits his ability to provide. Advice of medical doctors is not enough, especially when abortion is recommended. My daughter and her husband were advised by two specialists to abort their baby, but after prayer they chose to deliver him, and their son is healthy, attractive, and a very capable Christian. The parents of Tim Tebow, the renowned Christian football star, were advised to abort. Parental convenience and prosperity are not valid reasons.

Marriage and Parent and Child Relationship

Love of Marriage Should Have Priority over Children

It is important to see that the *love of husband and wife should be above that of the children, as the general rule.* This does not mean children should be less loved, but they should never be allowed to supersede that to distort the oneness of love in the marriage union. God created Eve and brought her to Adam to complete his life. They were the only two in the Garden and their oneness was the condition resulting from God's initial created work. That was the ideal original condition of the man and wife in marriage in the Garden before man sinned. Thus the two aspects of God's image joined in marriage was the primary condition before there were children. While children were in God's plan, the children were secondary.

Moreover, before Adam and Eve had children they were told that their children when grown should be united in a monogamous marriage and *grown children should leave the home for forming their own union* (Genesis 2:24). Jesus and the apostle Paul refer to this statement by God as the ideal, so that the union of the husband and wife is the primary unit in God's plan (Matthew 19:5, 6; Ephesians 5:31).

Unless the husband and wife intimately know each other, and grow in trust so that they achieve intimate and satisfying love, they will not demonstrate that love to their children. The greatest security for children is to know that their parents love each other. I mentioned this in teaching on marriage, and had people in the class repeatedly confirm this. In mentioning this recently, a young man came up to me and shared an experience he had with his two-year-old son. He said he kissed the boy and then his wife kissed the boy. Then his son put his hands behind both their heads and drew them together to kiss each other. This illustrates the point

When a man and wife put their love for each other first, they will try to transfer their power over the child to be shared with the other spouse. The mother has a very strong bond with her children from birth and due to nursing them, which by nature, the father cannot have. Men are denied that powerful influence on children that is afforded to women. Little children continue to have a strong affinity for the mother from her early nurture. Until recently (with DNA tests) man's recognition as the father had to be given to him voluntarily by the wife. For this reason, almost all societies have designated children's identity by their father. In the Bible the genealogies lists the child as "the son/daughter of" Abzug etc. In the western world this has been done by the mother and child having the father's last name.

Love for the father seems to be intuitive. Even babies seem to gain security by love and affection from the father, and sense his difference and abilities. As kids grow, they like to have their dad play with them, wrestle, and throw them around with his superior strength. As the child grows, within the stable marriages, the father establishes the controls, and supports his wife in enforcing these. In adolescence, boys and girls tend to act independently, and their father must see that they respect not only him but their mother. Children find a sense of protection and look for provision from the father. A selfish father can buy gifts and give them from him, rather than joining his wife in giving the gift. The mutual gratitude and affection of the husband and wife for each other communicates appreciation for the two sexes.

As children grow to puberty, the submission of the mother to her husband *sets the example for them to obey* and recognize authority. While respect for her husband is commanded, the mother must exemplify her respect in word and acts, but involve the children in respect. When there is a major question a mother can do this by saying, "Your father is the head of our home, let's go ask him what to do." These acts and others of the primacy of the husband and wife as belonging to and supporting each other give tremendous security to children, and encourage the acceptance of the male and female differences of the image of God in their parents.

After children are born, if the husband or wife is selfish, the result will be that the either of them may seek to possess the child, and play the child against the other parent. This creates insecurity for the child and the marriage. Continued strong conflict in a home between husband and wife where children are played against the other sex can produce homosexuality.[23] Conflict, divorce, or loss of a parent is very disturbing to children and can cause psychological problems. Both parents are needed for discipline. Many gang members and imprisoned criminals come from dysfunctional or single parent families. Of course, God can give special grace to single parents who have lost a spouse to overcome absence of the other sex. But these are exceptions.

Violation of Primacy of Husband and Wife Marriage Love
Either fathers or mothers can wrongly tend to put a child or children first in their lives over their spouse. Feminist movements have violated the primacy of the oneness in marriage, and selfishly tended to put women's rights to the children even to exclude the fathers. In modern America, the Supreme Court ruling on women's independent rights to abortion was extended by a Pennsylvania court so that the father could not have a say in the aborting of the child. That court ruling set a standard for a complete denial of rights of fatherhood by the courts. Such extremes of feminism have resulted in men not wanting to marry some women they have gotten pregnant. In other cases, men often are not willing to pay child support to women who divorce them. All government efforts to pass laws to make men responsible can only partially solve the

---

[23] cf. Wilson, *Man Is Not Enough*, Chapter 19 for research on this subject.

problem. Such rulings for feminism have not been a victory but a loss for women themselves as will be shown in a later chapter.

The mother's great dependence on the father has usually caused her to desire his help, but in modern America that is being denied because of economic prosperity and welfare help where others supply assistance to care for the young child. In early colonial America, rights to children in the courts went to the father and an orphan was one defined as "a child not having a father." This changed with the feminist movement. Under modern secular thinking women tend to think of the children as primarily theirs; however, children belong to God for both parents to raise. Women should encourage their children to be with their fathers and love them, and should encourage men in caring for and loving their children.

The individualism of the old sin nature causes husbands and wives to compete for the affection of their child. Women may act selfishly by spending more time, giving more affection, and doing special things for their children to gain their affection over the husband. These individualistic women are selfish and insecure, and want to be sure their children love them more than their father. When women are possessive and protective of their children from their fathers, men will react and compete more. Women may seek to gain their children's affection subtly by tending to blame arguments on the husband, or exaggerate on his absence or failures. Men may then give less attention to wife and children and turn toward greater involvement in their jobs or business where they gain greater sense of self-worth, or to sports that exalt the manly strength of men, or to pornography, or to the conquest of another woman. These attitudes move husbands and wives further apart. The children are the great losers, but so are the man and wife who miss the great pleasures of marriage.

Even without the wrong attitude or lack of primacy of the mother toward the husband and father, men can also selfishly seek to gain the affection of the children over their mother. Men can actually be jealous of the child's normal affection for the mother by bonding and nurture. Because men usually have more money, they may try to gain affection by buying and giving a child more things or opportunities. Or the husband may call attention to failures or inadequacies of the mother to exalt himself. Men often are too zealous to want their boys to be manly, and focus heavily on manly pursuits, or even will try to succeed in sports through their sons of daughters. In these selfish expressions, all lose, and God is dishonored.

Men who are not treated with a high regard and received little love from their wife and children, will tend to be too demanding of their children and are more likely to discourage their children. Women who do not experience a deep love from their husbands will compensate by focusing on the children.

A husband and wife who are in competition can find many devious ways to seek to gain the children's affection over their spouse. In either case, mothers and fathers can play the children against the other parent by their selfish desire to have their affection and to feel important to the child. It is easy for parents to be critical of each other and to dominate the child. The degeneration of a civilization by sexual perversion usually accentuates this problem. Individualism produces sexual promiscuity and homosexuality.

In America, when the husband and wife do not see the children as God's gift from their love for each other, or the importance of children and the family, it may lead to one or both parents focusing too much on their children. Parents want to protect their children, and modern psychology has emphasized the importance of *self-esteem* for the child. This has been carried to the point of almost *worshipping children,* and doing too much for them. The most important thing for a child is to understand their great value in Christ and feel *Christ's esteem from his love*. This comes best from parents who show their supreme love for Christ and for each other. Then their sacrificial love for their children will be seen in such a way as to make them secure and hold them accountable.

There are many cases in the Bible where we find people's desire for and love of children superseding the love of their spouse.

Abraham's wife Sarah wanted a child so much that she encouraged Abraham to give her a child through Hagar, her maid servant. The result was painful to her and Abraham. Rebecca showed favoritism for Jacob while Isaac was showing favoritism for Esau. These abuses are also seen in many other cases. The Bible shows evil consequences from these.

Proper Response to Abuse, Suffering Love

The definition of New Covenant love is one of willingness to suffer abuse from others. When one member of the marriage puts children, work, or anything else in first place over the other, the tendency is to react selfishly, and fight back against what is seemingly the injustice. This is the opposite of Christian love, and always makes matters worse. The only way to allow God to change the situation is for the offended partner to respond with sacrificial love that is expressed first by confession, and then request forgiveness. First the person feeling unjustly treated should examine their own heart, and ask God to show them how they have been selfish toward their partner. They should then confess this and pray that God will reveal the offense. No marriage partner can successfully tell their spouse they are wrong. Often a third party can help intervene, and point out problems from putting children first. Christian husbands and wives will repeatedly fail, and must repent as evidence of suffering love.

Whether or not there is any change, the person feeling offended should recognize that their suffering is for Christ's sake and not to gain self-justification. This understanding of *suffering for God's glory* and not in self pity removes the reaction, and allows a continual forgiveness and love for the spouse. God honors this, and does in time and through patience help the spouse see and correct the abuse. Often the Spirit of God uses the offense and suffering for the person to grow in Christlikeness. This reduces the conflict before the children and helps them.

Ordinary Training Responsibilities According to Gender

Women and men have different roles in training and developing children according to the different aspects of the image of God in both genders. While men and women have equal intellectual abilities, they naturally use them differently, and in varying degrees according to personality differences. Women have the power to communicate emotion through stories. The normal communication gift of women in the church is that of prophesy and prayer (1 Corinthians 11:4, 5). The word for prophet meant "to flow forth." Women are great at recounting what they have experienced and seen, and can "flow forth" with emotion in telling these. Thus women can best recount the biographical stories of the characters of the Bible. They intuitively see results of emotion. Mary of Bethany foresaw the crucifixion of Christ because of the emotional hate of Jerusalem authorities. Mary Magdalene and the other women were given the privilege of first seeing and telling about the resurrection. Teaching Bible stories to children builds a sense of history. Stories about great missionaries are best done by women.

On the other hand, men are more factual and issue oriented. They see moral implications, and want to respond. Teaching doctrine, and motivating to action on major issues are important to men, and they best teach these matters. They are the ones who are most concerned to keep law and order for love in the family. Women love "in spite of" and men often love with "tough love." There are exceptions where women are good at this too, but usually men are best.

Teaching children God's truth should be shared in a loving and caring way, so that the parent communicates his or her love for Christ. To legalistically force children to listen can lead to rejection of the truth. However, all children are sinners and parents must make God's will clear and hold the line for obedience to God as tough love.

Conclusions about Extending the Kingdom by Children

It is very important for the church to see that having and raising children in the suffering love of Christ is vital for the witness of the church. We should seek to have more children, but husbands and wives must demonstrate the image of God from their gender perspective. The evangelization of the world is linked to this, and Scripture shows this is God's will. However, for it to be powerful, the primary focus of God's love must be in the oneness of marriage of the husband and wife.

Children are to be loved as equally valuable, also as an expression of love in marriage oneness, and as future witnesses of God's love to the world. Those who grow up in a home which reflects the sacrificial love of God are most likely to be called of God and believe. The miracle of love that produces a miraculous birth of a child is compelling, for the children in the family, but also for the world at large.

When union in marriage love is practiced it expands the witness of the church to show God's love. The first commandment is to love as he has loved, and then the second calls us to love our neighbor as he loved us. There is none nearer, more neighborly than our husband or wife. Jesus taught that by your love for one another as he has loved you, they will know you are his disciples, and the world may believe. For Christ, the most powerful influence is to produce covenant children and to spread the gospel through them. In time, this will lead to the cultural change of laws to conform to God's will. Legal efforts without this will be unsuccessful. Love for our children can be experienced by others.

A woman who is one of my closest friends recently shared an experience as a child. Her home was dysfunctional with a dictatorial father who was constantly provoking to wrath and leaving all the family in insecurity. She had some neighboring childhood friends that she would visit. They were a devout Christian family who manifested the love of Christ. At times she would spend the night with her friends. The father and mother would come in arm in arm when they were ready for bed, tuck all of the children in, give them all – even her – an affectionate kiss, and pray for each before they said goodnight. My friend told me that experience gave her great hope and desire for a good marriage. Some years later she and her husband together accepted Christ and they found that kind of loving marriage.

Does this mean that we should diminish the sharing of the simple gospel of how to be accepted by Christ thought faith alone? Does it mean that we should not preach the gospel to every creature in all nations? Certainly not! But unless this is done in such a way as to show the love of God embodied in us, it will be of minimal effect. "By this shall all men know that you are my disciples, if you have love for one another" (John 13:35). That is God's designed plan. It should come first and primary through the love of a man and his wife.

Chapter 6
Conflict of Our Old Nature and Love in the Spirit

New Covenant Love Is Opposite to Selfish Desires of Flesh

In Chapter 4, the New Commandment of the New Covenant was shown to be highly important in applying it to marriage as the basic institution. The New Commandment of the New Covenant is to love those who sin against us as Christ sacrificially loved us. The implementation of the mutual submission of woman as helper and partner, and of man as sacrificial leader and provider, is seemingly impossible. Moreover, it is often undesirable for unbelievers and difficult for the Christian. Sacrificial love is an utter contrast to our old selfish fleshly nature. Loving another person who acts selfishly *seems unjust,* and therefore we react to such conduct. Christ showed his love in his willingness to suffer our injustice, and paid the penalty we deserved. He offered forgiveness and grace in spite of our injustice and unrighteousness toward him. Can marriage love really produce oneness that reflects the wonder of God's love to accept and forgive and be a witness of this to the world? How can this be, and is it desirable, powerful, and wonderful?

Our New Nature by the Spirit is in Conflict with the Flesh

The New Testament Scriptures tell of this conflict, and the importance of knowing the answer. The apostle Paul describes the battle involved against the deceptive forces of the world. He said,

> But I say, walk by the Spirit, and you will not gratify the desires of the flesh. For the desires of the flesh *are against* the Spirit, and desires of the Spirit *are against* the flesh, for *these are opposed* to each other, to keep you from doing the things you want to do. But if you are led by the Spirit, you are not under the law (Galatians 5:16-26).

> For those who live according to the flesh set their minds on the things of the flesh, but those who live according to the Spirit set their minds on the things of the Spirit. To set the mind on the flesh is death, but to

set the mind on the Spirit is life and peace. For the ***mind that is set on
the flesh is hostile to God***, for it does not submit to God's law;
indeed, it cannot. Those who are in the flesh cannot please God. You
however, are not in the flesh but in the Spirit, if in fact the Spirit of
God dwells in you. Anyone who does not have Spirit of Christ does
not belong to Him (Romans 8:5-9).

The conflict between the flesh and the Spirit is further
complicated by the created differences between man and woman
that involve not only our physical construction but all our
emotions, mental thinking, and feelings of the past. Also, marriage
partners bring different values and ideas from their families, which
many times involve learned anger and resentments against the
opposite sex that repeatedly reemerge and are used by the world
and the devil. When children are born, they have their own
temperaments, and more complications are added to the marriage
relationships. In addition the changes in the culture of the world
repeatedly offer appeals and desires that are often new and highly
seductive. All these things make living and walking in the Spirit
seem difficult. But precisely because of these things, the guidance
and power of the Holy Spirit enlightening us and empowering us
through God's word are all important. Living for Christ is in fact
impossible unless it is done in the Spirit. Why does our salvation
involve this conflict of the flesh and the Spirit to give glory to
Christ?

The Reason God Called Us as His Disciples in the Conflict

If Christ wanted us to be one in marriage, why did He not give
us a new body so these differences and old feelings and emotions
would not be there? Then we would be loveable! Why not? The
answer is that then we would not be ***a witness to his suffering
love***. The exact reason Christ gave us his Spirit in our weak fleshly
bodies is so that when we are wronged we can show that we are his
disciples and reflect his suffering love for those people who treat
us wrongly. The Garden of Eden was a place where Adam and Eve
could show God's goodness, but not his suffering love. There
would be ***no opportunity to reveal suffering love in a perfect***

world with perfect people. In a perfect world there would be no revelation of God's justice, because there would be no wrong to judge and punish. God's eternal plan allowed for angels and men who could *do wrong* to him and others so he could reveal his justice and then his love.

But more importantly, all natural men with a nature of self-wisdom since Adam have changed what God made to be good and evil to benefit them as good and evil. The Bible reveals there is *no one* who has chosen to live righteously and all in every nation, even his chosen Israel, changed God's good to be evil, and his evil to be good. So they all have deserved judgment (Isaiah 5:20; 29:16; Micah 3:1, 2). Read all the revelation of the Bible and in every book, in all the prophets, in every nation, God records there is *no one* who does good and sins not (Psalms 53:1-3). So no man can save, but only God who came as a man to make a new race by grace.

This condition of mind for self in the flesh is against God and all others (Romans 8:7). The just condemnation of all gave God the opportunity to reveal his suffering love of mercy and grace for those who repent. "For God has consigned all to disobedience, that he may have mercy on all" (Romans 11:32).

The church is the bride of Christ, so we as his elect can reveal his suffering love. Christ's death as a substitute sacrifice is sufficient for all, but efficient only for the elect. To these elect, God offers forgiveness, acceptance, power to live and love by the Spirit, and reveals his transforming power for heaven. These new men are called to be ambassadors, or disciples, to make that suffering love known, and become agents to bring men to repentance (2 Corinthians 5: 14-6:2). All the treasures and pleasures of the world that the devil offers in the flesh are now surpassed by the pearl of great price and the treasure found in a field. We have the surpassing greatness of Christ and his eternal kingdom that cannot be shaken.

We in the flesh are called to the wonderful task of revealing his amazing love "that passes knowledge" (Ephesians 3:19). And marriage is the basic beginning point to show his love. How this is done will be the subject of the next chapter. But how does this happen? How does the Spirit replace the lusts and conflict in the flesh for the wonderful fruit of the Spirit? How, when we are obedient to death, does he begin his powerful work within us for our salvation?

The Body was an Instrument for Sin, Now for Christ

We are left in our bodies with fleshly natures. We have both our weaknesses and strengths with which we were born. Our unique personality is designed for us as Christians to special works of grace through our walk in the Spirit (Ephesians 2:5-10). So God uses every event, even the bad, and the failures we suffer, for our good and his glory (Romans 8:28). The dying to self when others abuse us *is the opportunity for Christ* in us to be manifested. "By this shall all men know that you are my disciples, if you have love (*agape*, suffering love) for one another" (John 13:35). The mystery of God's eternal election in grace involves God's sovereign working, and man's willful response. The devil does not want this saving love to be known, and he seeks to distort truth in the world to keep us from showing that love by the Spirit. We can trust Christ to work mightily beyond "all we can ask or think, according to the power (of the Spirit) within us" in the church for his glory (Ephesians 3:2, 21).

The Mind of Christ in Us Enables Freedom for the Spirit

There are two things to be discerned about the mind of Christ regarding the flesh and the world that the devil does not want us to know. First, Christ *never thought the fleshly body is evil in itself.* The fleshly body was made to enjoy the sensual pleasures of food, sexual love, security, and comfort of the created world. Those desires were still there after man sinned and was put out of the Garden. Secondly, Christ never used the power and pleasure of the flesh to promote himself or use his body only for his own selfish pleasure and power. His body was always used to please the Father (John 5:19, 20).

But as an individual who believed he was wise as God, Adam who was in a mortal body and without hope of eating of the tree of life, only had hope for the things of this present world system. Thus, because natural men are always fearful of death, the devil keeps them in bondage to sin (Hebrews 2:14, 15). Christ's disciples who die with him are then freed to have life and hope of a resurrection to a new body and new heaven and earth.

Jesus Christ came incarnate in a fleshly body, and never lived according to and for his flesh, but according to the will of the Father in the power of the Spirit (John 5:19-24). We are told in Scripture that the eternal Word or Son of God, "the Word *became flesh* and tabernacled among us" (John 1:14). But the fleshly body of Jesus was not just any flesh — "His Son who was descended *from David according to the flesh*, and was declared to be the Son of God in power according to the Spirit of holiness by his resurrection from the dead" (Romans 1:3, 4). Christ lived holy and without sin, and so was raised from the dead. Thus the flesh is not essentially evil, but mortal without hope of eternal life. But by obedience to death, Christ's body was raised and transformed from the Adamic nature free from trials and temptations. He is the second Adam and life-giving Spirit.

As the promised heir of King David, Christ is now glorified in power; he now can enable us to be obedient which we could not be in our Adamic nature.

> Jesus Christ our Lord through whom we have received grace and apostleship to bring about the obedience of faith for the sake of his name among all the nations, including you [believers] who are called to belong to Jesus Christ (Romans 1:5, 6).

Because of God's grace, what does Christ do to enable us to escape the power of the devil through the flesh? Christ comes into our fleshly body by the Holy Spirit and his Spirit teaches our mind and empowers our spirit. Christ thereby enables us to be free to live unto God. Jesus said,

I will ask the Father and he will give you another Helper, to be with you forever, even the Spirit of truth, whom the world cannot receive, because it neither sees him nor knows him. You know him, for he dwells with you and will be in you" (John 14:16, 17).

This will be a result of our love for Christ — "If you love me, you will keep my commandments" (14:15). Paul said, it is "Christ *in you*, the hope of glory" (Colossian 1:27).

Mind of Christ Enables Those who Trust Him to Choose Spirit over the Flesh

Scripture repeatedly directs us to choose the Spirit over the desires and works of the flesh. Since the flesh and the Spirit are in conflict, how is the Christian to have the fruit of the Spirit? The repeated exhortation by the apostles is that the Christian must have the *mind of Christ* to be repeatedly *humble and die to self* to accept suffering in obedience to the Spirit. The apostles taught the mind of death with Christ is the way to walk in the Spirit's leading and power. The devil would have disciples deny that we are to die with Christ and lose our life now, living unto him and with eternal life in him now. That is the mind revealing one is a disciple. This is the teaching of Christ and of his Apostles.

Peter said,

"Since therefore *Christ suffered* in the flesh, arm yourselves with the *same way of thinking*, for whoever has suffered in the flesh has ceased from sin, so as to live for the rest of the time in the flesh no longer for human passions but for the will of God. The time that is past suffices for doing what the Gentiles/unbelievers want to do, living in sensuality, passions, drunkenness, orgies, drinking parties, and lawless idolatry (1 Peter 4:1-3).

Paul referred to the great mercy of God's acceptance of sinners and said,

I appeal to you therefore, brothers, by the mercies of God, to present *your bodies as a living sacri*fice, holy and acceptable to God, which is your spiritual worship/service. Do not be conformed to this world, but be transformed by the *renewal of your mind*, that by testing you may discern what is the will of God, what is good and acceptable and perfect" (Romans 12:1-3, cf. 11:30-36 referring to God's mind of sacrificial mercy to us).

Likewise Paul tells the Philippians that if they want Christ's encouragement, comfort of love, and participation in the Spirit, they are to put the interest of others above their own. He said,

> *Have this mind* among your selves, which is yours in Christ Jesus, who though he was in the form of God, did not count equality with God a thing to be grasped, but *made himself nothing*, taking the form of a servant, being born in the likeness of men. And being found in human form, he *humbled himself* by becoming obedient to the point of death, even death on a cross. Therefore God has highly exalted him and bestowed on him the name that is above every name. ...Therefore, my beloved, as you have always obeyed, so now ...work out your own salvation with fear and trembling, for *it is God who works in you (by His Spirit),* both to will and to work for his good pleasure (Philippians 2: 4-13).

The devil would distort the idea of dying to self into some kind of escapism or monastic withdrawal that treats the body and its desires as evil. He would have worshipers focus on rituals and self-efforts of obedience to commandments (cf. Colossians 2). The body is not in itself evil, but only the selfish use of the flesh is dishonoring to God, and harmful to others. Under man's sin nature, seeing himself as wise as God, all men use their body for selfish reasons and sin against God and others (Ephesians 2:1-3; Psalm 14:53). As sinners we all may even do good things for others to gain their help and benefit ourselves. But all acts of unbelievers are for self and not for God — "Whatever is not of faith (in God) is sin" (Romans 14:23, Hebrews 11). We are here to suffer in the flesh by the Spirit for witness to Christ's suffering love.

The Fleshly Body is the Spirit's Instrument for Right

The body has been an instrument for unrighteousness, breaking the law of God, dishonoring him, and harming others to get things for ourselves. After repentance, the Christian has the mind of Christ, and under the power of the Holy Spirit, the body is to become an instrument or member for righteousness unto God (Romans 6:5-14). Our bodies are to become the instrument of God to do His will and service as the Spirit guides and enables.

Secondly, Christ's **mind was one of complete trust in God's love and power** to provide all the needs and pleasures for his good, no matter what happened to him. When we **trust Christ** and die with Him, all our sin and its offense against God is forgiven, and our guilt and fear of him is removed. God's Spirit is in us and available to provide his guidance and power for our good. When we trust Christ's love and power, God will give us the right desires and direction to find our utmost fulfillment from the pleasures and provisions of the world and eternal life with him.

Freedom in the flesh for the Christian is not to do just anything the flesh desires, but freedom to obey God which is freedom indeed. Jesus said, "If you **abide in my word** you are truly my disciples, and you will know the truth, and the truth will set you free. ...Truly, truly, I say to you, everyone who commits sin is a slave to sin. The slave does not remain in the house forever; the son remains forever. So if the Son sets you free, you will be free indeed" (John 8:31, 34-36). So in Christ the believer does not see the flesh as evil, but good, and an instrument to be used to bear fruit of the Spirit. The unselfish use of our body brings amazing pleasure to God, to ourselves, and influences others to repent.

Unselfish suffering love for our spouse brings our whole sexual person into surrender to God and each other, which brings maximum long term pleasure. This is done by dying to self and living in the power of the Spirit of Christ in us, who can do exceeding and abundantly above all we can ask or think. More will be explained about this later.

Moreover, the flesh is not an instrument for liberty to indulge selfishly, but under control of Christ's Spirit to be free from sin. But to show suffering love, the Holy Spirit must at times lead us to deny our desires and be hurt by others. Jesus was repeatedly rejected, and told his disciples they would be persecuted for his and righteousness' sake. Enduring these times is what gives us greater rewards and pleasure in heaven. The Spirit then produces the fruit of the Spirit — love, joy, peace….

Faith or ***trust in his love and power gives us the freedom to do what the Spirit shows us***. Our bodies become his. When we try to do what we humanly want to be right and count ourselves righteous (by the law), we sin and end up guilty and doing evil (Roman 7:14 ff). Faith in the forgiveness of the cross, and the victory of ***trusting God*** is seen in that the resurrection *frees us to obey*. We know ***God*** will exalt us and give us success as he did Christ (Philippians 2:5ff).

Every problem becomes God's opportunity. We no longer worship mammon or wealth, but trust our heavenly Father to provide daily all we need as we seek his will and his kingdom (Matthew 6:19-34). Every use of food is for energy and pleasure to serve him according to his word. Our thoughts and desire for sexual pleasure is to show his love in union to our spouse, and not for individual self-gratification. We no longer have to fear God or the consequences of evil men in a wicked world. God is for us because we are Christ's, and he has all authority from the Father. We can believe, "All things work together for good, for those who love God and who are called according to His purpose" (Romans 8:28).

Mind of Faith Makes our Body God's Instrument of Power

As Hannah Whitall Smith has illustrated, just as the carpenter's powerful arm uses the instrument of the saw on the wood, the work is done. It is the carpenter's power that does the work; the saw is an instrument. But this illustration is inadequate, because we are not an inanimate instrument. We ***willfully respond*** to the love of Christ to repent and trust him by choosing to die with him on his cross. Christ's resurrected life enters us with transforming power. If a person does not experience the guidance and desires of the Spirit, he will continue to follow the fleshly desires to spiritual and physical death. Paul draws the contrast:

Now the works of the flesh are evident: sexual immorality, impurity, sensuality, idolatry, sorcery, enmity, strife, jealousy fits of anger, rivalries, dissensions, divisions, envy, drunkenness, orgies, and things like these. I warn you, as I warned you before, that those who do such things will not inherit the kingdom of God.

But the fruit of the Spirit is love, joy, peace, patience, kindness, goodness, faithfulness, gentleness, self-control; against such things there is no law. And those who belong to Christ Jesus have crucified the flesh with its passions and desires. If we live by the Spirit, let us also walk by the Spirit (Galatians 5:19-25).

The branch bears fruit because of the life of the vine. "I am the vine, you are the branches. Without me *you* can do ***nothing***" (John 15:5). Paul said, "We are the true circumcision (covenant people), who worship/serve God in the Spirit, and have **no confidence** in the flesh" (Philippians 3:3). Christ in us is the hope of glory. And the love of Christ in us by the Spirit bears much fruit. But the natural man and woman in the fleshly world's system for selfish reason believe changing the differences to be equal in kind is the way of good.

Selfish Sin Natures makes Any Difference a Threat

Male and female as sinners are under bondage to the devil, each believing he can be wise as God and know what is good and what is evil. Because they are offended by their differences, they believe it is good to remove differences, and enable both to be equally the same. Their self-righteousness rests on removing all differences of everyone; racial, class, ethnical and the foundational one is that of the sexes of male and female. All values for the flesh are based on material temporal wealth. The self-righteous mind of men and women lies in seeking to produce this equality

Man's wisdom is that women should be like men for success for material worth. Women's wisdom is that men should let women tell their husbands how to help them be equal to them. But to promote women's equality, women want men to assume some of their responsibilities. In trying to communicate with men to let them be like them as leader and earner, women have found an impossible barrier and great frustration in that men by nature continue to want to be the leader and principle provider. They can't have babies or bond like women do with their children, so that they can in their own rights claim ownership of the child. They can't find equal worth as surrogate mothers for the women to be free. So men fight the communication efforts to be like them. Becoming the same will only occur when public law requires men and women to be alike, and both resist this change until required.

Sexual Battle of Flesh and Spirit: the Mind of World or Christ

Different Sexual Abilities are Opportunities for Flesh

Because God created both male and female with different strengths to show two aspects of his image, the devil's temptation is to deceive by causing the misuse of each of these strengths and weaknesses. The differences of male and female were created by God for good. How sin involves these aspects in temptations to the flesh in relationships is important to knowing how the Spirit would have us respond. When a culture turns to material worship and away from God, the differences become more painful, and attention focuses more on them. In the last decade of the twentieth century when the fifth phase of the U. S. feminist movement reached a climax, [24] many books were written to better define male and female characteristics, and to try to give answers to the conflicts of the flesh. Qualities as observed are as follows.

Masculine Qualities

Some major masculine qualities and powers are: greater muscular strength, willingness to risk and to compete in order to win, and to dominate and lead. Men are oriented to goals for achievement for fixing things, for solving problems, and for setting rules and borders, desiring significant activity to create, and the desire to protect and control. Men want individual recognition, but find great satisfaction achieving through team work in sports,

---

[24] Carl W. Wilson, *Man Is Not Enough*, (bravegoodmen.org: Andragathia Books, 1998), 195-225, especially 213 ff.

military, or corporate ventures. Outside trade, fighting and war are mostly men's work. Most want outdoor activities, but many in modern tech cultures want to work at tech games and projects.

The male by nature is attracted and aggressive toward the female sex. One of his greatest powers **as a man is to choose or reject a mate.** The male's primary sex act is to have an erection and to give pleasure, and impart the gift of sperm for having children. Success at this activity is highly important for his identity. If this power is used in love for his wife it is a wonderful power. If used selfishly, it is will be result in suffering and a burden. A man by creation wants to claim ownership of his wife and children, and in most cultures the wife and child take his name. But the man can change relationships more easily than can a woman; he is more decisive and directive and has a stronger voice to gain control. Men want community recognition for community problems and leadership. For most men their primary desire is for justice and for fixing wrongs; secondarily their desires are for mercy.

Feminine Qualities

Women have broader sexual powers. The prominent sexual analyst George Gilder has said, "The prime fact of life is the sexual *superiority* of women."[25] While women have very unique powers, those of men mentioned above seem to also be strong. Female powers orient women toward nesting and home. Women are highly relational and designed with a brain to remember more detail, to communicate well to maintain relations, and are better at and are concerned about words. The female has a natural desire to help others, especially her husband and her children. Women have a *strong desire to attract a male* for a long-term relationship, and to be thought of by men and other women as attractive. But the greater attractive power that is within makes even the most common of women exceedingly beautiful (cf. 1 Peter 3:1 ff).

---

[25] George Gilder, *Men and Marriage*, (Gretna, LA: Pelican Publishing Company, 1986), 5. A revision of his book, *Sexual Suicide*.

Much of the female's world is broad thinking about sexual physical attraction as is evident in women's magazines and advertising. Beauty of hair, eyes, lips, clothes, hygiene, and smell of perfumes are of interest to most. Women have greater dexterity with their hands and fingers, and can do detailed work better. They strongly want to communicate for intimacy with others, especially in a long-range, close relationship with her man that then gives freedom for sexual pleasure and security of family. A woman has a broader sensitivity for touch and affection. But emotional difficulties relate to failure in her sexual role, which is not as obvious or profound as the male's. Her selfish desires in the flesh soon make her offensive to the man she may attract. Her female emotional concerns for her husband should involve helping with his work, helping with children and home, and financial support. Doing meaningful work of her own that is recognized as a contribution with her husband to the success of the family is important for her sense of value. This can come only by the Spirit, and she is revealed as great value to him.

The female alone has the sexual power to conceive. She has the power and pride in giving birth to a child, but pays with the price of pain in childbirth. She alone can nurse and best nurture young children, and all these powers give *her exclusive right to close bonding and claiming ownership of the child.* These powers also require help from her husband or, if not, from surrogates or the church or state for provision. She alone has the power to designate who her child's father is, which compensates for his power to choose her. If she has no children of his, and therefore does not have the influence of this power to give recognition of paternity over to her husband, she then focuses strongly on pleasing him through housekeeping, superior cooking, entertaining, and especially giving sexual pleasure. Only by the Spirit can she make these an unselfish effort as a gift of love to him.

Use of words and communication is of central power for control with a woman's mate and with friends. Women, being more careful about relationships, generally like to make decisions by consensus, while men often want the decision to be primarily theirs. This desire and power of communication will be more extensively discussed in Chapter 7 and following.

Men and women are essentially the same genetically, women being created from man and "being flesh of his flesh and bone of his bone." They are together set apart in kind to one another from all other animals. This is clear in Genesis chapter 2, where Eve was created when the animals were insufficient as a partner (cf. Genesis 2:18-23). But as previously mentioned, Louanne Brizendine has pointed out that every cell of the female body is different from the male.[26] The woman is a complement to the man to allow oneness for reproduction and extension of family, community, and civilization that relates to everything in the world. Their emotions and thinking are intended to complement. Therefore sex is not just an act, like eating a meal and drinking a glass of water for the physical benefit of pleasure. *Sex is the nature of the whole person uniting with a spouse in all of life.* Thinking of sex really involves the whole person.

The Sexual Mind Fits the Male and Female Nature

Studies have confirmed this difference of the female from the male in sexual perspective. Brizendine, in her book, *The Female Brain,* on several occasions mentions that men *are repeatedly often thinking about sex* while women only maybe once a day. But Brizendine is defining sex in the perverted way as the act of coitus, and not of sex as the whole person. Women are thinking of sex virtually all the time as the emotional and psychological attraction of men, not just as the consummating act. After the sin and change, God told Eve, "Your desire shall be to your husband" (Genesis 3:16). Examine the magazine racks and the novels, and they almost all address this sexual aspect of women seeking to be attractive. Frequently these magazines then give advice as to how to please their man in bed. This is fully explained to be true by Brizendine throughout the rest of her excellent book.[27] It is

---

[26]Louann Brizendine, *The Female Brain*, (New York: Broadway Books, 2006), 1.
[27]Ibid. 5, 91 et al.

therefore extremely important to see the sinful fleshly natures of man and woman, and why this selfish individualism requires *the New Covenant work of the Spirit as the only way real unity in love can be achieved.*

Fleshly Conflict and Rejection Used by Demonic Tempting

The man's drive to work, risk, achieve, create, provide, and lead, and the woman's desire to emotionally direct and control through her attractiveness and supportive help and to communicate in the family — both of their very natures — are turned by the devil into sin and into reasons to produce conflict, hate, and division. The sin natures of male and female are turned to pride to protect their individual wisdom of good and evil in order to have self-esteem, to selfishly enjoy the lusts of the flesh, and to own what is beauty in wealth. All the strengths become time bombs by selfishness. Their freedom of powers for dominion and happiness together in the world, become their sources of bondage, misery, and death to their sexuality.

In Chapter 10, the path of sexual destruction in a civilization will be discussed. This path is *initiated by men* who by their material achievements use their wealth to pridefully feel superior to the woman. As men become prosperous, the value of a woman's role in having children and helping her husband drops, since children hinder her earning ability. She must then in the flesh deny this great value and pursue worth in success for money. With this change in value established and led by men, women then must fight for material worth, which requires neglecting their partnership and motherhood for combat in the marketplace. This change in value, which causes women to seek more rights to become like men, results in fleshly-minded men claiming that they seek to gain women's favor by supporting women in their greater freedom to be like men and to be equal. These are subtle changes, and may have varying degrees of influence in the progress of role changing. This individualism resulting from materialism leads to sexual immorality and perversion. These perversions are described by Paul in Romans 1:24-27 and will be explained.

Every aspect of the sexual strengths of both men and women soon are joined for the combat to change the other sex and make them alike. The women want to be like men and the women want the men to change to help them and allow them to succeed and find worth. The end of the role of this sinful, selfish individualism is homosexuality. When homosexuality is universally practiced, this will end reproductive humanity.[28] The path to equality by becoming the same is suicidal for the human race.

Reactive Nature of Women for Conflict in the Flesh

Brizendine explains how the woman's nature works with anyone at the hint of conflict, especially with her husband.

> This is a trap that plays in the brain of every woman at the thought of conflict, even a small disagreement. *The female brain has a far more negative alert reaction to relationship conflict* and rejection than does the male brain. Men often enjoy interpersonal conflict and competition; they even get a positive boost from it. In women, conflict is more likely to set in motion a cascade of negative chemical reactions, create feelings of stress, upset, and fear. Just the thought that there might be a conflict will be read by the female brain as threatening the relationship, and bring with it the real concern that the next conversation she has with her friend will be their last.
>
> …As soon as a woman gets her feelings hurt, the hormonal shift sets off a fearful fantasy that the relationship will be over.[29]

The result of the threat of combat is that a woman tries to use her communication to get the man to hear her and agree, and it ends up in quarrels to try to change him from being a leader and provider, and become her helper.

Men want to love their wives, but this feminine reaction to conflict turns men off. When the wife is in conflict, men want to avoid communication, and quarreling shuts men off. Her irrational arguing is like a continual dripping rain, and men want to escape to the housetop or retreat in a field (Proverbs 19:13; 21:9, 19). They go into another room and shut the door or get drunk, or take any

---

[28] See my chapter 18 in *Man Is **Not** Enough.*
[29] Louann Brizendine, *The Female Brain*, 40, 41.

means of escape. Feeling rejected by his wife men seek to enhance their esteem by greater work and success. Or he may seek escape in alcohol or drugs. The more he is criticized the more he drinks or withdraws. This opens the door to using pornography or seeking someone else for an affair who will show him respect. While the man started this by exaggerating his role and power by mammon or Baal worship, the woman then focuses on feminist power to gain worth.

Women then accelerate their pursuit to be successful in worth as their goal, or in essence to worship Ashtoreth (meaning "to be rich"), the feminine Canaanite goddess for wealth. Equal pay and breaking the glass ceiling, or more welfare and help from government or church, become the objective. Also, she will want approval and the affection of other men to whom she has no responsibility, who are more compliant, and who have not experienced her anger and are less angry. When a woman is thus insecure, she finds ways to tightly bind her children to herself under her control, and to put her spouse down. Under trust in Christ by the Spirit, she will transfer her powers to her husband for him to lead the child in what he should do, and support the father as the leader. This trust in him as father makes the child more compliant to her.

The result of a woman's selfish control has been called *momism* and the increase in conflict then inclines sons to homosexuality.[30] When women and men emerge from families where one sexual parent is favored or hated, the conflict is more difficult and likely to repeat in the next generation. After women gained the right to vote in 1921, the period of the family was popularly called "Momism" in magazines.

Self-Righteous Women Feel Men Should Change

When a culture reaches this stage of efforts for sexual equality, women feel certain, for fleshly reasons, their husbands need to be more feminine in communication and caring, and less

---

[30] Cf. Wilson, *Man Is Not Enough*, chapter 19.

active and goal-oriented in male strengths. Women's ***major calling becomes changing her husband and her sons*** because they feel men need this. But since their husbands are males in nature, they do not likewise feel the need of this transformation, and women do not understand this resistance and resentment by most men. A woman feels to change her man is the right thing, not only for her good, but for all society to be better. At the height of the painful conflict for sexual change in the 1990s in the U. S., Daphne Kingma devoted her counseling skills to this crusading attempt to change men. She commented about women's desire for men.

> ***Women are brought inescapably to this task*** because men don't have what they need to do it for themselves. Indeed, it is exactly the thing men lack that is required in their transformational process. …On their own, men have no way to reach out into the emotional stratosphere and call in the feminine consciousness. Men are also hobbled in whatever efforts they might put forth, …effort to evoke the ***missing feminine*** in one another. They've had to live by the secret contract of competition which has required that at every level of social encounter with one another, they remain heroes or adversaries, staying emotionally guarded….[31] (emphasis mine)

The conflict to change men's natures leads beyond words to physical attacks on one another. While studies show women assault men about equally as much as men do women (men about 25%, and women 24%), even though men are stronger, and by greater strength they can do the greater damage, men are unwilling to publically admit attacks from their wives. Moreover, women are more likely to report attacks than are men. Thus the fighting and abuse by women is not clearly known.

The sexual conflict results in great efforts by secular and Christian counselors, to better define sexual roles and to help the other sexual partner feel greater understanding and self-esteem.[32]

---

[31] Daphne Rose Kingma, *The Men We Never Knew; Women's Role in the Evolution of a Gender*, (Berkeley, CA: Conari Press; 1993.) 192, 193.
[32] cf. Willard F. Harley, Jr., *His Needs Her Needs*,(Grand Rapids, MI: Fleming H. Revell), 1986, Dennis & Barbara Rainey, *Building Your Mate's Self-Esteem*, (San

But the loss of real love and affection, which both want, is strongly felt. Kingma described the situation.

> Although intuitively *we know it is* **only** love *that can bridge the abuses* within and outside of our own wounded psyches, very few of us have been taught how to practice the *true medicine of love*. Even more than that, however, because of the evolution of our society, women have a very incomplete picture of men, and men have almost no way of understanding their inner sensitive selves, nor, as a consequence, of understanding women.
>
> …When this drama between the sexes comes down to intimate relationships between men and women, we are all in a sense perpetuating the tragedy we fear is inevitable. We live our lives being endlessly at odds with one another, accepting our marriages or romances as the private battlegrounds in which these frustrating inevitabilities will be repeatedly played out. The deeper tragedy in this is not only that we have remained embroiled in the drama between the sexes, but even worse, that human intimate relationships have become not *an image of what is impossible in the world at large, but a despairing symbol* that harmony at any level between any two disparate factions will be difficult, if not impossible, to achieve.[33]

Paul Tournier's book on communication brings this out in a chapter, "My Husband Is a Mysterious Island!" In counseling, Tournier said one wife ended the session by blurting out, "My husband is a mysterious island. I am forever circling around it but never finding a beach where I may land." [34] Ordinary efforts to intimately communicate to change or get agreements may arrive at a truce, a giving up for peace, or result in ignoring the other. Women seek to gain freedom from being a woman as helper, but with no real intimacy.

In these statements it is admitted that men and women are unable to find and present an image of unity and love in marriage

Bernardino, CA: Here's Life Publishers,1986, et al.); John Gray, *Man Are From Mars, Women Are from Venus* (New York: Harper Collins Publishers, 1992;

[33] Kingma, *The Men We Never Knew*, vi, vii.

[34] Paul Tournier, translator John S. Gilmour, *To Understand Each Other*, (Richmond, VA: John Knox Press, 1968), 16.

in the flesh. But that is their great sexual desire that continues to elude them. Kingma offers her *solution as women changing men to be more feminine.* Her views are given approval of many men who seek to understand.[35] After women earned the right to vote, in the 1930s, a leading female psychologist, Marinia Farnham, warned that the competition of women with men would make love impossible. Marie Robinson, another leading female psychologist at the time, reported that for women, their way to power and happiness was only in sexual surrender. A generation later, George D. Gilder pointed out that the man was the beginner and chief perpetrator of this sexual suicide.[36] New Covenant love must replace the flesh as the only answer.

Conclusions

Christian disciples who have accepted Christ's death as theirs are now citizens of heaven and heirs of eternal life, but also ambassadors in the world in a fleshly body. Our bodies have been an instrument that has been under the control of the devil to fulfill selfish desires. As a disciple trusting in the love of Christ and the hope of new transformed body and heavenly rewards our knowledge or mind is being transformed, from that of the world to that of Christ's suffering love. Our body is now the instrument of God to serve him

Disciples are not only *forgiven* for the deeds done by sin in the body, but they each now have the *power* of Christ's Spirit to be free from the deceptions and appeal of the devil to react to competition with our spouses. Trust in our selfish fleshly ability is enmity against God, and we lose power and will die. But if we yield to Christ's Spirit, and renew our mind to be humble to please and obey God, then we are no longer under the law, but are God's children with his power of suffering love that changes us and others.

---

[35]E.g. John Gray, and many others.
[36] Marinia Farnham, in *The Way of Women*; Marie Robinson, *The Power of Sexual Surrender* , and George Gilder, *Sexual Suicide* and its revision, *Man and Marriage.*

Chapter 7
Communication by New Covenant Love

Only Daily Death with Christ Releases Heaven's Power

To communicate in the power of New Covenant love and have the fruit of the Spirit, "love, joy and peace," it is essential that a person have faith as a disciple. This faith now leads to death to self with Christ for eternal rewards instead of fleshly worldly rewards. A disciple needs to trust Christ's death as his to satisfy the punishment for him, and believe that all of his sins are now forever forgiven. He, by God's grace, is again a son of God and citizen of Christ's heavenly eternal kingdom with all his hope in a resurrection to the future life.

But a disciple must see that he now has the power of new life by the Holy Spirit to enable him to humble himself to be obedient in loving his spouse and all others as Christ loved him. A disciple's *whole power comes through Christ in him,* and his eternal life already is secure in that he is in Christ who is seated in the heavens. This faith as a son of God is what gives him freedom to overcome the power of the devil. He can now lose his life in the flesh, showing the love of Christ through his life. If you are a disciple you now no longer need to judge anyone in the flesh or defend your personal earthly kingdom.

This power can continue only by a disciple's daily walk in the Spirit and in prayer to Christ as your King-Priest. Christ can lead, motivate, control, and recreate you to be his witness as a heavenly citizen living as a pilgrim in the world. A married disciple needs to understand that union in marriage by suffering love is a major part of his calling for this life. That love now on earth in marriage is to reflect God's perfect love in heaven. It requires suffering abuse as one who had died with Christ.

Our communication of love to unify the two aspects of male and female in order to reflect Christ's image requires the Spirit's help in understanding and empowering us to act with the mind of Christ, that is in agreement with his word in Scripture. In the last chapter it was shown that male and female living in the flesh faced the impossible task of trying to make men like women, and men to make women like men. Union with Christ in death and resurrection is the only way to accept each other and communicate as one.

The Spirit gives us power to accept Christ's attitudes as in the Sermon on the Mount that can be summed up as loving your enemies as your heavenly Father loves you (Matthew 5-7). He will help us understand and appreciate our spouse's sexual differences, and their unique differences given by God to help us. The Spirit will enable us to use our differences to edify and help each other grow even when we encounter difficulties and tests in our faith.

This New Covenant of God's love and power transforms us from seeing others from our fleshly perspective to being his and fully accepted by him, so we can treat others differently. We can look at everyone differently, and communicate his love to anyone as his ambassador. This applies especially to the one closest to us in marriage (cf. 2 Corinthians 5:14- 6:2).

This way to communication New Covenant love is given in three chapters. This chapter is on communication Covenant love in daily words and conduct. The eighth chapter is on communicating by unselfish love by our bodies for true physical union. The ninth chapter is on communicating God's suffering love in marriage as witness for him to the world. While the implications for expressing love are logical, significant areas will be explained and illustrated to help you see areas of words and acts that you and I may overlook in our postmodern fleshly culture.

Appreciating Sexual Differences in Daily Communication

In dying to self and yielding to trust Christ's love, the Spirit needs to teach us *to accept the differences* of the opposite sex in the flesh described above so that we experience these as created for our good and his glory and not as a threat to our selfish happiness. In the last chapter, it was shown the devil gives the unbeliever an overpowering, consistent desire in the flesh to get our spouse to do what we want and think is best for our self-interest to be happy. It is critical *to yield to* Christ's heavenly perspective that these will glorify God and be for our good in the long run.

Examining Sexual Differences to Illustrate the Power of Love

These are some areas of differences to appreciate about the nature of women and men as observed by psychologists and seen in Scripture. Women want to please, and they want emotional acceptance before they want advice. They will even accept less material security if they feel emotionally loved. They want approval before knowing how to fix things. As men, we instantly want to get things straightened out or fixed. But dying to self to accept must precede leading to fix.

When a woman gives herself in marriage, she continues to want to feel the union is growing. Saying "I do" may be a commitment but is not a final negotiation. When the marriage counselor told this to the husband, he said, "I told her that when we married, didn't I. Why do I need to tell her over and over?" A woman wants her husband to pursue her all her life, not just until the marriage is consummated. She will yield this expectation when she knows she comes first. This is a desire for security in a growing relationship from and with her husband. Natural emotional dependence is probably reflected in the desire for close and long term relationships with all her friends. Also, most women are nesters and want their husband to help them make the home comfortable and pretty.

The husband's appreciation and caring of his wife needs to be a constant thing. While birthdays, anniversaries, vacations, dinners out and the like are helpful and important, the deeper desire of a woman is in everyday little ways of appreciation – of thanks for a meal, recognition of things well done, a hug or kiss or a loving word just to show she is greatly valued. Complements for saving or making money for the family, and for helping get things done on time are also appreciated. Giving a daily sense of being wanted and needed is more important than formal acceptance and recognition as her husband's wife. Just as it is not enough to simply know and accept that Christ died for us, we want to experience his love daily; so also a wife wants that daily experience of love.

Most women are made to be highly *verbal.* Since Adam found the animals were not companions, God created Eve so she would be able to talk to him for his good. Many women like to tell things in detail, unfolding the story to communicate the objective in the information. Women need to recognize that men want them to get to the bottom line and not react when they seem impatient. But men need to show suffering love by being patient to hear. Women want to give the details to make it clear, but also to be appreciated as helping. Since women are more emotional, they remember past abuses and neglects when the whole issue did not seem to be addressed. They are hurt and therefore want to bring up issues that are not settled from their point of view. One man once said to me, "Why is it my wife frequently goes back to things years ago?"

Men *are visual,* have logical objectives, and want to see and state the issue and make a decision. If the issue is not clear, they want to drop it and leave it for more thought. A wife should be patient. Women want to talk it through — right then. Some women want recognition for every detail of what they do, and until they are secure in their heavenly value in Christ, the husband must suffer hearing it all. Similarly, some men also have the need to convince their wives of the value of their work by constantly telling the details of their activities.

Men need the keen observation and detail of women to help guide them. Women need to see the man's long range desires, objectives, and help for the family. When this is not clear to a wife, she needs to trust Christ, and by suffering love go blindly with him as being led in Christ. These acts of suffering love seem ridiculous — or unreasonable — from the fleshly point of view.

Man's Suffering to Give Security in Loving Provision
A woman's emotional security does not comes entirely from her mate spending long hours at work and earning more money, but rather from his providing a sense of *emotional security* that can only come from a few words, even in a phone call, or from a

116

tender word or kiss. She values the time he spends with her just to talk and do little things, like a walk in the air-conditioned mall on a hot day or in the neighborhood in the cool evening. Closeness may also come from reading and discussing things.

A woman can usually accept a man's failure and defeat if he is still determined and committed to trust Christ for future success. Her knight may fall off his horse, but his spirit must not be killed too, so that he does not get back on. His long-term love and commitment is what is important for her to see. Many a divorce comes, not when a man loses his job, or is disgraced by wrong choices, but when he won't continue to try to work to lovingly provide even in a menial way. Most women cannot abide men who do not love enough to try to provide, even if they earn only a little. Taking a humble job paying less than before can show suffering love to her more than promotions to a higher pay.

Women have always worked to help husbands, and a man ought to encourage and appreciate his wife working to contribute to the family. But her work must be to help him and not to exalt herself. This has been shown in Proverbs 31:10 ff. These and other differences in men and women are important for communicating with suffering love.

Knowing and Appreciating Our Unique Spouse

Our attraction is to a particular spouse who will complement only us and no other person in marriage union. Not only are male and females different; every man is different and every woman is different within their sexuality. Therefore *each man and woman needs to communicate to know their own unique spouse* so they can better understand how to unite to serve together for Christ and his glory. As we know the gifts God gave to our partner and the ways they differ, we can see how we can better help each other in whatever the family needs and in the work God has called us to. We need to understand our spouse's different temperaments, ways of expression, and gifts.

Some spouses are people-oriented and are expressive extroverts, while others are quiet and withdrawn introverts. Some

117

are artistic doers; others are thinkers and planners, and need time alone. There are a thousand ways we can differ, but understanding these differences and having open communication to take advantage of them can enable us to help each other and appreciate that help. In our family, my wife is gifted in music and loves it, while I enjoy music but have little ability there. But this enriches my life and the lives of our children. She likes to save in small ways, which takes time like clipping coupons, but I like to just buy to get things done. We complement each other in these ways and constantly need to learn from each other. Many times our spouse's differences test us to help us grow. Sometimes we can resent these, but suffering love calls us to accept and learn. A fleshly, cruel reaction may incline us to also react, sometimes by showing appreciation for gifts of other women or men, when our spouse wants us to see their abilities.

It is important to remember that from heaven's perspective a simple activity may be more valuable than another matter seen as big in the eyes of the world. A simple word of praise or forgiveness at the right time may be more important than the costliest gift. Jesus pointed out that the least shall be greatest and the last shall be first. Jesus said the widow's mites sacrificially given were more important than the rich man's big gifts, and her act has inspired much more giving for the kingdom of God.

Love Offers Areas of Freedom
Communication of trust in each other's love in Christ should allow each to have broad areas for each person to do things. These things should aim to helping the other person, but each should be able to work without having to get permission or make decisions for approval. Every man and woman should have areas that are considered his or hers to do as they please. In Proverbs 31:10 ff. the wife is herself creative and acts, and her husband trusts her. Knowing that your spouse trusts and loves Christ and wants to show his love to you should offer freedom with only a few boundaries. Defined agreements on boundaries are not for laws to

judge each other, but are to show how far we can be free without causing each other problems.

Knowing each other's abilities and weaknesses helps the husband lead his wife, and together they set a minimum of these boundaries for family. For example, if a wife is frugal, she may pay all the bills and spend all the money without having to discuss these. In this case the husband will need to inform her if he needs to spend an amount beyond his usual needs. If the husband is inclined to work all the time, he needs to set times that he spends with his wife and with his family and know that his love requires that he try to keep these. When we fail, love forgives.

Edifying the Other Should Be the Aim of Christ's Love

All things should aim at edification, and this can involve negative and positive communication (Ephesians 4:29). Openness and truth should replace any falsehood or secrecy in our words and acts. The Spirit will enable each of us to know when we are being secretive about something. This is a lack of faith to trust God in our spouse. While injustice and selfish wrong-doing justly produces anger, faith in God calls us to let him avenge for us. Anger maintained leads to greater anger and self-vindication. The wrong should be suffered in love and lead to forgiveness. Anger can be used by the devil to produce hate and should be put to bed by the end of the day. When men or women hold resentments, these increase. The distance then between each other becomes ever greater, making intimate love impossible. Suffering love brings Christ's presence into the marriage that wonderfully unites.

Repeated devious doings are the devil's tool to reveal our naked differences and offend. "We are naked and we are ashamed." To take and use significant money for what we want without our spouse knowing, is stealing. While there should be freedom to trust each other to use funds, if we privately buy things that we think our spouse would question, this is an open door for the devil to enter and divide. To contact other people, especially a person of the opposite sex, and discuss matters to enhance our feelings about ourselves is a breach of love, and divides. First, prayerfully go and discuss the matter with your spouse for help. If your spouse approves for you to share with others, such friendly communication with others can be edifying. If we do things secretly, it is a work of darkness and it destroys love's power

Negative criticism to help improve our spouse is needed and should be helpful. But for us to correct others, we need to do it prayerfully to be sure the aim is love and not to justify self. Take the bean out your own eye first. We should always welcome negative criticism, even if we think it is unjustified. If we have died to self with Christ, we will want to see our wrongs and change to be more like him. If the criticism is not valid, the Spirit will encourage us and use this in our lives in the future. Genuine loving criticism is helpful and even unjust criticism can be accepted as suffering for Christ. No criticism can hurt us if we trust Christ. Most often we should first pray for God to show error. But if the Spirit confirms over time that we are right, we should proceed in love. If it is not favorably received, then the help of two or three others is needed. (Matthew 18:15-20).

Forgiveness is the Basis of Suffering Covenant Love

The New Covenant is based on the fact that "God has consigned all to disobedience, that he may have mercy on all" (Romans 11:32). The mercy to continue to offer forgiveness from all sin is based on the fact that to believe is to admit we in the flesh also still have a sin nature. While as a member of the New Covenant our desire is to please Christ from the heart, the Spirit will always call us to forgive our neighbor/spouse where there is failure. How many times should we forgive? "Seventy times seven!" That means repeatedly. We don't earn forgiveness by forgiving others, but we show we trust his love. We have eternal life and have God our Father to answer our prayers. Jesus taught the need to forgive in the last portion of the Lord's Prayer.

Forgive us our debts as we also have forgiven our debtors, And lead us not into temptation but deliver us from evil (or the evil one).

120

For if you forgive others their trespasses, your heavenly Father will also forgive you, but if you do not forgive others their trespasses, neither will your Father forgive your trespasses. (Matthew 6:12-15)

Paul instructed that anger should never go past the day of the offense. As New Covenant believers and the New Commandment we should ask for forgiveness and kiss each other good night to end each day. This is fundamental for continuing to have the power of New Covenant love by the Spirit to unite us.

Some Demonic Problems Can Require Greater Suffering Love
The final partition of the Lord's Prayer, "Lead us not into temptation but deliver us from the evil one/evil" makes it clear that as children of God in a world dominated by the devil, there is the possibility for us to fall into bondage from which we will need deliverance. All the writings of Christ's apostles warn against the snares of the devil against which we are constantly in combat (Ephesians 6:10 ff.). Jesus' teaching is that by prayer we can be led away from the devil's traps. Paul says,

Therefore let anyone who thinks that he stands take heed lest he fall. No temptation has overtaken you that is not common to man. God is faithful, and he will not let you be tempted beyond your ability, but with the temptation he will also provide the way of escape, that you may be able to endure it. Therefore, my beloved, flee from idolatry. (1 Corinthians 10:12-14)

When a spouse (or neighbor) has a weakness to repeatedly sin, the suffering required for the spouse to continue loving may be very difficult. If this is repeated, the question is raised as to whether the person is really in the New Covenant of Christ. John said,

Whoever makes a practice of sinning is of the devil, for the devil has been sinning from the beginning. The reason the Son of God appeared was to destroy the works of the devil. No one born of God makes a practice of sinning, for God's seed abides in him, and he cannot keep on sinning because he has been born of God. By this it is evident who are the children of God, and who are the children of the devil: whoever does not practice righteousness is not of God, nor is the one who does not love his brother. (1 John 3:8-10)

A true disciple of Christ has died with Christ as his sin offering and has lost his life, or given up the old man, to live by the Spirit with the power of eternal life. Paul promised that no temptation is too great to escape from, so if one loves and wants to please Christ, he cannot continue in sin and be a true child of God. Jesus himself warned that a true disciple is one who is now free by continuing in his word (John 8:31).

But there are hard situations that we must face in our marriage. Experienced counselors know that a person's family background can breed deep habits or sinful responses, the chains of which are extremely strong and hard to stay free from. Young men sometimes have fathers that have conflict with their mother. Some have fathers or older men that have involved them in pornography and immorality. Young women often have grown up in a home where their mothers have deep resentments and reactions to their fathers, or they are abused by men and have deep hurts. Today there are many families where drugs are given to children. Alcoholism is a prison the devil seems to repeatedly draw men and women back into. The demonic patterns are hard to eliminate and require much suffering love to help the person change.

We must hold that true children of God have the Spirit within them and they will want to continue in obedience and be free. But it is important to face the facts that not all Christians are equally strong, and some may fail more often than others. This is not an excuse to continue in sin. But it does mean that when we are married to a spouse who has been imprisoned by resentment for a long time, it will require greater and patient suffering until their freedom is secure.

Those who have such problems need to recognize that not only is this suffering for Christ's sake, but it is also a test of discipline given by God to enable the one suffering to be strong for his ministry to others in this world. Communication is harder, but brings joy when we are like Christ, who kept his eyes on his coming throne at the right hand of God (Hebrews 12:3-11).

Confession is important. Openness to admit our failures to each other sometimes gives opportunities for the devil to react and give pain or destruction. Our partner can see and use our disclosure of weaknesses and failures to accuse, advise, and in anger reject. It is important to recognize that there is the possibility of taking advantage and responding in revenge instead of suffering love.

I know of a situation when a man disclosed to his wife that when traveling in his job he was unwell and lonely. He showed affection toward a woman he met, and he was tempted. He did not commit adultery, but had failed in his heart. He was telling his wife this because he loved her and wanted her loving help. But his wife was so hurt with this intimate communication that she separated from him and lost her freedom with him. Their relationship and his health went downhill. This was his wife's opportunity to show forgiveness and great affection and love which would have drawn them together at a time when he would have wanted more intimacy. Her power with him would have magnified instead of diminished.

Growth in Knowledge of God's Love Increases Our Love

It is trust in Christ's love that enables us to die to self and communicate. Only by being rooted and grounded in Christ's love, and then by continuing to grow in the knowledge of the love of Christ that passes knowledge, can we increasingly let the suffering love of Christ be expressed through us (Ephesians 3:17-19). Use of all the means of grace from God's word in private devotions, and from the church will enable us to grow stronger and to communicate better. Growing in the knowledge of the love of Christ requires participating in and humbly accepting the benefits of the gifts of other members in the body of Christ, who help each other through exhortation, teaching, and prayer. Paul's great chapter on love (1 Corinthians 13) is in the midst of his instructions about how to use your gifts in communicating to edify and help each other in the body of Christ. "If I speak with tongues of men and or angels..." but I don't have love, *it is nothing*. "Love does not rejoice at wrongdoing, but rejoices with the truth. Love bears all things, believes all things, hopes all things, endures all things" (1 Corinthians 13:6, 7).

Conclusions

Trust in Christ's love for us enables us to trust each other. If we believe Christ can work all things for our good by his abiding love and his glory (Romans 8:28) we can go beyond the pain of self-pity, selfish defense, or vengeance, and truly communicate by words and acts those things that are really caring and meaningful to our spouse. This will enable us to truly know each other by experience and not by profession of words.

Chapter 8
Covenant Love Uniting
Male and Female in One Flesh

Alone or United, Self or Christ's Love

In the beginning creation the only thing that God said was "not good" was that man was *"alone."* To make all things good, God created a wife of his essence to complement him, being different to supplement other aspects of God's own image or character. The loneliness that could not be satisfied from the animals was ended by both Adam and Eve uniting their differences as one. The union of their different bodies to express God's goodness to each other was supremely expressed by Adam wanting to join his body to Eve's, and by her willingness to give her body to him. Each of their male and female whole persons, mentally, emotionally and in abilities were expressed through their different bodily natures. Therefore, the union of their bodies that defined their different natures was an expression of appreciation of the goodness God gave by making them different so they could united to be one, and *not be alone*. Each giving their body to the other to complement as one was the *ultimate act of union and trust in God*.

By believing the deceptive lie that they as individuals could, by eating the fruit of knowledge, own nature and be wise as God, they did so and fell into sin. As individual gods like him, their judgment was that their differences were evil (not good) and to be ashamed of, so the good would be to make each person perform the same. As shown in the previous chapter on works of the flesh, and the fruit of the Spirit, the natural effort of the woman is to want the man to be like her, and that of the man is to want the woman to be like him. This is to ask the other person to be who they are not. These perversions change the sexual purpose of physical union from an acceptance of the whole person as complementary, to selfishly using each others body primarily for an act of pleasure. Thus the man wants to use the woman, and she then also wants his body to please her. The male and female are thus thinking and acting as selfish lone individuals. While each selfish person will do things to please the other person to get them to let them use their body, the ultimate aim is selfishness. Thus in all they do they are *alone.* The limit of the individual selfishness changes as the whole culture degrades.

John T. Cacioppo, in his extensive study of this problem at the opening of his book *Loneliness* quotes a woman to illustrate the problem he found. In Part One, "The Lonely Heart," she said,

> In a crowd at work, even in a family setting, I always feel lonely. It can be overwhelming at times, a physical sensation. My doctors have called it depression, but there is a difference. I read once, you are born alone and you die alone. But what about all the years in between? *Can you really belong to someone else?* Can you ever resolve the inner feeling of being alone? Shopping won't do it. Eating won't do it. Random sex doesn't make it go away. If and when you find any answers, please write back and tell me.[37]

The obvious answer is expressed by her, in that one cannot end loneliness *without belonging to someone.* To have all social connections one must begin by belonging to another person in marriage and that only happens by giving yourself to be accepted by the other person, and them giving themselves to you. All children need to belong to a mother and father. Every family must belong to others in a group to worship, work or function together to extend belonging by marriage of the children, and to then extend further in work and culture.

The problem is that human nature of all men and women since Adam is selfish and they think they are wise as God (Romans 5:12). Each one wants everyone to be like them and comply with their wishes. If a person is willing to belong to someone else, this belonging is extended by like mindedness to others, and so on. Adulterers use sex selfishly, and homosexuals have rejected others

---

[37]John T. Cacioppo and William Patrick, *Loneliness: Human Nature and the Need for Social Connection* (New York: W. W .Norton & Company, 2008), 1. This is a professional detailed study. Cf. also Lisa Grossman, "The Ties that Bind," *Science News,* January 16, 2010, 26-29.

except those who satisfy them. This belonging can only occur when we repent and believe that God in Christ died as our sacrifice for our sins, and now he is raised and accepts those who give him their life now, and who trust his sovereign power to live in them and raise them from the dead. The power of New Covenant love is the only way to be united, and it must begin by faith in God's great love in submissive sexual union by Christ's Spirit.

God in his grace is known in his power and goodness by what he does for all men through his control of the natural working of creation. After man's sin and their exclusion as selfish individuals, God killed animals and clothed the man and the woman for them to accept their differences. Adam and Eve's understanding of God's accepting love is manifested in that Abel believed acceptance by sacrifice. Moreover, God changed their conditions. Eve was to bear more children and with pain, and Adam could no longer provide with ease as in the Garden, but all nature was cursed requiring him to work harder. Both these changes made Eve and Adam see that God was controlling all things, and that they had limitations in their knowledge and needed to be dependent on him to bless their efforts, and on each other for help. God's continued love of sinners is taught by Jesus, who said,

> But I say to you, Love your enemies and pray for those who persecute you, so that you may be sons of your Father who is in heaven. For he makes his sun rise on the evil and on the good, and sends rain on the just and on the unjust (Matthew 5:44; Matthew 5:45).

All previous civilizations have believed in a sovereign God who accepts by death in a sacrifice, but this is a shadow of the only effective sacrifice that is the voluntary death of God's incarnate Son.

In chapter 10 Paul's description of the pattern of God in his grace enables a nation of people to know and trust him, and through loving marriages they build a prosperous civilization. But then in unbelief they become ungrateful and turn and worship that which is created in nature, and turn again to selfish treatment of sexual roles that destroys marriage and all relationships that emerge from ungratitude (Romans 1:19-28). In chapter 9, the influence of Covenant love through marriage will be seen as spreading power of God.

The amazing paradox is that the only way to find acceptance of our differences is not by trying to change and equalize others, but to repent and return to trust God's love in Christ, and then with faith, let him show his love through us with the power of New Covenant love. His suffering love for us then can be experienced and shown to others by union of our two different aspects of his image, male and female.

More will also be revealed about what is happening in the United States, and how only the power of New Covenant love can renew our civilization. This chapter is written to help the reader understand how Christ's love can give intimacy to the whole person that makes joining together man and woman a wonderful blessing in marriage, and in doing so, reveals the image of God.

Biblical Meaning of "One Flesh" in Marriage Love

Right Meaning of Word "Love"

What does the Bible mean by God's love in Christ? The world uses the English word "love" for many things and in many ways. We love ice cream or skiing, or in regard to many other things we like. But it most often is used to express the love of a man and woman, and primarily regarding sexual relationships. The early Christian world wrote and conversed in the Greek language as well as Aramaic. Most of the New Covenant scriptures were written in Koinē or popular Greek. The Greeks had five words which more clearly defined ideas about love than does English. One that is translated into English is *erros* from which we get the word erotic, usually suggesting the sensual. But **erros** in Greece had the idea of **romantic love** or desire to see and have a person who physically and emotionally appeals to you.

I saw a lovely and brilliant young woman who needed help in arranging an organic chemistry experiment, and after helping her I wanted to be with her, and soon wanted to marry her. That was over 64 years ago, and the beginning of something wonderful. That was romantic love. Such romantic love (*erros*) then often involves the idea of love as *passion* in sex which was the word *epithumia*. Invitation to sexual passion is what is promoted and used to sell things by sex, and it is what describes a brief overwhelming emotional boost of temporary sensual pleasure. Another Greek word is *philos,* which expresses familial affection for loyal responsibility to each other. *Phila*delphia is a city known as "the city of *brotherly love*." A fourth little used Greek word was *storgē,* which expressed likeness for another person that you are comfortable with – like an old shoe; with them you seemed relaxed and you like to be around them.

The fifth word was the one that God used to express His love, or *agapē*. This word meant *to care for intensely as a fixed choice of character*. It is used to express God's care for the world in sending Christ to die, but it also means the choice and fixed desire of the world for darkness, even when God has revealed his light. "God so *loved* (*agapē*) the world, that he gave his only begotten Son" (John 3:16). It then said light has come into the world and, "Men *loved* (*agapē*) darkness..." (John 3:18). This contrast is throughout the New Testament in showing that God chooses to care for those who have rejected him or do not love him. The love of Christ is therefore a love of his choice that is made effective by faith of those in spite of offense and suffering. This is given clear definition by Paul in 1 Corinthians 13:4, "Love suffers long, is patient and love is kind ..." By trusting his love for us, we are enabled to accept offenses and to love each other in marriage. This was shown to be the essence of the New Covenant of God with his people in Christ's death for us (John 13:34, 25).

The Greek words are explained to help you see the importance and difference of meaning given by God in contrast to the world. *Erros* or romantic love may soon be disillusioned when the person acts selfishly. Sexual *epithumia* or passion can become hot as fire, but can be put out or killed by a selfish act or harsh words. Passion may be no longer desirable when the partner seeks selfish passion only for themselves without considering the other. Familial love or *philos* will soon die if the person does not care and neglects responsibilities to the family on which we depend. A wife who never does her share, or a husband who refuses to work and provide, may bring to an end a willingness for meeting obligations. Self-interest may overtake the desire to participate. The feeling of comfort in being together (*storgē*) and mutual acceptance also will be disrupted when a person ceases to feel cared for, is ignored or is offended and manifests resentment. It is therefore the **unselfish choice to care even if it causes suffering which is the love** (*agapē*) that makes all other expressions of love of abiding value. This **gives all these kinds of love an abiding meaning and worth**. With *agapē* love, romance can develop, passion intensifies to intimacy, mutual helpfulness has meaning, and comfort together grows.

It is God's love in us that transforms marriage and sexual relations for self-giving, and allows pleasure in sex to grow and produce the deepest marriage love. Joining our bodies is the ultimate act of giving oneself to another, and therefore communicates our caring in the most final and absolute way. But that is why experiencing the vertical view of our marriage oneness with Christ in his death is critical to promote all the other benefits of physical union. In a sinful world of selfish people, becoming "one flesh" should be the best expression of Christ's love (***agapē***). Without this all physical love is a passing fancy that is soon lost. That is why "love" is usually sought for selfish purposes with alcohol, psychedelic drugs, and in unnatural ways to hide the pain.

Submission to One Another as to Christ: Love that Unites

The Scriptures spell out how suffering love is to be practiced by each sex for marriage oneness. The achievement of "one flesh" in God's purposes for covenant people involves the "***submission*** of one to another" as described in Ephesians 5:22 ff., and as discussed in Chapter 4 in this book. Submission to one another proceeds from the fullness of Spirit in submission to Christ, and for His glory. Mutual submission to Christ and each other is the key to real union and great pleasure.

The whole idea of sexual oneness in the flesh is based on the understanding that the man and woman are each giving their body to the other partner for him/her to use for their benefit. Paul's instruction to the churches was as follows.

> Let each man have his own wife and each woman have her own husband. Let the husband fulfill his duty to his wife and likewise also the wife to her husband. The wife does not have authority over her own body, but the husband does, and likewise also the husband does not have authority over his own body, but the wife does. Don't deprive one another, except by agreement for a time that you may devote yourselves to prayer, and come together again lest Satan tempt you because of your lack of self control (1 Corinthians 7:2-5).

These instructions were given in a time of growing tribulation for Christians when extraordinary devotion to Christ and much prayer was recommended. Paul here sets forth what he considered the normal sexual relations in marriage. The husband and wife are to **give authority over their body to the other partner.** The adage, "It is more blessed to give than to receive," is true in sexual relations. The giving of oneself brings the greatest blessing of pleasures back from each other and from the Lord. It accomplishes a progressive long term love for union under the presence and power of God. When experienced as caring love from Christ to us, it achieves the deepest intimacy and pleasure, uniting the male's aggressive sharing and giving with the woman's delight in submissive helping and receiving. Such sexual surrender is the source of power.

In discussing the New Covenant love of Christ for his bride the church, it was emphasized that *knowing* God through Christ's revelation to his elect disciples was the basis of them experiencing trusting Christ's love and becoming one as a church. Christ looked forward to their eternal union together in that love (cf. John 17; 22, 23, 26). Jesus repeatedly emphasized in his prayer that he had *made known* to them God's person; he had *manifested God's name* to them, and they had received the word, and believed, giving them eternal life. It was this intimate *knowledge* that produced *trust*, which would lead to experience his *great love* and *produce oneness*. God's love properly understood and trusted is the power that produces a oneness in those of us who are Christ's bride with him. It also gives us love from above by the Spirit.

In the manner that Christ builds love in his bride, a man and woman must communicate, *know each other*, their needs, and their deep desires including sexual ones. As they sacrificially meet these, they will grow in trust that enables them to give themselves to each other. "Adam *knew* his wife, and she conceived" (Genesis 4:1). The "one flesh" is the completion of the *process of knowing* each other to be one with each other in life's goals, purposes, in ways for mutual cooperation to show his love, and in intimate sexual oneness.

Narcissism Rather then Knowledge and Care of Others

Psychological hindrances from offenses and lack of understanding and appreciation of the sexual partner are the chief obstacles to complete enjoyment of sexual oneness. It has been accurately and repeatedly said by sex counselors, that "the most important sex organ is the brain." When the brain is turned off or hostile to the partner, pleasure and true union dies. This often includes major anger or resentment passed on to us by mother and father against the spouse in our upbringing as mentioned above. Or selfishness may be from the natural tendencies of our old natures. Failure in attitude and communication are said by Ed Wheat, a Christian counselor, to be half the problems hindering sexual satisfaction in marriage, while other counselors say it is 80%.[38]

Women's Selfishness Causes Sexual Resistance

According to Marynia Farnham and Marie Robinson, two leading women psychologists, offense and fear of men were the main cause for being "frigid" or for lack of full intimate pleasure

---

[38] Ed Wheat, M. D., and Gaye Wheat, *Intended for Pleasure* (Old Tappen, New Jersey: Fleming H. Revell Company, 1977 et. al.) 127.

by women.[39] Many women don't even know if they have experienced full pleasures – which would indicate they haven't. Many men and women approach union selfishly, even with resentment, and have no idea beyond efforts at mechanical titillation to help achieve any greater pleasure than their own individual selfish climax and release. Therefore, Shere Hite's research for the feminists concluded that masturbation was as satisfying for most women as heterosexual acts.[40] Masters and Johnson concluded that homosexuals had greater satisfaction.[41]

Subconscious fear or hate by a woman is an almost insurmountable dam against responding and lovingly giving herself to her husband, and she has a hard time allowing him to give her anything. Above all, her sinful nature tells her she must be independent! Many men look at the bed as their privilege, and they go to have their pleasure and leave. Many men and women cheat themselves out of real pleasure by being unwilling to give or yield themselves which allows emotional union. Many women resentfully allow themselves to be used in fear of losing financial support for them and their children or losing respect socially. Only dying with Christ and trusting his Spirit to enable them to love an unlovely man or woman gives change. How does this work?

Man's Selfishness Encourages Women Toward Rejection and Unfaithfulness

Man's ability to work hard, provide, to boldly take risks, and his intense desire for intercourse are all manly aspects of God's plan to help woman and should be appreciated. But if a man is selfish in these, manliness alone does not bring the intimacy that a woman wants and needs. She may then seek that affection elsewhere. The wife of Potiphar, the Egyptian general, had luxury

---

[39] Marynia Farnham and Ferdinand Lundberg, *Modern Women: The Lost Sex,* (New York: Harper, 1947) and Marie Robinson, *The Power of Sexual Surrender,* (New York: A Signet book of Doubleday Publishers, 1958).
[40] Shere Hite, *The Hite Report,* (New York: Dell, 1963) p106.
[41] William H. Masters and Virginia E. Johnson, *Homosexuality in Perspective,* (Boston: Little Brown, 1979). Cf. Carl Wilson, *Our Dance Has Turned to Death* for this and other studies, p71.

and protection, but he was constantly gone, and the faithful and conscientious Joseph who managed the house was attractive to his wife (Genesis 39:1-10). The beautiful woman who becomes an adulteress has a husband who goes on a long journey with much money, and will not be back until the new moon, leaving her alone (Proverbs 7:19, 20). But these beautiful women were seeking love for their own attention and pleasure.

Selfish men make it hard for women to love. Only by trusting Christ to love a man who is unlovely can she find oneness. It is easy for a man to be independent, to seek success for self, and neglect his wife. Moreover, Scripture reveals more promiscuity and abuse by men toward women. He can walk away from a casual affair and leave a woman with a child and long-term responsibility. New Covenant suffering love where both spouses die to self with Christ is essential to progressively yield intimate love.

Different Submissions Produce Oneness and Pleasure

Understanding Submission and Destiny
In discussing New Covenant love in Chapter 2, it is said, "Wives, be subject your own husbands, as to the Lord." The emphasis is the husband's headship over the family and the wife's extent of submission to him is "in *everything*" *as to Christ*. The way the wife is to yield authority to her husband is to not just allow, but to submit fully to him, since he is Christ's head over her. His responsibility is to know Christ's will and share it with her.

A life of growing to know each other should lead to experiencing the deepest physical knowledge. Her mental attitude of respect and practice of submission always in everything becomes the key to her attitude in physical union to completely give herself. This leads to the most exhilarating union of one flesh. As shown in Chapter 4, the submission of the man is to sacrificially give himself in love as Christ has for us, his church, or to love her as the husband does himself. To submit as to Christ, makes union an act of worship.

Trust is Key to Love, Pleasure and Transformation

A woman's attitude often is influenced by her family or from other experiences with men, for good or bad. As mentioned earlier, the findings of Seymour Fisher's experiments, showed the *only consistent factor* for women who most regularly reached full satisfaction was that they had fathers whom they respected that were in strict, loving control.[42] The view of men by these women was of a man who cared and who exercised control because he cared. This was a surprise to these who approached the matter as scientists. Also, bad experiences with men cause wrong attitudes.

Dr. Marie Robinson, a Diplomat of the America Board of Psychiatry and Neurology, and a Fellow of the American Psychiatric Association with a broad hospital and private practice with women, was regarded as a major authority on women. She was made a member of the National Academy of Science. In her book, *The Power of Sexual Surrender,* she found that for a woman to consistently and deeply experience maximum physical pleasure was for her to appreciate and respect the contribution of her husband's manliness to her and her family. In this book Robinson spends many pages explaining that a woman should delight in her husband who complements her by assuming difficult and daily responsibilities of providing for and protecting her and children.[43]

Robinson and her team found that when thousands of women who were restrained from pleasure in the physical union received such an understanding of men, and changed their attitude toward their husband, they were liberated to ecstatic sexual pleasure. Thus gentle patient love from her husband, and her complete submission, gives her the most power and pleasure. Since he wants to see her pleased, her response gives him great satisfaction. Thus the wife who surrenders gains greater and greater power to control her husband. More importantly, their *intimate union manifests to God the complementary joining of their two aspects of his image revealing his Covenant love.* This intimate love will be seen in all

---

[42] Seymour Fisher, *Understanding the Female Orgasm* (New York: Basic Books, 1973).

[43] Robinson, *The Power of Sexual Surrender*, chapter 25 *The Male Sex: a New Horizon,* 297-308.

their relationships, from daily life with their children, and even to the entire community. The realization of her glorification of Christ in trusting him through her husband, gives the woman a sense of Christ's daily presence. Yielding to him gives her freedom and power as a woman. Competition is bondage, fear, and loneliness.

After helping hundreds of women, Dr. Robinson wrote,

> For a woman requires a trust in one's partner that is absolute. Recall for a moment that the physical experience is often so profound that it entails the loss of consciousness for a period of time... There must be a sensual eagerness to surrender; in the woman's orgasm the excitement comes from the act of surrender.[44]

This deep sensual sexual desire is explicitly presented as good from the woman's and the man's point of view in *The Song of Solomon* in the Bible. All good sensual excitements from the best foods, wines, good-smelling anointing oils, and fragrant spices are associated to illustrate and give excitement. Men and women need to see the man's appreciation of woman's sexual beauty and the woman's appreciation of his strength, aggressive agility, and desire for her. This book of the Bible should be read along with other passages, such as Proverbs 5:15-19 which present the good for a man to love his wife. Proverbs also reveals the bad effects of seeking immoral pleasure. These passages plus Robinson's book have been helpful to many. But because Robinson's language is more explicit than most Scripture, I have chosen to give her teachings as Addendum B at the back of the book to be read as you might choose.

Women's power by surrender is transforming. Dr. Robinson emphasizes the transformation this surrender has is profound, extensive, and powerful in her book's third chapter entitled, "The Not Impossible She." It is not just that a woman then enjoys such an ecstatic and amazing relationship in union with her husband. It is that *she realizes her created feminine nature and the power*

---

[44] Ibid, 157, 158. Read Chapter 2, The Normal Orgasm, *The Power of Sexual Surrender,* given here for reading at your discretion in Addendum B, pages 265-275.

that she has as a woman. She can now appreciate the power to give this great pleasure to her husband, and how this makes him want to please her. Moreover her realization of his great worth changes her attitudes toward him and others to express her amazing ability to use all her gifts to serve. In Chapter 16 on "The Nature of Surrender," Dr. Robinson said,

> With this kind of acceptance of her central role, changes now come rapidly to a woman. As she feels the unity of need and good between her husband and herself, any remaining contention leaves her. In the marriage, consensus now becomes her aim. She is no longer by losing an argument, fearful that she will be forced to do something that is repugnant or humiliating to her, for she realizes that to her husband her welfare is the dearest of all things. And conversely, his happiness and peace of mind become her first desire.
>
> And now she has tapped in on the greatest psychological joy of women – her capacity to give. …We have called this the "essential female altruism," a characteristic root in every woman's biological nature. Women who are really secure within themselves and in their roles have an inexhaustible store of this altruism.
>
> At this juncture, or closely following on it, a woman begins to feel her full power, the power that comes to her for her destiny. She now realizes that, far from being in a weak position in relationship to man, her position is so strong that she must be careful not to exploit it. One of the deepest and strongest psychological needs of man is his poignant desire for immortality through his children. She could deny him this or she could make his life miserable while granting him it. Or she can make it the most beautiful and meaningful thing in her life and in his.[45]

By discovering the sexual power of her womanhood to influence husband, children, and others, Robinson explains how this even changes her physically. She said,

> As she reaps the rewards of her new capacity to give of herself unstintingly and fearlessly to her husband and her children, the very appearance of a woman often begins to chance. Drawn expressions

---

[45] Ibid., 155-156.

relax, anxious forehead wrinkles disappear; thin-lipped mouths soften. Indeed, her whole body rounds and softens, taking on the look associated with a tender and giving femininity.

She also describes how often intense pre-menstrual and menstrual pains and irregular periods are changed and pregnancy, which before was very difficult, becomes "a highly accelerated feeling of pleasure and well-being."

Trust in God for Marriage Comes from Creation and Bible
This self-giving of man and woman to each other comes from the knowledge of God in creation (Romans 1:19, 20) and natural desires, which come from the need for each other (Genesis 3:16-19) and can be accepted as good by all people. But in societies of material competition, this rational view ends.

The abiding change can only come to any woman from faith in God and accepting her natural purpose in creation. But only the woman who has accepted God's New Covenant suffering love for her in the cross, and the power of that love by the Holy Spirit, can also find the joy of giving suffering love to her husband, and thereby revealing God's image.

Physical Union becomes Sacred Event for and with Christ
Moreover, the whole sexual experience of becoming one is changed into a great realization of God's presence and achieving his purpose in her as a woman. Robinson quotes from a letter of one of her patients who had come to appreciate her husband and having surrendered to him, experienced exciting sexual climax.

> This feeling of power was quickly followed by an intense feeling of humility. I thought of how I held within me, within my body, the power to bring him (my husband) the greatest of joys; or to deprive him of it. And then I realized the terrible thing it would be to ever misuse this power. And now I felt really for the first time, despite my former lip service to the idea, the reason why marriage must be considered sacramental. The relationship between husband and wife which results in the unsolvable mystery of birth goes beyond human understanding. To participate in this mystery really requires a

consecration by both. Any lesser attitude toward it is like the laugher of mockery in a holy place.[46]

I must go beyond Robinson, by saying that the act of giving pleasurable intimacy with a sense of God's presence can produce the most profound love between two people. The woman's participation by complete submission to her husband for his pleasure is because of Christ's love and is in obedience to him. And the husband's love as a gift for her has implications for all they do.

Submission in Love Gives Freedom to Act

Submission in love does not mean inactivity or lack of affection by a wife. It does not mean she cannot initiate by kiss, touch or hug, nor does it mean she cannot suggest and invite in various and even explicit ways. Most men like this and it should be a part of her giving her body to him in love. But it means that her mentality throughout is one of respect and yielding to his leading – of unreservedly giving herself to him.

There is an old nature in every woman and she will never do this perfectly in this life, but for Christ she commits herself to this end. Preoccupation and previous fears may be used by the devil to hinder. Too often a woman has other things on her mind, but she must ask God to remove these distractions, give victory over previous fears of men which she imputes to him, in order to desire to be his completely. Many women feel hesitant to tell their husbands they love them or to give them a hug and kiss or show special evidences of caring. Some fear he will use this as an opportunity to take advantage of her. Some women do not want their husband to see and know her pleasure. They hold back, consciously or subconsciously, and deny themselves their pleasure rather than have him feel he has pleased her. Other women may strongly resist making love. A woman has to die with Christ to these attitudes to obey Christ. Most of all, a Christian man wants to know that his wife has been blessed and enjoyed his love.

---

[46] Ibid., 155.

The Husband's Submissive Sacrificial Role

The husband's submission by sacrificially giving is equally satisfying. The husband is instructed to "love his wife as Christ loved the church and gave Himself for her" and "to love his wife as he loves his own body." As her leader, he is to submit to Christ and sacrifice himself for her good. He must realize this leadership in giving her his body is part of his bigger role to know Christ's will and love her. This calls him to see this act as part of his duty to know Christ's will and share it with her. Adam was instructed about their mission and work in the garden, and the command not to eat of the tree of good and evil before Eve was created. Men today have the responsibility to know and share Christ's love. This giving is communicated in the gift of his body.

This is to be the husband's lifestyle in daily relationships *in everything.* Christ was Lord and Master of heaven and earth, but he illustrated his death to cleanse his disciples by washing their feet as their servant. By a man making his power and as her leader available for her good as she pleases for Christ's sake is his act of humility to show his love. The husband as lord should daily be washing the feet of his bride. This is to be extended to the marriage bed. Men are prone to think that sexual relations are for them. Many women complain that their husbands forget them, and once they have their pleasure are not patient. I have had women tell me that their disappointment often is that when all is over, the husband does not continue to kiss and express love and appreciation.

In the western Christian civilized world, real men used to be called "gentlemen" – men who are *gentle* towards women. Much is said about foreplay which usually refers to physical touching, but as Dr. Laura once mentioned, vacuuming the house and every evidence of daily caring is in a way preparation for the bed together. No man is worthy of the gift of from his wife's body, and he will never give himself to her perfectly. However, it is most important to see that a life of growing understanding and mutual giving builds the foundation for a woman to be free to respect and respond. Kissing, hugging, and giving thanks often in many things when no full sexual intimacy is intended or possible is good preparation for the bed at a later time. Of course, patient affection and physical touching is also desirable immediately to prepare. But to think a wife or husband will be ready at every moment is unreasonable and unbiblical.

Generally, it is the husband's initiative to submit his body to the authority of his wife. Throughout the process he is to be aware that in his control as leader he is to seek to know her pleasure and response, and *proceed as she indicates*, and not according to what he wants. An understanding of her needs at the time of initiation, and feeling her desires throughout are to guide his giving of himself. He therefore focuses on *controlling his desires* to help meet hers so *she can yield complete control*. He is the one leading, and is in control to sacrificially care for her. The husband uses his control to help his wife achieve her blessing, and to give her children. In their union, all of the husband's body is to be under the power of her womanhood. Her communication by word or evidence of physical response is her request to which he should respond.

Again, the husband's supreme desire should be to glorify Christ by sacrificially loving his wife in becoming "one flesh." As the giving of Christ on the cross was to bring his disciples to experience love that unites, so the giving in all life and physical union aims at communicating deep love for each other for Christ's sake. The *physical pleasure is a motivational means* to that end, but by this sacrificial attitude the ability to give and receive, and therefore enjoy *the pleasure will be greatly increased*. The pleasure is greatly intensified because this caring assists her to be fully receptive physiologically to his manly power, and then he can know her at the deepest point of her being. Because there are many circumstances involved, every experience will not be the same.

Transforming Power of Man's Humble Suffering

There is a tremendous sense of humility and gratitude created in the husband when a wife completely surrenders to him. The immense pleasure she gives him along with this tremendous act of trust in him humbles him to better realize his responsibility to her

141

and to children. Her surrender gives her power over him. Moreover, the realization of that immense responsibility to care for them humbles him to seek and depend on God's wisdom and help to provide and protect. The greatness of her love and the idea of the miracle of a child also introduce the sense of sacredness and closeness of God. A husband can afterwards lead his wife in prayer of thanksgiving for the blessing so that making love becomes more sacred.

This act of the husband's self-giving for his wife results in a transformation of his own self-image and his purpose in life. He goes to work with a new desire and greater purpose to provide for his wife and children out of love, and not to gain recognition, personal self-esteem, and wealth. He has a new motive to act honorably for his family so they will not be ashamed. She has a new motive to want him to be "honored in the gates." He becomes deeply concerned to protect and keep her safe and secure and to be ready to help her in every way. While other women may seem beautiful, his thoughts and heart are toward his own wife and the children she may give.

His strength becomes devoted to producing a family for the glory of God, and he wants to develop and increase it for that purpose. His propensity for risk is wisely directed by God to protect and provide. No longer does he want to show off his manly courage, by foolish and dangerous acts to show manliness. He wants to use that strength and courage to risk for serving his wife and children, and to give to the glory of God.

Control of the Old Nature Requires Christlike Suffering
The husband and wife are exhorted, "Be angry and do not sin, do not let the sun go down on your anger" (Ephesians 4:26). Uncaring words and acts do not prepare for good response, since trust builds love in the experience. When the man or wife are unresponsive or not capable at the moment, tenderness toward each other is the evidence of Christ's suffering in the relationship.

Because of past experiences, some men and women have difficulty showing affection or giving themselves. Willful trust in

Christ can overcome fear and inward selfish resistance. An unaffectionate man or woman can overcome this by willfully making themselves break the demonic barrier by recklessly saying "I love you," or giving a hug or kiss to their spouse even when they don't feel like it. Soon this will not be an effort, but a joy. Willful acts of trust can break barriers where there is no feeling, and bring feeling.

It is highly important that neither the husband nor wife express expectations for performance, but allow freedom for complete or partial failure to be accepted and appreciated. Freedom of love is important, and opens the door to the most fulfillment.

Expressive Submission Will Grow the Pleasure

This kind of sexual union will grow in pleasure, desire for, and trust in each other over time. The night of a Hebrew wedding began with the bride veiled, to allow her to be comfortable in making herself known and knowing her husband without sudden bold new acquaintance and fear. Adam and Eve said, "I was afraid because I was naked" (Genesis 3:10). The old Hebrew wedding chamber came after a feast with good wine. Gradually the two could know how to freely claim all the body of the other as theirs to fully enjoy. Learning more about our bodies and what pleases each other is part of *knowing* each other, and allows each to give a greater gift. This should be progressively meaningful: even in old age the experience can become more intimate, more wonderful. A well know resource on technique is by Ed and Gaye Wheat.[47]

The world's way of instantly jumping into bed fully exposed, and using various techniques for manipulating more self-satisfying pleasure may occasionally give greater thrills. But seeking self-pleasure will not give growing and long-term intimacy and meaning as being "one flesh" in Covenant love. It actually dulls the satisfaction and brings fear, hate, and loneliness. This often leads to greater perversion in techniques and to different partners.

---

[47] Ed and Gaye Wheat, *Intended for Pleasure* is competent for Christians to explain physiology and technique.

When seeking new techniques and postures for fleshly pleasure becomes the objective, then selfishness will often obscure the objective of a life of love that should consummate in the bed. Technique for pleasure should always be secondary to building New Covenant sacrificial love. The whole body should be available to the other person as a gift and various touching and kissing is acceptable, provided it is sacrificial for the other person and acceptable to Christ who is present to guide. Genuine giving to each other pays the higher dividends that far surpass the best techniques. This union in love for each other goes beyond and is more satisfying than all feelings communicated by the body.

Since the body and sex is God-created, and nakedness is not evil, most (but not all) agreed upon techniques are permissible, although even all the right ones may not be desirable. The husband and wife should reject practices condemned by the Scriptures that are unhealthy and humiliating to the partner.[48] Communicating about what is pleasurable is highly important and unintended acts that may be offensive must be forgiven. Fathers should explain to their sons the basic physiology and technique for showing love and mothers should teach their daughters.

God's Expansion of Union by Multiplication

The greatest consummation should come when the physical relationship is fulfilled by the husband giving his seed to his wife to combine with her egg under God's working to produce a child. The true union of "one flesh" is seen in a child who by both genes produces a new individual bearing the resemblance of both. More importantly, the child will also bear the image of God. This leaves an indelible reminder that God was present in the union.

This is dramatically illustrated by the conversion of a nationally known Black Panther gang leader in San Francisco. He

---

[48] All is to be done as unto Christ. Self masturbation apart from the partner or pornography promotes selfishness and actually will diminish closeness. Sodomy includes several perversions, including anal sex which is productive of VD. Oral sex may be humiliating or offensive, but study shows six out of ten men want this of wives, and some wives want this. Bestiality is evil.

and his wife had a son. One day as he looked at the little boy, he recognized features resembling his wife, and how his son's ears and nose were like his. He suddenly was overwhelmed with this miracle. It could not just be by chance. God had to be in the act and produce this union. He broke down and confessed his anger, asked for forgiveness, and expressed his faith in a prayer of thanks to God.

Throughout becoming "one flesh," the vertical participation from God is involved. The great pleasure that draws the man and woman together results in the amazing miracle of a new human being. Producing children in marriage can extend the work of God in the world.

Only Real Suffering Love Produces God's Eternal Reward
Men and women know intuitively the needs of the other for sexual satisfaction, and can adapt these for selfish gain. Men learn that women want a mate that is tender and women learn men want respect. A divorced woman who had a man living with her and her children came to me for counseling because of a sense of insecurity. I asked her why she had accepted this relationship, and continued in it when she knew it was wrong. Her response was, "He is so tender and patient in our relationship." But he was a Casanova who had learned the art of seduction, and in time her fears were realized. He left her for another woman. My wife learned from her beautician of a man who had a beautiful, capable wife, but also had another woman besides her. The shop keeper explained what the man said was his reason for his other female companion: "My wife uses me; my other woman companion respects me." Both the "tender man" and the "respectful" consort learned to fake and use what the other sex wants.

Conclusion
But the real "gentleman" (gentle man) and the caring, respecting woman are those who chose to love because of Christ's suffering love for us, knowing this Covenant suffering love alone really unites and glorifies God and shows his image. A man may

accept rebuke and quarreling often with the hope of freeing his wife from self to find the deepest pleasure of union. They should never cease being willing to suffer to help their spouse find full release and freedom in their whole relationship. A wife may often react and not show respect. A woman may obey and respect her husband and not find tenderness. But they are called to suffer for Christ's sake in hope.

Like Christ we are to lose our life in this world and in our marriage, to find it again eternally. Only the disciples who die to self point to its source in heaven, where it has eternal meaning. And maybe by God's grace, they will find freedom in trusting God's calling and blessing in their differences. In such a marriage a man or a woman will not be alone, but united by his love. In heaven, marriage and all differences will end, because our love will be perfected. The revelations of suffering love will no longer be needed to show Christ's love to the world. Jesus said, "I made known to them your name, and I will continue to make it known, that the love with which you have loved me may be in them, and I in them" (John 17:26). Jesus never married because he always experienced perfect love with the Father. Others, like Paul, chose the single life and found that love, though not perfect, was adequate until the resurrection. Then there will be no one lonely.

Chapter 9
New Covenant Love as Mission

New Covenant Love: Method to Extend the Great Commission

Jesus had stated that the New Commandment of the New Covenant was based on the witness of his love through his disciples. He said, "By this all people will know that you are my disciples, if you have love for one another" (John 13:34, 35). It was shown that the apostles applied this to the way the wife and husband submitted to Christ in marriage. After Christ's obedient death, resurrection, and sending of the Holy Spirit, the Church began the efforts to carry out the Great Commission to proclaim God's love to all people of all nations. Paul said, "God has consigned all to disobedience that he may have mercy on all." Moreover, he stated this was from God's "depth of the riches and wisdom and knowledge…" of his eternal plan (Romans 11:32, 33).

Through his ministry, Christ had led and trained his disciples in the method the Great Commission was to be carried out so that new disciples would be taught "to observe all *that I have commanded*" (Matthew 28:20). The design of Christ's ministry methodology to build his kingdom through his disciples was based on the plan of God that had progressively unfolded from the time of man's sin. This included marriage as a central part.

Jesus and Paul both accepted the **Hebrew premise** that *the family of believers was to be the center of expanding the gospel from the house churches to their community.* In the preceding chapters I reported that the union of husband and wife was central to God's plan for his kingdom in ruling the world. After creating man and woman in his image, he blessed them, "And God said to them, 'Be fruitful and multiply and fill the earth and subdue it and *have dominion* ….'" (Genesis1:28). After the sin of Adam and Eve, Eve was promised that her seed from Adam would crush the head of the serpent (Genesis 3:15). God, by grace, added trials of pain in childbirth and toil in earning, causing greater dependence on their desire for union, and he continued his blessings of provision through nature. But in time all men in the world violated God's plan for marriage and lustfully, "they took as their wives any they chose." Giant mighty men of renown bore children by adultery. The result was that "every intention of the thoughts of his heart was only evil continually" (cf. Genesis 6:2-5). The indiscriminate marriages and children from such marriages ended God's plan through union of male and female to make him known and have dominion.

This failure of man to extend God's rule over all animals and earth sorrowed God, leading him to eliminate the whole system (cf. Genesis 6:6-7). Only Noah and his wife were righteous, and God saved them through the flood. Afterwards it was reaffirmed that "God made man in his own image," and Noah and his wife and their children were told "And you, be fruitful and multiply, increase greatly on the earth and multiply in it" (Genesis 9:6, 7). Later, the center of God's covenant with Abraham was to have a miraculous child who would through them bless all nations (Genesis 12:1-3; Galatians 3:16-18). God's plan to rule the earth through man clearly involved their union and the children born from this.

Chapter 4 of this book showed that the New Covenant of his love through his disciples was the primary way for spreading his witness. From their humility to die to self and love as he loved, they would communicate this love to each other, to their children, and to all man's relationships in community. Even in the worst relationship of slave and master, God's love could remove abuse. The master was to receive the servant slave as a brother (cf. Philemon). With Christ's presence in every New Covenant disciple, and each one using his gifts in humble suffering love, Christ's bride, the church would witness his love to the world (Ephesians 4:7-16).

Two Aspects of Witness to Extend Great Commission

When the husband and wife unite in suffering love they demonstrate to their children and to the world the suffering love of God seen in Christ. It is astounding that Jesus linked the New

Covenant love of disciples, married or single, to the expansion of the ministry to the world, and to the final unity of the elect in the eternal kingdom of God in heaven. Shortly after giving the New Covenant and the New Commandment he said,

> The glory that you have given me I have given to them, that they may *be one even as we are one*, I in them and you in me, that they may become perfectly one, so *that the world may know that you sent me and loved them even as you loved me.* Father, I desire that they also, whom you have given me, may be with me where I am, to see my glory that you have given me because you loved me before the foundation of the world. O righteous Father, even though the world does not know you, I know you, and these know that you have sent me. I made known to them your name, and I will continue to make it known, *that the love with which you have loved me may be in them, and I in them*" (John 17:22-26).

As the man and the wife are united by showing suffering love, they reveal the love of Christ and extend the knowledge of Christ to the world. This enables the church to fulfill the Great Commission by showing God's love *in their local situation*, and by having more children who know this love, the family perpetrates and spreads the gospel. The church as Christ's bride was important for manifesting God's eternal purpose in the suffering love and grace of God even before God and his *heavenly rulers* (Ephes. 3:8-13).

The Reason Witness through Marriage is Omitted

The understanding of the churches in their mission have not adequately acknowledged this second of the two aspects of the spreading the Gospel to fulfill the Great Commission. The reason is that it was accepted as a fact among God's Hebrew Old Testament people that the family of believers was an important way God's kingdom was spread and continued. Jesus had in view two aspects in his method of : missionary individuals or apostles who go out, and families in local churches. He emphasized that the children were to be accepted and included in the kingdom of God (Matthew 18:1-6). Jesus chose and *sent apostles/missionaries to go into towns to preach the gospel and evangelize.* They were to stay *in the home* of a worthy or believing person where they were to gather the people they evangelized to form local churches as a continuing witness (Matthew 10:11; Luke 11:5-9). This second aspect was that *the local churches through the families* of believers would continue and *extend the witness* to the local community, and give continuity by having and raising believing children. In this second aspect, the marriage union in love of men and women showed both male and female characteristics of God's image by consistently exemplifying his humility, and teaching obedience to children and the community.

Paul followed this pattern of two aspects of witness. He and his teams of apostolic evangelists went out to new towns/cities (e.g. Antioch, Philippi, Corinth, Ephesus) and preached the good news, or evangel, of the grace of God. They formed local churches from which the families of members witnessed the gospel of his glorious reign and *extended and maintained* the church in that region. This is seen in Paul's missionary journeys, and is reflected in comments in Paul's epistles.

To the Thessalonians and Colossians Paul commended the witness of suffering love through the families in the local churches. This is reflected in the following and other references:

> And you became imitators of us and of the Lord, for you received the word in much affliction, with the joy of the Holy Spirit, so that you became an example to all the believers in Macedonia and in Achaia. For not only has *the word of the Lord sounded forth from* you in Macedonia and Achaia, but your faith in God has gone forth everywhere, so that we need not say anything (1 Thessalonians 1:6-9).

> Of this you have heard before in the word of the truth, the gospel, which has come to you, as indeed in the whole world *it is bearing fruit and growing—as it also does among you*, since the day you heard it and understood the grace of God in truth (Colossians 1:5, 6).

From Abraham of the Old Testament to the New Testament, the men as fathers were to be the leader and teacher, and their wives equal partners, following their husband's sacrificial lead in oneness to demonstrate faith and love in Christ. Israel's men were to observe this throughout the generations (Deuteronomy 6:1-9; Psalm 78:2-7; Proverbs 1:8, 9; 4:1-6 et. al.). In turn the family leaders or elders were to represent the kingdom in the community. By the work of the union of man and wife in love, the Spirit would extend God's love to bless the world as promised through Abraham. We forget the seed for the Savior through the Covenant with Abram and Sarai was through the miracle of their union and that of their children.

Conditions in Roman World and in Roles of Women and Men

Marriage union in the Roman world of Jesus and Paul was in crisis and decline. The women's movement in Rome was a result of materialism from Roman conquests and trade that had resulted by the early second century B. C. The beginning of the women's movement in the Roman Republic was recorded by Livy during the time of M. Porcius Cato as head of the Senate in 195 B.C. The women protested for full legal authority for woman to be free and equal with men in earning and in sexual freedom. Otto Kiefer said,

> It is not by chance that one of the first complaints [of women] dates almost exactly to the period when the emancipation began. The elder Pliny (N. H., xvii, 25 [38]) tells us that the consul L. Piso Frugi lamented that chastity had disappeared in Rome. That was about the middle of the second century B.C. .... Similar complaints continued for centuries.[49]

For feminists, freedom from their husbands and sexual immorality had become dominant and undermined the ideal of marriage by the time of the Christian movement, or by the time of Caesar Augustus.[50] The immoral relationships were so bad that Augustus had to divide the women from men to the main floor and on the balcony in the theatres to prevent sexual immorality that was publically occurring. Women were leaders in everything. It is

---

[49] Otto Kieffer, *Sexual Life in Ancient Rome (New York: A.M.S. Press, 1934) 45.* See all of Chapter 5, Wilson, *Man Is Not Enough.*
[50] Carl W. Wilson, *Man Is Not Enough,* Chapter 5 on degrading of the Romans, 82, 83.

known that at least seven liberal synagogues were led by women and the orthodox Jewish reaction was to force segregation of women from men in the synagogues and in relationships with legal controls.

For the witness of the church, it was important to show God's plans for union by suffering love by created roles. As started before, the roots of love grow, and are manifested and spread through marriage. The early churches met this breakdown in marriage and indiscriminate sexual acts, not by open criticisms or by trying to pass laws in the corrupt senate, but by their example of the power of Covenant Love in sexual union in their marriages.

Appreciation and Love for Women by Jesus and Paul

Many assume that the teachings of Jesus and Paul as single men were reflections of the Orthodox Jewish male prejudice against and segregation of women. Because of the difficulties and burdens for women that resulted from feminism, the apostles were counteracting the conditions, and were in fact establishing the created differences of the sexes in the churches, which readily accepted women to serve, ***but with great respect for the created differences***. These New Testament functions of creation assured women of the maximum sexual power and freedom, and upheld the creative sexual differences in the face of the radical feminist demands for individual sexual liberty that prevailed in Roman society. Feminism was a reaction to change from faith in Jupiter the one sovereign creator, to materialistic values. The shift to trust in nature for prosperity by man's wisdom began after the First Punic War.[51] The greed in worshiping or seeking creation's wealth had produced individualistic pride and resultant in selfish sexual abuses of men.

Paul's respect and appreciation of woman is repeatedly referenced in the book of Acts, showing the response of leading Greek and Roman women to Paul's teaching in establishing the churches: Thessalonians (Acts 17:4), Berea (17:12), and Athens

---

[51] Wilson, *Man Is Not Enough*, 76.

152

(17:34). In the leading Roman city of Philippi, Paul began the church in what was mainly a woman's prayer meeting (Acts 16:13 ff.). One of the women was Lydia, a prominent and well to do business woman from Thyatira. Lydia responded and hosted Paul's team that began the church in that city in her house. Her household is mentioned, so she probably was a widow who carried on her husband's business to sell the dyed garments that were famously produced in Thyatira of the providence of Lydia in Asia Minor across the Aegean Sea.[52] Whether her name was related to the providence's name is not known.

Also, Paul highly commended the woman Phoebe to be helped by the Roman church. She had moved from Cenchreae to Rome. He said, "She was a servant of the church in Cenchreae …who has been a patron of many and of myself as well." Paul also gave great commendation to Prisca and her husband Aquila for risking their lives for Christians, and serving Christ, and having a church in their home (Romans 16:1, 2, 3). The restrictions of Paul to women in the church's worship require understanding how these biblical principals were protective and beneficial for the church, the family, and the women themselves at that time.

All Gifts, to Men and Women, Were to Show Love

It was in the midst of the corrupt Roman culture where there was a breakdown in marriage and all human relationships that the church was to be a witness for God's love and union. Paul indicated this as the purpose of Christ giving gifts to every member of the church to help it grow. He said,

> And he gave the apostles, the prophets, the evangelists, the shepherds and teachers, to equip the saints for the work of ministry, for building up the body of Christ, until we all attain to the unity of the faith and of the knowledge of the Son of God, unto mature manhood, to the measure of the stature of the fullness of Christ, so that we may no longer be children, tossed to and fro by the waves and carried about by every wind of doctrine, by human cunning, by craftiness in

---

[52] The establishment of the business by her husband is only a reasonable speculation. Why she is named for the province is not known.

deceitful schemes. Rather, speaking the truth in love, we are to grow up in every way into him who is the head, into Christ, from whom the whole body, joined and held together by every joint with which it is equipped, when each part is working properly, makes the body grow so that it builds itself up in love (Eph. 4:11-16).

Paul's instructions on marriage that immediately follow this indicate the way the sexual roles should function for the practice of these various gifts.

Roles in Church Practices Upheld Covenant Love

The apostles consistently maintained the importance of roles of male and female in the churches to reveal the image of God in love for union. Paul's instructions for the churches were very similar to Peter's. If properly understood they fit with the roles of suffering New Covenant love in marriage. The individual gifts to members of Christ's body are given to show loving care to help others, and make the whole church grow in love and union for Christ the head to accomplish his redemptive purposes.

> I desire then that in every place the men should pray, lifting holy hands without anger or quarreling; likewise also that women should adorn themselves in respectable apparel, with modesty and self-control, not with braided hair and gold or pearls or costly attire, but with what is proper for women who profess godliness—with good works. Let a woman learn quietly with all submissiveness. I do not permit a woman to teach or to exercise authority over a man; rather, she is to remain quiet. For Adam was formed first, then Eve; and Adam was not deceived, but the woman was deceived and became a transgressor. Yet she will be saved through childbearing—if they continue in faith and love and holiness, with self-control.

> The saying is trustworthy: If anyone aspires to the office of overseer, he desires a noble task. Therefore an overseer must be above reproach, the husband of one wife, sober-minded, self-controlled, respectable, hospitable, able to teach, not a drunkard, not violent but gentle, not quarrelsome, not a lover of money. He must manage his own household well, with all dignity keeping his children submissive, for if someone does not know how to manage his own household, how will he care for God's church? He must not be a recent convert,

or he may become puffed up with conceit and fall into the condemnation *of the devil*. Moreover, he must be well thought of by outsiders, so that he may not fall into disgrace, into a snare of the devil (1 Timothy 2:8- 3:7). (Emphasis added)

Paul presents the aspects of the created roles of men and women in the light of the spiritual conflict with the devil as in Genesis 3 (cf. 1 Timothy 2:13-15; 3:6, 7), and asserts these roles should be practiced in the church as a witness for Christ to the world (cf. 2:3-7). Adam was created first and he gave the word of God to Eve, who was created afterwards. But she was deceived. For these reasons women are to learn Christ's will from their husbands, and not take authority over and teach him. By attention to the important role of wife and mother in having children, she will be saved *from the power of the devil*, and "continue in faith, and love and holiness with self-control."

Peter, Paul, and John teach salvation is first of all from the power of evil in this world (Acts 2:40; Galatians 1:4; 1 John 2:8), and by the power of the Holy Spirit they have eternal life. The man's role is leading the family in prayer and teaching (2:8; 3:7ff.). Thus, a man in a monogamous family where he manages his family well is likewise qualified to be an elder or overseer in the church.

Also, Paul's instruction to Christians in Corinth about how to operate in the churches maintains the same roles in witness. Having dealt with personal matters about marriage, vocation, and how to relate to the world (1 Corinthians 7-10), Paul turned to instructions about how to conduct worship and witness in the church, including expressions of gender roles (1 Corinthians 11-14). Throughout this whole passage he expresses how love is to be shown in practicing the various gifts (Chapter 13). He begins with the standards which he has repeatedly taught to them of how *the man and woman* are to pray and prophesy in the church. He indicated cultural procedures were different for men and women based on created headships. "But I want you to understand that the head of every man is Christ, and the head of a wife is her husband, and the head of Christ is God" (11:3).

When a woman married, she adorned her head with a bandana or headcloth (probably was the Hebrew, *kishshûrm,* which means "to bind"). When she was in public this headband indicated her commitment of union to her husband (11:4-10). This public policy showed she was joined to her husband. As man was created first, his wife was second from him. Her husband was her leader under God. The public practice demonstrated *the union* of the man and woman before God and his heavenly hosts of angels (11:10). All subsequent men being born from woman likewise made them equal in value but different in function and not the same. This headcloth was a symbol of a binding union, and was not like the Muslim burka that implies shielding the whole woman's person as an object of sexual temptation. Muslim men in lust had polygamous marriages.

This interdependence of man and woman in union with one another was from God. "In the Lord, the woman *is not independent,* from man nor man from woman; for as woman was made from man, so man is now born of woman and all things are from God" (11:1, 12). In early western Christian culture the symbol of this union was indicated not by the binding bandana, but by a wedding ring which the bride accepted from her husband.[53] Paul associates the tradition of the headcloth with the fact that women see long hair as her glory, and a head covering before her husband. But Paul does not insist on contending on the practice of women having long hair in the churches (11:15, 16).

Paul continued emphasizing to the Corinthians the suffering love for union in the church as the bride of Christ. He had scolded them for selfishness instead of showing caring unity in their love in their feasts before eating of *the Lord's Supper.* That sacramental sharing should reveal Christ's dying love that should unite them (1 Corinthians 11:17-34). He followed this (in Chapter 12) by applying love for unity by *the gifts* which the Spirit of Christ gives to each (male and female) for help, and thereby care in love for each other as members of one spiritual body, his bride. These were

---

[53] In the twentieth century the feminist movement led to men also receiving a ring in marriage.

illustrated to be like a foot, hand, or eye, which were different organs to participate as one under the head's direction. In Christ everyone has partaken of, and is united by, the Spirit (Jew, Greek, slave or free, male or female equally cf. 12:11, 13; Galatians 3:27-29). Paul then said the use of the individual gifts from Christ's Spirit is *useless* to the body unless they are practiced in *New Covenant sacrificial love* that unites them (1 Corinthians 13). *This great chapter shows unity in love is the great objective in the church's witness by the various gifts.*

Paul concluded these instructions on worship to the Corinthians by emphasizing that we imperfectly see and have this love like children now, but we grow in faith and hope toward the perfect love in Christ. We only know partially now, but will have perfect love in Christ at his coming (cf. also 1 John 3:1 ff.). Therefore we should pursue love earnestly (13:8- 14:1) and seek the gifts that most edifying each other in love (14:1-25, cf. also Ephesians 4:10-16; Romans 12:3-10 ff.).

Paul ended this discussion to the Corinthians with *directions to the moderator for controlling the house church meetings,* again pointing to how individual members should act in caring love. The fact that he is giving instructions for leaders moderating church meetings is seen in that five times he uses the word "let," directing how to control the participation of the members using the gifts (14:26-30). The gift of prophecy was reporting an experience from God, and was not the same as authoritative teaching that was exclusively for men.[54] Even in Old Testament, the prophet was not a teaching authority, but reported a message given to him or her from God. Here Paul is excluding selfish *individual* use of gifts.

Paul has instructed that husband and wife should not participate as separate *individuals* for they are one flesh (11:11). In this context of what Paul has taught, he is giving instructions for

---

[54] See my article on "Women..." *Baker's Dictionary of Theology*, (Grand Rapids, MI: Baker Book House, 1960), 557 for more on New Testament prophecy, and Carl W. Wilson, *From Uncertainty to Fulfillment* (Fayetteville, GA: Worldwide Discipleship Books, 1992), Chapter 16, "The Holy Spirit on Miracles," distributed by New Life Resources, Peachtree City, GA.

the moderator in all the churches. The practice is that the women should keep silent, they are not permitted to speak, and it is shameful for a woman to speak in church (14:33-36). Paul is not saying the women could not participate, but that that they should not take over the meeting and share their gifts until called on by the moderator. Paul has **already said women can participate** in prayer, use tongues and prophecy, which is revealing an experience with God. But he said she is to do it with respect for her husband by having her head covered (11:5). The gift of tongues was also practiced by women, as was public prayer, showing their equal individual acceptance by God as a member of the church, his bride.

The Roman world was highly individualistic. It was dominated by radical feminism and individual sexuality. The policy for the moderator in the church was to **avoid confusion,** which meant not exalting the individual value of women and a desire to be like men (14:33). Women's participation was to be only by invitation of the male moderator. He was not to let them initiate and take individual control by asking questions or using their gifts of prophecy and prayer to take over. The word of God for the leadership in their marriage was through the man, and therefore a woman should look to her husband for guidance. To let the women take over and teach in the church would contradict the role to be practiced at home.

Scripture shows that Paul respected and freely worked with capable women in the churches. This consistency of church practice with love to unite the two aspects of God's image in marriage makes the powerful witness to the love of Christ and his bride in eternity. In these instructions to the moderator he was showing how to avoid demonic perversion of roles that gives them freedom *in marriage.*

Women were to have leadership roles under their husbands in the household, to train and **teach younger women** how to conduct themselves and how to love their husbands and children. This is not exercising authority or teaching their husbands. It does **involve teaching their sons until they are adults,** along with other women.

They are doing this in accordance with what their husbands have taught them (cf. Proverbs 1:6; 4:3: et al). These designated opportunities to teach indicate the women are equally made in the image of God and granted teaching intelligence. This is indicated by Paul's statements as follows.

> Young women should marry, bear children, manage their households, and give the adversary (the devil) no occasion for slander (1 Timothy 5:14).

> Older women likewise are to be reverent in behavior, not slanderers or slaves to much wine. They are to teach what is good, and so train the young women to love their husbands and children, to be self-controlled, pure, working at home, kind, and submissive to their own husbands, that the word of God may not be reviled (Titus 2:3-5).

Example of Role of Wife as Partner and Manager of Home

This ideal of a biblical wife in value and ability as serving with her husband as a partner in marriage is shown in the wisdom of Proverbs 31:10-31.

> An excellent wife who can find? She is far more precious than jewels. The heart of her husband trusts in her, and he will have no lack of gain. She does him good, and not harm, all the days of her life.

> She seeks wool and flax, and works with willing hands. She is like the ships of the merchant; she brings her food from afar. She rises while it is yet night and provides food for her household and portions for her maidens. She considers a field and buys it; with the fruit of her hands she plants a vineyard. She dresses herself with strength and makes her arms strong. She perceives that her merchandise is profitable. Her lamp does not go out at night. She puts her hands to the distaff, and her hands hold the spindle. She opens her hand to the poor and reaches out her hands to the needy. She is not afraid of snow for her household, for all her household are clothed in scarlet. She makes bed coverings for herself; her clothing is fine linen and purple. Her husband is known in the gates when he sits among the elders of the land. She makes linen garments and sells them; she delivers sashes to the merchant. Strength and dignity are her clothing, and she laughs at the time to come. She opens her mouth with wisdom, and the teaching of kindness is on her tongue. She looks well to the ways

of her household and does not eat the bread of idleness. Her children rise up and call her blessed; her husband also, and he praises her.

"Many women have done excellently, but you surpass them all." Charm is deceitful, and beauty is vain, but a woman who fears the LORD is to be praised. Give her of the fruit of her hands, and *let her works praise her in the gates.*

The picture of the attitude and role of an excellent wife is more likely the ideal wife, rather than one individual. She is a great shopper for even imported foods; is a gourmet cook for husband and many others. She is successful at real estate, grows a prosperous vineyard, makes wine or useful beverages, is profitable in business deals, and she weaves and manufactures cloths and sells them. She is involved in charitable giving, tailors and dresses herself and her family, is psychologically sound in not worrying about the future, shows kindness in relationships, and manages the household of children and servants for the family. This shows she is an intelligent, dignified, and capable individual on her own. The city leaders "in the gate" recognize and praise her as a person of worth in the community *for what she herself is and does.*

But most importantly, the excellent wife is doing this not as a selfish individual, but as partner with her husband, having *his complete trust, and exalting him as the leader* of the family that gives the family respect in the community. The elders sitting in the gate were the recognized and chosen leaders of the city. Her husband trusts her as caring for him foremost, and also for the family and household. This trust grows out of her respect and worship of God.

Union of Suffering Love in Marriage as Mission

Loving the sinful world as Christ loved us, and dying with him to love those who are sinners, is the mark of a New Covenant disciple. Paul said,

For *the love of Christ controls* us, because we have concluded this: that one has died for all, therefore all have died; and he died for all, that those who live might no longer live for themselves but for him who for their sake died and was raised.... From now on, therefore, we regard no one according to the flesh. Even though we once regarded Christ according to the flesh, we regard him thus no longer. Therefore, if anyone is in Christ, he is a new creation. The old has passed away; behold, the new has come. All this is from God, who through Christ reconciled us to himself and gave us the ministry of reconciliation; that is, in Christ God was reconciling the world to himself, not counting their trespasses against them, and entrusting to us the message of reconciliation. Therefore, we are ambassadors for Christ, God making his appeal through us. We implore you on behalf of Christ, be reconciled to God (2 Corinthians 5:14-20).

When a husband loves his wife as Christ loved the church and gave himself for her, when he loves her as himself, she can respond, and want to humble herself and follow his teaching of the Lord's word. When a women is humble and respects her husband, sharing with him and listening to be obedient, she exerts power that makes him want to hear her and give himself for her. This sacrificial love enables her to transfer her power to him in bonding with the children so that he shares and truly leads. This gives her greater power within herself and with her children. Suffering love is the greatest power on earth that a man may have with his wife and that she will have with him. Their union of both aspects of God's image reveals God's love to the children. It becomes the most powerful witness to the community. The apostle plants and nurtures the church, such love spreads it.

Conclusion

The word of Christ when preached may always forward Christ's kingdom. But unless the public preaching of the Gospel is attended by the evidence of suffering love, the message of the cross and resurrection of Christ soon becomes meaningless. Organized efforts of personal evangelism and the many words of public teaching and preaching of the Bible on radio all will be rejected by the sinful mind. Even repeated information without obedience, no matter how insightful, becomes like sounding brass and a tinkling symbol. The world is less and less listening to the many words of even good preachers. The creation of big church buildings, organizations, and communication networks for groups and individuals who build them, soon become negative influences.

Much of youth work today is in their own groups, and they are never integrated into or participate in church activities. More than 65 % of youth who leave for college never become involved in the church. Married love that produces family unity and expands the witness of the church is missing.

The whole church should be one of love. "By this shall all men know that you are my disciples, if you have love for one another" (John 13: 34, 35). Marriage of man and wife is the foundational beginning point to expand and truly build the church, and make disciples that obey what Christ commanded.

Chapter 10
Good Sexual Roles for Marriage Union
Destroyed by Change from God's to Man's Wisdom

God's Wisdom of Justice and Mercy

Every civilization began with faith in God, and then turned by intellectuals to trust in nature and worship creation. The folly of man as male and female self-righteously claiming to know good and evil, and turning to individually worship creation, was eternally designed by God's infinite sovereign wisdom so he could reveal his justice. He then could also show his unbelievable mercy to forgive and graciously accept. By "the deep riches and wisdom and knowledge of God... God has consigned all (every nation of Jews and Gentiles) to disobedience, that he may have mercy on all" (Romans 11:32, 33).

All men and women in all nations have gone through a pattern of faith in the goodness of God's help in creating great civilizations, and foolishly changed their attraction for a loving union in marriage to individual competition and destruction. The civilization of the West, the United States, and the whole world is now experiencing that pattern of folly. The apostle Paul, drawing on the prophetic past, and reviewing the history of the Greeks and Romans, has outlined this pattern and proclaimed that by faith in Christ there is salvation from the demonic destruction unto eternal life with God (Romans 1:14- 3:2).

In this chapter we will review Paul's description of the steps of moral decline's pattern, and explain while this deceptively seems reasonable, it turned marriage into conflict in most national civilizations. The next chapter will review the sexual changes as folly. Chapter 12 will give the facts of what appears to be the coming world crisis of following this pattern worldwide.

Christ's Salvation for the Degrading Greek and Roman World

Paul proclaimed Christ's salvation from the sins of the brilliant, powerful, and evil Roman world. His offer of salvation is also for those of us today who are in this world, which is still degrading from man's sin nature. The Roman civilization began about 500 B.C. by a manifestation and renewal of their faith in the sovereign Creator, Jupiter, who they believed was the son of Uranus, or the God of heaven. After over 200 years of trust in God and his blessing on their work, they had built a large, successful civilization incorporating much of the knowledge of previous nations. Then their intellectual leaders stopped worship of the one sovereign God, and began to believe in nature, and to worship that which was created rather than the Creator. Then trusting in their own wisdom, they foolishly changed the sexual roles that destroyed marriage and led to anarchy and judgment. In this change they accepted knowledge of the degraded Greeks.

This chapter will present the steps to increasingly greater evil and rejection of God. It shows how man's sinful nature is deceptively drawn to follow these steps

Christ's Salvation is from Evil Now for Eternity

Salvation is from Evil in the World unto Eternal Life

Paul's context for interpretation is not just to be saved from religious works to receive forgiveness in order to gain eternal life in heaven. That would be limiting the meaning, which was focused on by the Reformers in the sixteenth century. Paul's is a picture of deliverance from the demonic power that controls all men's hearts in every nation in this world. This demonic power has imprisoned men in pain, destruction, death, and hell. It separates them from, and dishonors, the only living and true God of heaven, earth, and under the earth. That salvation is now by grace unto obedience as his children in his eternal kingdom. The picture of Romans 1:18 ff. is on what is happening in this world that has eternal consequences.

Paul said any other Gospel was a distortion of the gospel which is that "the Lord Jesus Christ...gave himself for our sins to deliver us *from the present evil age*, according to the will of our God and Father" (Galatians 1:4, 7, 8). This is what Peter taught in initiating the church on the day of Pentecost saying, "Save yourselves from *this crooked generation"* (Acts 2:40).

Salvation is not Only from Guilt, but Demonic Control

The first promise of a Savior was the seed of the woman who would crush the serpent (Genesis 3:15); Jesus' first act as Christ was to defeat the devil (Matthew 4:1-11); the evidence of his kingdom was using the Holy Spirit to heal demonic influence (Matthew 12:25-30); the disciples showed they were extending Christ's kingdom by casting out demons (Luke 10:17-20). All New Testament writings refer to power and conflict with the devil. John said the Son of God came into the world to defeat the devil (1 John 3:5-9). The saving work of Christ is repeatedly said to be deliverance from the power of the devil (cf. Ephesians 1:18-2:10; 6:10-12; Revelation 12:7-11, et al.).

The traditional *roles of men and women in marriage are specifically referred to* by Paul as important in Christ's saving work from the devil in their ministry in the world now (1 Timothy 2:8-13; 3:1-7).

Proclamation of How Faith in Christ's Power Saves

Paul claimed to the Romans that the power to escape demonic destruction in this life is in Christ. In the beginning of the book of Romans on the salvation of God, the apostle Paul presents the great power of God's saving work in Christ by explaining the terrible sin of man, and sin's destruction to the civilizations of the Greeks and Romans.

Paul declared that for such a world, he was bold to proclaim the answer in the good news of Jesus Christ, bringing saving work by telling men that "the just shall *live by faith.*" This was the message that the prophet Habakkuk gave to the people in Judah when they were facing the destructive evil of their world (Habakkuk 2:4). As in Habakkuk, Paul's primary message is how, through Christ's justification and forgiveness to go to heaven, men can escape and be saved from the serpent's evil.[55]

It is important to see how the devil has worked to destroy marriage, and thereby civilizations. As our marriages are being destroyed, this destruction is then spread to the world. That is why this chapter is so relevant to promote the power of New Covenant love. By seeing the importance of sexual union for civilization we can grasp how Christ now can save by witnessing to his love through our marriage union. Hope and faith in his eternal life is the only way of salvation today to find greater meaning in the eternal future.

Decline by Sin Corrupts Sexual Relations that Destroys

Paul described the decline of the Roman Republic civilization. He showed they went through the following steps which had occurred before in Greece (Romans 1:18 ff).

1. *Elite Lead in Rejecting God Intellectually*: "When they knew God they did not honor him as God or give thanks to him, but they became futile in their thinking, and their foolish hearts were darkened" and "Claiming to be wise, they became fools" (1:21, 22). "They exchanged the truth about God for a lie" (1:25). "By unrighteousness they suppressed the truth" (1:18).

2. *Turned to Idolatry of Worshiping Material Creation*. They worshiped and *served the creation/creature* rather than the Creator (1:25). Man considers himself the highest of other animals (1:23).

3. *Perverted Sexual Roles and Turn to the Sensual:* "God gave them over to the lusts of their hearts to impurity, to the dishonoring of their bodies …to dishonorable passions." (1:24, 26). "For their *women exchanged their natural use/role to that which is contrary to nature*, and likewise the *men gave up natural relations with women*

---

[55] Wilson, *Man is **Not** Enough*, Chapters 3-5.

and were consumed with passion for one another, men committing shameless acts with men..."(1:24, 26).

4. *Rejection of God to be Free for Anarchistic Thoughts and Acts*: "Since they did not see fit to acknowledge God, God gave them up to a debased mind to do what ought not to be done. They were filled with all manner of unrighteousness, evil covetousness, malice ..." (1:28-31).

5. *Conflict and Judgment of Each Other and Judgment by God*: "Passing judgment on another you condemn yourself, because you, the judge, practice the very same things. We know that the judgment of God rightly falls on those who do such things" (2:1, 2).

These steps are demonically deceptive leading to degradation because *they are a logical progression appealing to the fleshly sin nature of all men and women.* For that reason mankind in every nation everywhere has foolishly and repeatedly traced these steps to his ruin. The perversion of the knowledge of God for trust in natural creation has released the power of human desires to sin. The process described by Paul is as follows.

Explanation of the Logical Process of a Civilization Decline

Pattern: Civilizations' Rise by Faith and Fall by Apostasy

Each new civilization is begun by a work of God's Spirit producing repentance and return to faith in one sovereign God and his love. Until the fulfillment in Christ, general revelation with God's law in man's heart is used by the Spirit to motivate. A remnant has been given faith in acceptance and forgiveness for eternal life as was Abel. This has occurred by unusual workings of the Holy Spirit in different ways to motivate men. Before Christ this occurred by the Spirit being *with* the leaders to motivate them but not *in* them. Faith in God enabled them by grace to build a prosperous civilization. All previous faith of the nations began by general revelation as shadows of the real salvation. Israel was chosen as a people through whom the salvation would come.

Only in Christ as Savior do men of all nations understand God's gospel in Christ for eternal life by his suffering love. That suffering love is manifested through his disciples who have died to self with him. I have reviewed this emphasis of salvation in Christ presented by Paul in Romans to explain why the union by suffering love in marriage of a man and a woman is so important. As described in previous chapters, it is the most important way the suffering love of Christ is manifested in the world. This chapter and the next will make this clear.

The Demonic Process to Change Values and Sexual Roles

In my book, *Man is Not Enough*, I show how this process in a national culture played out and it is briefly described here. In the beginning of each civilization, the faith in God led people to be cooperative and do creative, hard work with the hope God would bless their efforts. This was done by men and women who were different from each other. These men and women of different abilities allowed some to profit more, but added more to the growth of the civilization. The children learned from their parents, and generally also had good work ethics, which led to creative productivity resulting in commerce with others. Their intelligence given by God's creation for them to help rule the earth (Genesis 1:26-28) led to their ability to see the regularity of the laws of nature, and how to better plan. After about 250 or 300 years, nations created brilliant cultures with much prosperity and freedom for most of the citizens. The growth of prosperity by faith then attracted immigrants from other countries. During that time the people saw themselves as valuable to God, because of being created by and for him.

Demonic change of values then occurred. When the civilization developed so that the needs of production, provision, and protection were met, there was less need to pray or to look to God, and thankfulness diminished. Then an educated elite, who had begun to see God's regular working in nature, started to speculate that they could know how nature worked, and believed they would make progress on their own. This led to the men especially feeling they were adequate and wise as God. Their individual wealth enhanced the feeling they were important, and each individual sought to gain more for his own security and self-esteem. Soon the men as leaders were caught up in more greed, which is idolatry, the worshiping of the created rather than the Creator.

The men led in changing values and roles for women. They had the money, and were gone in business and war, and increasingly felt their power as individuals. Men then began to treat women who were dependent upon them as inferior. The men could hire help in the home. In pride of sufficiency, they felt free and more important than women, and sought sexual relationships with other women when convenient for selfish pleasure. Their patriarchal leadership of the family became harsh and abusive. Marriage faithfulness diminished. Devotion to their wives and family in monogamous marriage began to be lost. The more able, hard working men began to oppress the poorer people to gain greater wealth, and developed an oppressed class. This caused some intellectuals to see an opportunity to appeal to the oppressed people to gain all the power and political control for themselves. The sin that developed inequality was used by some to *promise equality for all women and the poor* to gain power to govern.

The whole society soon followed the views of the educated elite leaders (as Eve followed the serpent) because the value of each individual was thought to be in material wealth represented by money, and not in value given by God. The created equal value of women had previously been accepted by faith in God to have children, nurture them, and as an intelligent partner be able to assist their husbands in production and marketing. But when trust in material prosperity occurred, which the men controlled for their own self-interest, *the value of women changed to materialism created by the men.*

For women to be equally valuable materially, they logically want to be free to earn and possess for themselves, and to successfully compete with men. To do this, they had to be free from having and nurturing children. Moreover, when competing with men, especially their oppressive husbands, this ended love. The women wanted to be free from control of their husbands, and to also find pleasure for themselves with other men who appreciated them. In this desire to change, women have called for help from the individualistic greedy men who were promoting freedom of the lower class to gain political power. These very men who wanted control by promising equality for more individual power are the ones they turned to. Also these women, who proclaimed the right for equality, are the women who selfishly were seeking progress toward being superior over others including other women.

The greed for material values that had become the god of men and also women progressively increased. As a person gained material power for self, there was an accelerated rate to promote individualism and claim the right to selfish fleshly pleasure. These motives from materialism changed the natural role of women to be free to earn, and be free as men. In turn it also changed the role of men. Sex changed its meaning from the whole nature of a person for giving love, to an individual act of pleasure. This growth of individualism increased promiscuous adultery, promoted divorce, prompted individuals to live together without commitment, and finally, it encouraged homosexuality. The individualism creates evil hurt to each other, and dishonor to God, whose image men and women bear. Their individual zeal for self leads to judgment of each other. Therefore God sends judgment to end it.

Once a people leave faith in God, and in their wisdom trust in material creation for their value, the next logical step man thinks is good is to make all people equal. This requires roles of women and men to be alike. This motivation destroys marriage and the family, and the civilization becomes anarchistic and destructive. *The point of folly*, as Paul said in Romans 1, is to *change from faith in God to that of creation.* After that, limited human reason cannot but follow the path of degradation. Those choices are passed on from one generation to another at increasing rates of successive human authorities until men proclaim themselves as gods and women as goddesses. Many civilizations end with one man and woman accepted as the wisest and most powerful with dictatorial power, ending the liberty they sought. [56]

Idea of Equality as Same and Each as Superior is Irrational

While our sex of male or female is the most basic difference (and the only one existing for Adam and Eve) each individual has different abilities and characteristics. Every human by their sin natures (male or female) believe they know what is good and evil, and each judges themselves the best. With that we align ourselves with others like us to also claim superiority, sex, race, wealth, and the like. Our sexual orientation is the most obvious, and therefore the most threatening or shaming universally. Most basic of all is our difference from God. Each as an individual in their fleshly nature feels shame, and also causes fear of God. The other sex becomes a threat, and therefore must be made equal to be controlled. These self-righteous attitudes as sinners in every culture are then passed from generation to generation. This causes anti-Christian and sexual conflicts to progressively increase.

The law of God to love our neighbor is written in every man and woman's heart. Since this is in every conscience there is a sense of thought that every person *ought to be treated as equal.* This leads man to know equality is right and to be accepted by others, so he must profess equality of others as his objective. This presents a paradox. On the one hand our selfish pride is driven by the temptations of the world and makes us want to be the best and believe we can transcend our limitations to be supermen or superwomen, and better than any other, even better than God. On the other hand we say we want everyone to be equal and to get the best education and opportunity to improve. But we are threatened by any differences and abilities of others, and we want to change others to be alike. This desire to promote equality is true not only of sex, but of those in a higher class, the dominant race etc., to have control to make all equal.

---

[56] Cf. the observations of French liberal Lexis de Tocqueville, in Wilson, *Liberty in an Evil Age*, Chapters 1, 6; or Wilson, *Man Is **Not** Enough*, Chapters 4-6.

In contradiction, we want to compete to see who is best or superior to others. We demand the best education for all, yet we are constantly seeking to be or to find and select the best: IQ ratings, most educational degrees, and superiority in competitions such as spelling bees, music, singing and dancing contests, games such as *Jeopardy!* and *Wheel of Fortune* etc., and athletic contests. There are inner drives to find superman or the perfect powerful man or woman that Adam and Eve failed to be. Men who are strongest, women who are most beautiful, etc., maintain some aspect of sex. If another person can become like god, however, we honor this because he or she seems to be the ideal son of man without God, which we think we also might become. This exaltation of man as superman or superwoman is the aim of our sin nature — to be as God. This drive to be God is the basic reason for jealousy, hate, and murder; furthermore, it is the reason man was excluded from paradise and why there is a final exclusion into hell. As the civilization becomes more individualistic and divided, a dictator generally emerges to give order to chaos, and fulfill the idea of superman. At the time in history of achievement of a man as dictator, the feminist movement would produce goddesses symbolic of superwomen. Women are given leadership roles, while the men usually still have control. On occasions when there is no male leader, women gain power to help the confused nation.

As the efforts progress to make men and women alike, more women are put in power or advisory positions to men to give a sense of equality. In the last days the youth rebellion results in them gaining leadership, because there is no adult man or woman who wants to lead in the chaos and disorder. Homosexuality becomes more rational in such extreme civilizations, even though if all are homosexuals the culture will end. Therefore, the civilization's collapse is generated by change to material values that change the values from what God created. The key to marriage and social disintegration is competition for material equality caused by individualism that *changes sex roles.* The key point of change is from worshiping God to worshipping mammon, from trust in the Creator to the created. Secondly, when all value is material, the role of sex must be changed so women can be equal like men, and men must be more feminine to please women.

Contrast of Value Changes and Results to the Sexes

The effect on marriage and family from the shift in values from faith in God to materialism may be reflected in the following illustration which shows the changing relationships from *equal value in the sight of God* and oneness in marriage to *competition under mechanical materialism.*

I give the illustration on the following page to make clear that the shift of value from God's created worth to materialism is the cause of the collapse of marriage and of social civilization.

The stick figures on the left hand column show the attitudes toward each other when living before God with faith in Him. These show how they accept each other's differences, see wealth as a common goal to have, and care for children. The right hand column shows that individuals, who see themselves as independent and equal as God, must *compete against each other*. The women must therefore postpone or *deny having children,* neglect them, or turn them over to surrogates or the state to be free to compete for money.

There is one factor in the decline and death of a society not illustrated. That is the way this progressively removes the middle class, and the only answer for women who reject submission is infertility. The roles of women are changed by men. Individualistic men want sex without responsibility, and are able to have it, because many women want the same thing. But by their nature women also want to have children and nurture them. So they have them or adopt them. As individualism grows the men leave the individualistic women, then the women are left with the responsibility of the children with less and less income, putting the responsibility on the government. The children in women's single parent families have less attention, and less educational opportunities as they grow up. The increasingly lower income of the mother causes her to live in poorer neighborhoods.

EYES OF GOD

ONENESS

INTELLECT

ACCEPTANCE

**GOD?
NO GOD!**

**MORTAL INDIVIDUALS
EACH WISE AS GOD**

**NAKED-DIFFERENT
FEAR**

MATERIAL

STEWARDS TOGETHER

MATERIAL SELF ESTEEM

COMPETE

Sexual

DEPENDENT FAMILY

SEXUAL DEVIATION

SELF ACHIEVEMENT AND PLEASURE

UNITED IN MARRIAGE

ANARCHY

There the children are more and more individualistic, and frustrated with less and less education and opportunity. These youth turn to drugs, alcohol, gangs and violence, and the next generation is less able to produce. The middle class progressively becomes a part of the poorer lower class. Only the upper and lower class remain. Women's offense toward men further reduces the level of childbearing that weakens and ends the culture.

This illustrates how when a society progressively rejects faith in God, the resultant individualism that then is based on material values changes the role of both the man and woman, and progressively results in greed, sexual immorality, and the reduction of the number of children. This removes the sexual commitment, and causes greater and greater individualism toward indiscriminate sexual immorality, and toward homosexuality. Each logical step to the individual leads him and the whole society to the decline of the civilization and judgment by God.

Truthfulness in History of this Pattern of Degeneration

The study of the vast history of civilizations would be defeating of our purpose in understanding the theme of marriage in this book. But the evidence of the pattern can be more extensively studied for those who want further research.[57] The breakdown in marriage and the destruction of civilizations from conflict over sexual roles is the main objective here.

Early efforts at comparative religion of intellectual unbelievers began with the view that cultures started with gods and goddesses from nature, and man by evolution produced one monotheistic God, which resulted in a patriarchal hierarchy with the traditional religious family. But these speculative ideas gave way to a science of cultures by the German ethnologists. The world-leading comparative religionist J. Schmidt, using scientific methods of the German ethnologists, found the reverse was the fact. All nations began with a faith in a monotheistic, sovereign, and loving sky God, and then degenerated into a religion of multiple gods and goddesses. The findings of archaeology also support this fact of the trend. [58] In the end of the civilization a dictator emerged claiming

---

[57] My whole book, Wilson, *Man Is Not Enough*, is devoted to this and has many references to major documented books. So does my book, Wilson, *True Enlightenment from Natural Chance to Personal Creator*, especially Chapter 30.
[58] Wilson, *True Enlightenment*, 437,438 on beginning and scientific facts in Chapter 30, pages 509-521.

he was God, and he was often heterosexual and homosexual and sometimes even a transvestite. The dictator god had a goddess or goddesses. I have traced these facts back to the earlier historic writings in the Bible and elsewhere until ancient times, and show how in zigzag fashion, this pattern of civilizations occurred.[59]

For example, the early Sumerian peoples of the Akkadian civilization in Mesopotamia (ca. 2000 B.C.) began with a faith in An, the sovereign sky God, and worshiped his son Enlil ("En" meaning ruler and "lil" as Hebrew "el," meaning power) who created and ruled. After many years with several successive city leaders, the city state organization rose to prosperity and greater urbanization. In time under King Lualzaggisi writing and wisdom of man was exalted, and a great bureaucracy arose, and finally ended with kings as god and, a goddess Inanna. I have shown how Greece began with one God of heaven, Uranus, and Zeus his son, and ended with Alexander the Great, a heterosexual and homosexual, who called himself Zeus-Amon, or god of the Greek empire and of the Egyptian-Mesopotamian Empire. Of more modern times Germany began with faith in the Lutheran God of the Bible, and ended with the Nazi dictator who had himself addressed, "*Heil* Hitler," or savior.

Most important is how the nations collapsed because of the change from paternalistic, monogamous marriage to a change in sexual roles with a feminist movement that has caused the breakdown of monogamous marriage. When change in sexual roles became an issue in England in the first third of the twentieth century, J. D. Unwin made an extensive study of the history of change in marriage and in sexual roles. About a generation and a half later, Pitirim A. Sorokin of Harvard researched the issue from Unwin when the feminist movement was beginning a new threat in the United States. Unwin's studies omitted all religious changes in faith, and the change of economic values that proceeded, and focused only on the marriage and sexual aspects in the history of eighty primitive cultures, and most of the ancient and modern

---

[59] Wilson, *Man Is **Not** Enough,* 34.

civilizations. Unwin, therefore, did not perceive the change from the long early years of growth to prosperity, but found the alarming change in sexual roles that led to the collapse of the civilization.

In this detailed, difficult study for objectivity, Unwin said,

> Owing to the egocentricity (individualistic) in our historical outlook, to which I have already referred (par. 159), it is often supposed that female emancipation is an invention of the modern white man. Sometimes we imagine that we have arrived at a conception of the status of women in society which is far superior to that of any other age; we feel an inordinate pride because we regard ourselves as the only civilized society which has understood that the sexes must have social, legal, and political equality. Nothing could be farther from the truth. A female emancipation movement is a cultural phenomenon of unfailing regularity; it appears to be the necessary outcome of absolute monogamy. The subsequent loss of social energy after the emancipation of women, which is sometimes emphasized has been due not to the emancipation but to the extension of sexual opportunity which has always accompanied it. In human records there is no instance of female emancipation which has not been accompanied by an extension of sexual opportunity.[60]

Had Unwin seen the earlier history of beginning with a faith in God that produced a loving patriarchy with a united family working together for prosperity, and the change in values to individualistic materialism reducing the value of the nature of the female role, he would not have blamed patriarchy and monogamy. The main issue to see from his study is that every major culture has regularly died after men changed the value of women, which motivated the change and dominance of feminism.

Sorokin refers to the studies of all these societies after the male turned to materialism and changed to a "stern" role. He said,

> With the expansion and growth of these societies, however, the stern regulations of sex relationships were progressively replaced by weaker ones. Sexual freedom widened until it encompassed the whole society, and eventually turned into anarchy. Wives and children were emancipated from the absolute power of the *pater families*, and their

---

[60] J. D. Unwin, *Sex and Culture*, (London: Oxford University Press: 1934), 344,345, 161

newly won equality brought with it sexual freedom. *Within three generations* from the moment of significant expansion of sexual freedom, the culture and creativity of these societies began to decline.[61] (Emphasis mine)

Conclusion: Degradation of Marriage Progressed to the World

The earliest civilized kingdoms that ended with perversion of the sexual roles and exalting and identifying the men and women as gods **were regional nations**. Because each successive civilization drew on the brilliance of the former ones, or "stood on the former ones' shoulders," they also grew more complex as empires. Earlier the northern Sumerian culture joined in the Mesopotamian area, and at that time the southern Egyptian one had joined upper and lower Egypt. This was followed by the Amoritic culture that was in Mesopotamia and Palestine, and the New Kingdom of Egypt extending into the Sinai Peninsula. Then the Israelite kingdom dominated much of the whole eastern Mediterranean area. The Babylonian and Persian empires extended over all of Mesopotamian, Palestine, and Asia Minor. By the time of Alexander the Great, the Greek Empire claimed all the eastern Mediterranean area and Egypt with other North African areas. The Roman Empire covered all of these areas, and Europe.

All these nation-kingdoms followed the path of rejecting their one God and perverted the sexual roles. The indication is that the sin nature of man turned from trust in God and worship of God to worship of natural material creation. This materialism was called by different names for God (Baal and Asteroth, etc., for each nation) and progressively has involved a larger and larger part of the world's people under demonic destructive influence of marriage and the family. The next chapter will look at the modern world of the West (1500 A.D. to the present), especially the United States, in order to observe the change of sexual roles and the effect this has had on marriage.

---

[61] Pitirim Sorokin, *The American Sex Revolution* (Boston: P. Sergeant, 1956), 111–12.

178

Chapter 11
Insanity of Sameness of Equality:
History of Sexual Perversion

Introduction: A Nation Begun by God for Faith and Love

The early American colonies that later formed the United States were no chance of nature, or act of human choice and will, but of divine leading and providence. When Christopher Columbus sought a new land, he claimed he was called and motivated by the Spirit of God, and when the crews were on verge of mutiny he asked for three more days, as with the resurrection hope of Christ. When on the third day land was found he named it San Salvador in thanks to the Savior. In those days ending the fifteenth century, the light of the Reformation was beginning, and by the time the world had found routes to the New World the genuine persecuted biblical Christian believers were able to migrate and form those colonies.

The state of marriage of man and woman in the colonies at that time reflected the equality of value from the Creator that was still powerful at the forming of the nation. In the mid-twentieth century when the humanistic forces were militant for equality of human rights, and Chief Justice of the Supreme Court Earl Warren was their advocate, he researched the charters of the colonies in 1954 and addressed the International Council of Christian Leadership and reported,

> I believe no one can read the history of our country without realizing that the Good Book (the Bible) and the spirit of the Savior, from the beginning, [has been] our guiding genius…. I believe the whole Bill of Rights came into being because of the knowledge of our forefathers had of the Bible, and their belief in it: freedom of belief, of expression, of assembly, of petition, **the dignity of the individual**, *the sanctity of the home, equal justice under law,* and the reservation of the powers of the people….[62] (emphasis mine)

---

[62] Wilson, *Man Is Not Enough*, 129, cf. Jim Nelson Black, *When Nations Die* (Wheaton, II, Tyndale House Publishers, 1994), 253.

A generation after Warren's statements, which had involved the feminist movement at its height, research indicated the truth expressed in Warren's comments, that equality given by the Creator in the early Christian colonies was confirmed by others to have been good. At the time of the nation's beginning, the families had no harsh oppressive patriarchy, although the biblical roles of men and women were the accepted practice.

In fact, the historian Arthur Calhoun commented on the wonderful family life saying that in colonial days to be sure this continued, "Every town has select men who by law were to enforce family morals and that family government was upheld."[63] Rosemary Radford Reuther and Rosemary Skinner Keller, in their introduction of their book *Women and Religion in America: Volume 2; The Colonial and Revolutionary Periods* (1983)[64] said their research objective was to support the women's rights movement that had challenged all traditional views for women for about two decades. Their stated thesis: "In what ways did each vision [of women] offer conflicting messages, at once encouraging and representing new egalitarianism?"

While seeking to represent the individualistic feministic views, Reuther and Keller conceded that women in the colonies were content, and said that they "accepted their subordination without question." These researchers say that Carol Karsen found worth and dignity of women in the home because of Godlike positions in the family, and a well-ordered hierarchical society. Referring to the early Puritans led by John Winthrop in the Massachusetts Bay Colony and his wife Margaret, Reuther and Keller also stated they were examples of how the man and wife had their own separate spheres to meet the family needs, and they shared a "love of each other as the chief of all earthly comfort in

---

[63] Arthur Calhoun, *The Social History of the American Family, Vol.1: Colonial Period* (New York: Barnes and Noble, 1960), 72, cf. 74-76.
[64] Rosemary Radford Reuther and Rosemary Skinner Keller, *Women and Religion in America: Volume 2; The Colonial and Revolutionary Periods* (San Francisco: Harper & Row, 1983), xiii, 138,163-165.

which their first and ultimate commitment was to God."[65] At first the colony had sought to grow a common garden, which failed. The leaders changed to gardening with each man and woman, and even children cooperating as a family had its own plot; each was given freedom to use their different abilities. This allowance for each family to produce resulted in amazing productivity and new prosperity for all, and together they even generously helped their former enemy. The structures of marriage with a hierarchy in the family were what enabled and encouraged the man and wife to be free to express their abilities and desires for which they were differently made able by creation.

But what is not mentioned by secular researchers about the colonies was the fact of faith that dominated, and that was what held the man accountable to God, and also the women to God through him, and the children under them. It was the traditional hierarchy of love that we have shown in the chapters on covenant love that gives power and joy to both sexes in union with each other. This was what controlled the marriage and family in the colonies. It was precisely the motivation produced by faith in God that produced spiritual values, and their love for union in a hierarchy that the secular disbelievers were trying to remove. Women had to be free from submission for childbirth and nurture, and work like men to gain equal success in material prosperity. The disbelievers *began their research* by omitting the most important factor of faith of male and female to accept their differences as good. By beginning with materialistic values they had no other way to make women equal with men than to deny the feminine to be like men.

The perversion in our cycle of Western civilization began with a shift from trust in the Creator God, to trust in a pantheistic power of nature as the turning point to claim *mankind as the highest power of the evolutionary process* of nature. The shift to worship creation was an inevitable result. I have traced in detail how this rejection of God, which began in 1750, occurred in my book, *True*

---

[65] A broader discussion of the facts about our nations beginning are found in my book, *Man is Not Enough*, Chapter 8, especially 136-139.

Enlightenment from Natural Chance to Personal Creator. This rejection occurred after over two hundred and fifty years of faith in God as Creator established in science and theology by the Reformation. At the end of the seventeenth and eighteenth century, unbelieving and unrepentant man who did not have God's Spirit rebelled against the truth of the Reformers. He began to trust man's individual reason based only on sense perceptions as the only real standard to know good and evil. The story of how men led the shift in this worship will be first reviewed and then that of the women. The Western civilization of the Reformation began in Europe and then those ideas found acceptance in America about a generation or two later.

Modern Western History of Efforts for Material Equality (Viewed Sexually)

To help understand the efforts to define and promote equality in the Western world and in the United States the following is my summary, and that of others, including that of feminists. This reveals the dominant view in the steps of decline under materialism and the progressive rejection of faith in God.

1. Material *Equality for* **all** *Humans* (1760-1850).
   Male conceived and led individualistic Enlightenment claims for equality and rebellion against God and all authority.
2. *Group Militancy for Equality* for female sex, slavery, and other rights (1850-1959).
3. *Protests for Social Equality and Freedom*, Women Central Feminism (1959-1979). Women's protests, racial protests, student protests. Neo-communists or postmodern efforts to remove traditional hierarchy.
4. *Women and Minorities Claim Ascendency to Irrational Power Demands* (1980s to present).

Male Efforts for Equality through These Steps
Material Equality for All Humans by Nature without God

At the end of the seventeenth and eighteenth centuries, there was a spirit of rebellion against leaders of the churches and political powers because of their corruption. This motivated men who did not have the Spirit of God to want more material wealth and freedom to enjoy the flesh equally for themselves. The demonic idea that man could be wise *as God, and like him know* what is good and evil, arose out of this failure of the previous dying culture. In this book on marriage it will help to understand at least the highlights as given in detail in my book, *True Enlightenment,* to show how men and women in their claim to be God to rule over nature, changed the sexual differences. [66]

This spirit of rebellion was put together by a German philosopher, Immanuel Kant, in 1755. He was an aggressive, 5-foot tall man with a deformed shoulder. He never married. Kant proposed a theory called *the nebular hypothesis* whereby all things began by a cloud of atomic dust and developed into stars, galaxies, planets, and then life up to man and everything else. He got his ideas, first from Lucretius (95-55 B.C.), a deranged and suicidal Roman Epicurean philosopher; then Kant got more refined ideas from Emanuel Swedenborg, a Swiss scientist who received voices and visions leading to religious heresy. Kant also got additional astronomical speculations from observations of Thomas Wright, an astronomer. Kant put these views from eccentric sources together from his own beatific vision, and described how it all developed by the pantheistic god of nature. To claim scientific credibility, Kant claimed a link of his theory of evolution of all things to the regularity of nature demonstrated by Newton's laws as determined knowledge, but contrary to Newton's faith. Kant then developed his view of knowledge that put God and morals in a separate category of thought that might be desired, but taught that only what is derived by sense perception is real. [67]

---

[66] For full details see Wilson, *True Enlightenment from Natural Chance to Personal Creator,* Chapters 4-6.
[67] Wilson, *True Enlightenment,* Chapter 4, 47-59.

183

Thus Kant excluded God, not from science, but by his philosophy of knowledge and by a pantheistic view of nature. According to him only what is learned about what is created is real, removal of spiritually revealed values required a change of all created differences. This was necessary to gain equality by material values. The natural power of evolution falsely promised progress. Kant claimed all men should be equal as did his successor.

This evolutionary concept was then spread by a young German man, William Herschel who became an English astronomer. It also became known in France and all of Europe. Pierre-Simon Laplace, who accepted Herschel's theory, claimed to mathematically prove how the planetary system that was being discovered was developed by nature without God. This evolutionary theory of cyclic progression, first proposed in astronomy, spread to all sciences, including geology.[68] An essential part of the theory was that only regularly known working forces of nature could be accepted, and all catastrophes were to be excluded. The uniform regular working of nature could be guessed and this required millions of years for development.

In the next century the Enlightenment's claim for human wisdom produced the French Revolution for democracy based on natural rights in *The Declaration of the Rights of Man and the Citizen,* and pursued equality of all against the rich and powerful by violent revolt as designed by Rousseau and others. While the views for equality were considered for women, this was a male controlled effort. It failed and led to the male domination by Napoleon's military dictatorship. Earlier, The Declaration of Independence in America occurred declaring equal rights based on all men being ***created equal.*** Alexis de Tocqueville in 1835 had observed the American democracy had succeeded when the French one didn't because of the common faith in Christ in the colonies.[69]

---

[68] Ibid. chapters 5-7, 60-94.
[69] Alexis de Tocqueville, *Democracy in America,* written in 1835 and translated by Harvey C. Mansfield and Delba Winthrop (Chicago: the University of Chicago Press, 1992). See my discussion in *Liberty in an Evil Age,* Chapters 1, 6.

This determined view of natural development required rejection of Christ's creation and God's cataclysmic judgments that are said in the Bible to have caused most of the geological changes in short times. Charles Lyell had been influenced by William Herschel's view through his son and by James Hutton. Lyell rewrote the geological history of the earth and re-dated all the strata in millions of years, to support change over long ages. The theory of evolution of all things was then substituted for the Bible as an explanation for the interpretation of how creation occurred. These views of evolution became popular and spread in acceptance for 100 years.

Group Militancy Claiming Rights of Class, Race, et al.

In 1859, Charles Darwin, with a theory of inherited changes but no known evidence at the time, added millions years more for the evolution process of life. Later, in 1871, Darwin claimed the evolutionary development of man and thought *males were superior to females by natural evolution*. There were discovered micro changes in species within natural genetic controls, and new unusual species, but there was no valid evidence of how a process of evolution occurred. Because the theory promised material progress for humanity within man's understanding, and without God, it gained wide acceptance by educators in the West.[70]

Also, the evolutionists had no measuring standards of age in development at the time they estimated these. One hundred years later there was the effort to give "absolute dating" from radioactive elements and "light years." These claims to dating were later found invalid because of a rate of decline of earth's forces.[71] But all human history was rewritten to portray modern man as developing toward superman. But by deceptive claims of an evolutionary process, the educated elite slowly promised progressive prosperity and equality for all from nature. The anti-slave movement, first begun by Christians, became a major effort of those who believed all had natural rights to equality. At the time of Darwin, Karl Marx

---

[70] Wilson, *True Enlightenment*, Chapters 4-6 for extensive details, 47-94.
[71] Ibid, Part VII, 387-430.

was also an atheist who sought to *promote social equality by communism* for the proletariat or common worker through governmental removal of any class.

The documented evidence reveals these men developed a faith in the power of nature to specifically dispose of God. They believed ideals evolved and made claims to discredit the Bible and remove any cataclysmic judgments for sin by attributing all to slow changes in nature to millions of years.[72] These and many other claims as scientific to support evolution were later discredited. [73]

By the end of the nineteenth century, the disbelieving critics had discredited the Bible and the supernatural evidence for Jesus Christ and promoted the idea of brilliant progress in man's knowledge. The educated elite believed man would progress to superman. The belief was that man had outgrown the childish belief in God, and he was now a mature man in understanding.

Following this thought process, Friedrich Nietzsche began with the idea of entering the ministry like his ancestors, but he gave up his faith after reading D. F. Strauss. Strauss believed the miracles of Jesus to be myths. Nietzsche then determined he could progress to be superman (Uberman) and ended up writing *The Antichrist* (1895). He then went insane and had to be cared for by his sister for his last ten years of life. She re-edited some of his works and gave them an anti-Semitic slant. While Nietzsche was not a social advocate, his views were used by Hitler and the Nazis to claim the Germans were the master race to be supreme.

In America the progress to man claiming to be God had been hindered by the Civil War, and later by the two World Wars. But the brilliance of science and management of some men produced the greed and wealth of the tycoons. Their accumulated wealth and their oppression of the poor required labor unions and the intervention of government anti-trust laws to promote equality. John Dewey's ideas of pragmatic instrumental social *communism* in teacher training schools and by required standards, resulted in the takeover of education by secular elite men, and the

---

[72] Ibid. parts VIII, IX , 435-540.
[73] Ibid, Part IV, Chapters 11-15, 159-240.

organization of the teachers union. Advancement of women's equality in 1918 by electing a woman president of the National Education Association, helped promote women's suffrage in 1921. The swing of most educators to the evolutionary view of man followed the fake Scopes "monkey trial" which had been promoted by the media.

Men's Modern Insanity Continues to Motivate Reaction

According to Daniel Bell of Harvard the leadership of men as gods was insane.

> Modernity …is more than the emergence of science, the explosion of technology, the idea of Revolution, the entry of masses of people into society — thought it is all of these. Modernity is the inchoate Promethean aspiration, now made flesh of men to transform nature and transform themselves *to make man the master of change and the redesigner of the of the world* to conscious plan and purpose.[74]

Two world wars under male leadership, followed by Marxist takeovers to build a world of equality or of supermen exposed the insanity of modern men. Dictators in Germany, Russia, and China, using modern weapons, killed millions in war and cruelly imprisoned and destroyed millions to control and make a better equal world.

Protests for Social Equality and Freedom in Everything

The apex for rejecting God, for seeing man as god whose trust in nature could produce wealth, health, and pleasure, was reached in the 1960s. Intellectuals then declared the death of God theologies, the removal of God from the public schools, and implemented the government's civil rights laws to correct racial injustices and women's rights to succeed as men and earn as much. With the male thinking he was brilliant, he had ended the Second World War introducing nuclear power and hydrogen bombs with a new threat between the West and the brutal communism of the

---

[74]Daniel Bell, *The End of Ideology: On the Exhaustion of Political Ideas in the Fifties*, (Cambridge, MA: Harvard University Press, 1960), 436.

Soviet Union. Man now as god, offered scientific knowledge that could end humanity in a fight for power and materialism.

Modern Women's Pursuit for Individual Material Equality

Material Equality for All, Males Leading (1760-1850)

The European Enlightenment which denied the reality of God and the metaphysical was man's self-righteous effort to remove all material and physical differences. The claims for equality of all by nature gave intellectual ascent to equality for women. The Enlightenment leaders promised opportunity for equal material and pleasure benefits by male wisdom for all in democratic government. This concept of Enlightenment for rights by nature produced the French Revolution that defined equal rights materially as political for all citizens. This meant removing the ruling, priestly, and royal class of hierarchy. As mentioned, Karl Marx protested the inequality from the Industrial Revolution, and the use of the common people, or proletariat. Theoretically Marx was advocating equality for women independently. But Marxism was mainly focused on opportunity for material equality for male workers with only few fruits clearly defined for women.

Earlier in 1790, Marquis de Condorcet in France extended the idea of equal rights to women by nature in a brilliant, but short, thesis. This received little attention. But a larger work from a woman's point of view written two years later by Mary Wollstonecraft of London, *The Vindication of the Rights of Women*, advocated for individual rights that initiated the feminist movement in England and France. However, the feminist effort for equality ended in Napoleon's male-led dictatorship as superman.

Group Militancy for Equality for Females and Slaves (1850-1959)

The movement for equality at this period involving natural material worth in the anti-slave movement became a time for women to also seek material equality from nature. The idea of equality of women was revived in France with the slave issue in the mid-nineteenth century. Some American women were involved in these social efforts in France, and helped motivate the promotion of equality for women in America. In 1848, the first women's rights conference at Seneca Falls, New York, was promoted by Elizabeth Cady Stanton and Lucretia Mott. (Both of these women had been involved in the slave issue in France.) At the conference, the *Declaration of Sentiments and Resolutions* was passed with about 300 women involved. They not only demanded the abolition of marriage as a form of slavery, but the women also demanded children be named for their mother, they boldly added the right to vote, and they later made demands for removal of men from public office. A woman had previously been defined by her bodily powers of giving birth and nurturing, and a man by business and politics. Most of the feminists' documents are still available.[75]

The women's efforts became political for material rights, and for the right to vote by the first quarter of the twentieth century. There was a backlash from women psychologists after the suffrage law was passed. Women's new sense of equal power caused the effects of *momism* on children in the home.

Marynia Farnham, a prominent woman psychologist, reviewed the results of the *Declaration of Sentiments and Resolution* and its results. While acknowledging the frustrations of women from the wealth and sense of superiority of men, she said that these demands were irrational and suicidal for women, and a hostile assault on men in keeping with the world's rebellious spirit of the times (anti-slavery, Marxist revolt against industrialization, etc.). She stated, "The real goal of the feminist movement was to eradicate men."[76]

While these feminist efforts gained legislation for financial benefits, divorce, child benefits, and the right to vote in the early twentieth century, the backlash of women psychologists pointed out the feminists' efforts were suicidal for women.

---

[75] For many details, see, Alice S. Rossi editor, *The Feminist Papers: from Adams to de Beauvoir*, (New York: A Bantam Book, 1979).
[76] Wilson, *Man Is Not Enough*, 201. Cf. for a review of the five waves of U. S. feminism, cf. whole Chapter 11.

Protests for Social Equality and Freedom, Women Central Feminism (1960-1979)

The third and modern effort came in the prosperity after World War II. Women had participated in male jobs, and the war and college education for many more people included more women. This opened many doors, and promoted the desire for women to have more individual material opportunity.

The mid-twentieth century revival of the modern women's movement came from the previous generation in Europe. There the women's movements was launched primarily by Simone De Beauvoir in her book, *The Second Sex*, published in France in 1949, and spread a new search for women's equality in Europe at the time, attracting interest from American women. Simone De Beauvoir, an educated and brilliant woman, wanted to know and define herself and women in general, and she turned to existentialism.

For many years, Beauvoir was the mistress of and influenced by Jean-Paul Sartre, the noted French atheist and existentialist. The French movement from Beauvoir envisioned women sharing in doing what men do, and men doing what women do in the home, and with child care. This sought to change men to accept women to share their areas of power; and while not as militant an effort, it was designed to remove male hierarchy in the family. But this inevitably led to a more militant feminism.

In America in 1963, Betty Freidan's book *The Feminine Mystique,* did not intend to pit women against men, but to "have women and men break out of obsolete unequal sex roles."[77] But she certainly was intending to change men's roles by making women's roles central in the equality issue. She anticipated a second future effort to redefine all aspects of male and female roles, but she did not want to get into politics. Freidan's book and her promotion of modern feminism led to forming the National Organization for Women (NOW), and many other related feminist organizations. The NOW movement initiated thousands of books,

---

[77] Betty Freidan, *Life So Far,* (New York: Simon & Schuster; 2000), 275.

departments of women's study, and many writings by women and some men. Attempting to review all of this would be a detailed diversion. Women became very aggressive as they desired more power.

Women Central Feminism was a social force trying to displace men and gain educationally and politically the same equal rights, and challenged men's nature and positions. Freidan's associates in NOW, Gloria Marie Steinem, editor of *Ms. Magazine,* and Bella Abzug, a lawyer and congress woman, along with others declared any job in business, industry, or politics should be open and pursued by women. The movement found itself involved in politics for women's rights. In 1970, Kate Millett's book, *Sexual Politics,* promoted this movement. Major efforts involved the Equal Pay Act, and ten years of efforts to pass a Constitutional Equal Rights Amendment in 1972, which failed in 1982. This was a time women sought equality in control in all areas of life, including acceptance of freedom in sexual matters like it had become for most men. Women were paradoxically supported in their efforts in congress to promote their freedom by men, most of who abusively dominated their wives and were known for having adulterous affairs.

Claim for Ascendency to Irrational Power Demands, by Women and Minorities (1980s to Present)

These times of the 1980s and following turned financially more conservative under Ronald Reagan. The Equal Rights Amendment was defeated, and the cold war with the Soviet Union discredited Communism and the neo-Marxist Postmodern efforts of the 1960s and 1970s. Women, therefore, saw this as a crisis time from "men's science" of nuclear threats. Women were in a stalemate, and their role and definition were in confusion from a reaction to the radical breakdown of morals, an increase of children out of wedlock, and crime from men without fathers. The difficulties of women mounted, as they experienced about a 70% in loss of income from divorce and increased child care; as a result, the growing dependence on government welfare abounded.

191

Feminists blamed *Christian tradition* and *the new male secular order* that still did not give way to changes in most men, and they accused men of "repeating the rule of the father and of the power of one will."[78] In these conditions the feeling was that women "would be ruthlessly crushed" in man's world.[79] Brilliant and powerful men still dominated and women despaired, seeing this time as "the terrifying domination challenging the age of man's maturity."[80] If this was maturity for men, what was the future? This motivated women to find a new definition for power.

New Non-rational Definitions of Women

The search to remove the unresolved conflict of difference from the biological or material realm came in two ways. These were a return to philosophical and metaphysical ways to try to solve the problem of male and female natures as equals.

French feminists appealed to Jacques Derrida (1930-2004) who removed all tradition and normal reasonable understanding. He taught that the language you speak determines the way you interpret the world around you, and makes no distinction between the natural and the artificial in experience. Words once spoken or written can be changed and misinterpreted. Therefore there is a constant deconstruction/de-realization (change) from the essential meaning.[81]

The French feminists advocated that sex is not something completely determined and definable, but sexual roles are a part of a changing system produced by language. Therefore the idea of woman or *feminine is really a state of becoming*, and not to be defined as "other." By claiming constant deconstruction for essential meaning, the French feminists claimed to treat the differences of women and men as transient with a different future.

---

[78] Marilyn Chapin Massey, *Feminine Soul: The Fate of an Ideal*, (Boston: Beacon Press, 1985), 181.
[79] Ibid, 183.
[80] Ibid, 183.
[81] cf. Carl W. Wilson, *Postmodernism, Threat or Opportunity?* This is my booklet of 20 pages explaining Postmodernism (bravegoodmen.org, books).

This linguistic argument of Postmodern deconstruction is a denial that the Word of God, *logos,* is the Creator who upholds all things with regularity in nature by the word (logos) of his power which gives abiding meaning (Hebrews 1:1; Romans 8:22, 23). This Postmodern path of constant deconstruction change, used to erase certainty in sexual differences by the French feminists, was an effort to remove definition of difference. This philosophy offered only an excuse to remove female submission, but gave the feminists no path for action.

The other desperate path of search to free women as equal was a return to a limited metaphysical ideal. Marilyn Chapin Massey and her Harvard teachers, as in most graduate institutions, had definitely **dismissed God and the metaphysical** for rights to compete with men for equal material benefits. But nearly half a century after de Beauvoir, the existential definition of women was still missing. Limited sharing of equal functions, positions, and power together had rarely occurred. No real definition had been found or given in efforts for men or women to be free individually. Kant had defined freedom from God, Marx had defined freedom of men to produce and claim goods, but there needed to be a final definition of women as reproducing human individuals.

Massey and others in seeking answers were attracted to Einstein's suggestion of the **fusion of women's body with their intellectual abilities** to produce humans and nurture them. Men and women's intellectual abilities are the source of meaning and a mystery. As C. S. Lewis once argued, human intelligence is the one link in the world to the transcendent God, but it is a limited aspect in humans. Yet sinful mankind had denied his limited knowledge was from God. Therefore, Massey considered this union of woman's intellect with her body **as soul** was not a return to faith in the supernatural, but to her, she proposed it as a limited transcendence in this world that hopefully could be transforming.[82]

The answer of Massey in uniting women's designed natural body with her intellect had to be a different definition to use her

---

[82] For this presentation of Massy, see her Chapter 8, Religion, Gender, and Ideology: A New Theory, in *Feminine Soul.*

abilities from those given by men. Massey's effort to find and define herself and other women was by uniting the intellectual with the body to be free, and she found the only answer was **woman's soul**. While therefore declaring a transcendent mind or soul as the answer, and not admitting woman was a creature of God, she declared woman as a god or goddess. She speaks of looking into a "divining mirror" to discover who she was. Just as Nietzsche and other male "death of God" theologians had seen themselves in their "divining mirror" as "superman" or the ideal man as a god, so, Massy declared this is the meaning of women.

This is exactly what God in Eden had declared was the result of the sin of Adam and Eve after eating the fruit of the tree of knowledge. The devil promised what the fruit of knowledge of good and evil would do when he said, "You will be like God" (Genesis 3:5). The result of this knowledge brought death, and God put Adam and Eve out of the garden saying, 'Behold, the man has become **like one of us** in knowing good and evil" (Genesis 3:22). Therefore, man and woman were put out of the garden lest they eat of the tree of life and live forever in this condition of destruction to death. This individualism of each with their differences, believing they were wiser than God, cannot resolve the differences and produce equality. As individual gods, they are left in competition and conflict.

Massey realized that in her solution of an individual feminist god/goddess by uniting her body and mind as a soul, she could not by her transcendent, rational intellect remove differences from man and produce equality, because her rational ability was linked to and defined by her material female body. Her thinking was different from man's because her natural body was different from his and a complement to his.

All previous feminists' efforts to produce material equality had required to compete materially to cause some degree of suicide to her nature that was designed for birthing and nurture. The unity of the body with the reason or intellect for a definition of woman as soul to free her from male domination still offered conflict or difference in reason. This route to transcendence in a material body confronted her with the fact that *she had to commit suicide to reason.*

Previous efforts to escape women's submission to man in her natural functions in the past had meant delayed marriage, birth control, abortion, even infanticide (in Germany), and on occasion murder of children. The issue confronting Massey was, were these extreme acts valid for feminist equality? Adrienne Rich reviewed the acts of infanticide and murder of infants, and suggested that this was to move beyond sanity.[83] Massey saw the issue of women's freedom to be goddesses to escape being women and the pain and suffering of women, and she dared to declare what was necessary for woman's equality. She said,

> What passes for sanity means conforming to the laws and ideologies of those who have been privileged to define the order of the good society and of the good mother.
>
> Naïve belief in the truth of post-Reformation Western ideology of the good mother or of the *morally superior* feminine soul *is not an option for women.* We must not forget the reality of maternal infanticide as a part of history nor deny the potential of and impulse to infanticide that arises from a fettered body. On the contrary, *women need to dare to be mad*, to dream, to envision the soul that might emerge from a free body. We need to speak and write the words that knock the winds *out of the codes of the good society* that have restrained us. To empower ourselves we need to use our own divinizing mirror that reflects *our truth as "ultimate."*[84]

Massey is saying that for women to be free to be like men, they must act against reason or act insanely, concerning who they are. To be individually god, man or woman, all past reason in civilization had to be rejected. They must make victims of anyone who hinders their freedom. As men in war, for this motivation to be equal as alike, she and other women must find a definition that

---

[83] Adrienne Rich, *Of Women Born: Motherhood as Experience and Institution* (New York: A Bantam Book, 1977), 283.
[84] Massey, *Feminine Soul*, 187

requires insane acts for equal kinds of power. Any who stand in the way of freedom of their individualism must be killed.

Was this not the result of men as supermen that was the male insanity that caused the Holocaust? Massey and other women were now advocating superiority to men who by science had invented weapons who could easily destroy humanity. They observed that the male sexuality as independent gods in a cold war was threatening the possible destruction of the whole race, and all women and children. But they were advocating infertility by birth control, abortion, and even child killing that could reduce replenishing the population and end the human race as well.

The irrational views of the French Postmodern feminists, and those of Massey and others of the Feminine Soul as goddesses, left women convinced they must compete, and require men to accept their character of nurture as guide. Formerly the appeal of women was de Beauvoir's idea of a gender neutral society of sharing. In private relationships women were settling for a kind of truce from the fight of male and female, which left room for selfish enjoyment of sex with each other. Even for men arguing for the importance of restoring manliness there has been an acceptance of this neutral gender ideal truce prevailing *in the private* practice. The conclusion was for women to be women and men to be men. [85] But this gave no personal intimacy and left loneliness.

But *in public*, women as goddesses wanted to run things or at least be advisers to men as gods in leadership. But do gods ever yield to other gods? As a group women were saying they were committed to do whatever is possible to be free to be first, and in full control in family, business, and politics. The feminist theory allowed marriage out of wedlock, sexual relations, and one night hook-ups as long as they were neutral, and with every effort to avoid having or caring for children in order to avoid responsibility that would hinder women. These feminists were attracted by the 1960s Communist ideas or revolution that promised equality for all, and by the later modified neo-Communist teachings for

---

[85] Harvey C. Mansfield, *Manliness*, (New Haven: Yale University Press, 2006), 237-244.

deconstruction of all standards with the strategy of taking control of institutions and organizations from within by rules for radicals.[86] Such rules for radicals pragmatically allowed anything necessary to gain the desired end.

Natural Development of Differences Shown to be Untrue

The claim of feminists has been that gender practices are mainly learned, and that men and women do what they do only because these are social traditions. Steven Pinker, a leading Harvard psychologist, says he is a gender feminist. He traced the many studies on the differences of male and females as socially learned and reviewed the findings of all claims. He gave the conclusion saying,

> Things are not looking good for the theory that boys and girls are born identical except for their genitalia, with all other differences coming from the way society treats them... Finally, two key predictions of the social construction theory – that boys treated as girls will grow up with girl's minds and the differences between boys and girls can be traced to differences in how their parents treat them – have gone down in flames.

Feminists have attributed many evils and oppression to patriarchy in order to gain advantages from men in control. Christina Hoff Sommers, also a moderate feminist, found the research and writings of modern feminists revealed many distortions and outright lies against men.[87] She is of the opinion this was different from earlier feminists, and believes this is harmful to the earlier feminists who only wanted equality.

---

[86] This is a complex process of development for gaining control with left wing Democrats, extensive labor groups, Liberation Theology churches, the State of Islam, and also importantly with the Muslim Brotherhood that organized in over 100 American universities that interacted with European and Eastern Asians and Africans. This has resulted in spreading the feminist movement and reducing the fertility rates of women with long term consequences for many nations. Cf. One long chapter in my *True Enlightenment, Volume II* to be published 2014.

[87] Christina Hoff Sommers, *Who Stole Feminism? How Women Have Betrayed Women,* (New York: A Touchstone Book,* 1995). Cf. Wilson, *Liberty in an Evil Age.*

In her research she shows that the emergence of feminist studies in academia resulting from the 1960s movement *was constructed on bias against men*, and not objective. Many of the accusations toward men and patriarchal society about discrimination and abuses to women have been false. She disclosed this about the claims of feminism about men being more violent against women, about most rapes, and oppression causing anorexia and bulimia from depression. She exposes false claims that women have been discriminated against, especially in education. While Sommers' reports were attacked as inaccurate, there is no question that her main claims of male abuse of women by the feminist are untrue, and their claims were false.

In addition, other unbiased research shows the feminist claims against men have been false. The accusation of feminists that women earn less, have less leadership roles in corporations, and have fewer leadership positions in science because of discrimination has been shown to be untrue.

Claim of Male Bias Cause Women to Be Less Successful

William Farrell is the only man who has been on the board of directors of the organization founded by Betty Freidan to promote feminism, National Organization for Women (NOW) in New York City. After the end of the century, he researched why women still earn less. He found that the women with the same qualifications as men in 1950, before the current women's movement and since, have actually made more when being equal in qualifications. Men have traditionally earned more because they take jobs of greater risk, work longer hours, and do work requiring greater strength.[88]

Also the claim of a glass ceiling has been found to be incorrect. *The Economist* did an extensive survey of recent history in corporations in America and Europe and found that corporations had actually sought women for executive positions with little success so that women still hold only one tenth of top positions.[89]

---

[88] William Farrell, *Why Men Earn More* (New York; American Management Association, 2005).
[89] "Helping women get to the top," *The Economist*, July 23-29, 2005, 11.

There was no "glass ceiling" of bias that kept women out of higher management positions. The same was true of women in regard to leading science positions. The problem has been and is that **most women want a family,** and prefer not to take or continue in those positions. These facts actually show that women's created natures are different and in generally don't change.[90]

The modern feminist movement has claimed that in ancient societies there have been matriarchal societies that were peaceful and prosperous, and women in political control produce peace and prosperity. Publication of articles in *Ms. Magazine* et al. claimed that up until 5,000 years ago, matriarchy was prevalent. Cynthia Eller, professor of Women and Religion of Montclair State University, wrote *The Myth of Matriarchy: Why an Invented Past Won't Give Women a Future* refuting these claims because she saw this as a fabrication that actually was detrimental to women's causes. This is not, however, a denial that in rare conditions women emerge to give significant and good leadership.

Consistent Feminist's Evidences of Dependence on Men

A review of the **women's movement shows a dependency on men,** and a desire to be owned by them. Elizabeth Cady Stanton married a successful business man, and had seven children. With his money she hired a Quaker woman who cared for them, and she was able to spend time and money traveling for the anti-slave cause as well as her campaigns for equality of women. In launching the women's movement the women leaders relied on male leadership. When Stanton and Lucretia Mott drew up a consensus for the promotion of the women's movement to present *Declaration of Sentiments and Resolutions,* they used as their model The Declaration Independence, which was written by men. They had James Mott, Mrs. Mott's husband, moderate the meeting. The Sentiments and Resolutions were presented and women were

---

[90] Cf. Pamela Stone, *Why Women Really Quit Careers and Head Home,* (Berkeley, CA: University of California Press, 2007); Patricia Roehling and Phyllis Moen, *The Career Mystique: Cracks in the American Dream;* and Phyllis Moen, "It's Constraints, Not Choices," *Science,* vol. 319, 15.

reluctant to act on them. These were passed by a narrow margin only after Fredrick Douglas, whom they had asked to attend, stoutly defended them from the floor. At this time, male promotion for equality was popular for anti-slavery, and also equality for the common worker by Marx's *Communist Manifesto.*

Men's Ideas on Equality Basis of Most Women's Thoughts in the modern final feminist movement. De Beauvoir drew from the ideas of Kant, Marx, Nietzsche, Freud, Hegel, and especially from the existentialist, Sartre. Harvey C. Mansfield in his book, *Manliness,* in tracing the male and female controversy refers to and even mentions at times that the women's movement drew originally on the ideas of men. Marilyn Chapin Massey's book *Feminine Soul: The Fate of an Ideal,* reviewing the modern development of feminism, often shows the same thing.

Feminist Leaders Desired and Submitted Sexually to Men
For years, Mary Wollstonecraft was in love with Henry Fuseli, a brilliant older married man. She later lived with Gilbert Imlay, a former American military man, and then married William Godwin, before she died in childbirth. While calling for rejection of marriage as bondage, Elizabeth Stanton married, and her rich husband provided a maid to care for her six children while she traveled. De Beauvoir was Jean Paul Sartre's mistress for over twenty years. Freidan was married for years and had children, though she later divorced. She said, "My involvement with the women's movement was also not exactly good in a sense for my life with men, which continued to interest me a lot. I never felt as alive, if I didn't have a man. And I love sex."[91] This indicated she enjoyed that submission for pleasure and worth. Her NOW associate Gloria Marie Steinem, while promoting feminist independence and equality in *Ms. Magazine,* boasted of her affairs with prominent men with whom she lived and submitted in sex. Kate Millett was married for years to a Japanese husband before

---

[91] Freidan, *Life So Far,* 313.

her divorce, and then had affairs with other men before she ended with lesbian affairs. These desires and acts of many of the most zealous leaders for feminine independence involved a relationship with a man that required submission.

Feminist who compete report a loss of sexual pleasure from men. This report on casual sex conforms to the research that showed women who respect men and submit gain the maximum pleasure. NOW rejection of men for sex pleasure is growing. Shere Hite writing for NOW said that women without men get as much satisfaction out of masturbation.[92] The prominent feminist art historian Amelia Jones and others have recognized that post-feminist text books in the 1980's and 1990's favor feminism as a monolithic entity, and accept lesbians and bisexuals. Single women are often lonely, and when they are the head of the family, they are burdened with providing for children, and frequently feel guilty for leaving the care of children to others.

Consequences to Marriage and Society of Sexual Competition

Conflict for equality of the sexes is causing oneness in marriage to disappear in the United States. The report on the status in marriage has reached a place where the family is crumbling.

According to Carolyn May, in February 2012, she wrote,

Now more than half of all births to American women under 30 are born out of wedlock, and the trend in marriage-less births is becoming an accepted reality of American life. While the middle class is seeing a rise in illegitimacy, 59 percent of all American births are within marriage for that class, but illegitimacy is increasing rapidly for them. The rate is rising fast among white women with high school and some college education. Indeed, it is college graduates and the upper class which have been able to stay within the bounds of tradition and marry prior to reproducing. Outside of the educational differences, there are distinct differences in the marriage rates between different races: 29 percent of white children are born to unmarried women, 53 percent of Latinos, and 73 percent of [all]

---

[92] cf. Wilson, *Man Is Not Enough*, 218, 219 discussions on Shere Hite and Jocelyn Elders as Surgeon General of the U. S. under Clinton, etc.

black children. Some causes are economic factors that have thinned the number of available, marriageable men; a larger social safety net; and a more promiscuous society.[93]

Other studies also document the trend of unmarried women with children being forced out of the middle class into the lower class for economic and other reasons. W. Bradford Wilcox has documented the fall from the middle to lower class of those "moderately educated" (high school and additional post-secondary training) is close to 60% of ages 25 to 60 years old. Four decades ago, in the 1970s, women of this education were married and were in the middle class.

Barbara Dafoe Whitehead said, "The change in unwed motherhood happened very quickly." Moderately educated women in 1980s had only 13% of children born out of wedlock, but in late 2000s this was 44%, which is an increase of 31%. The increase for the lower class least educated showed a 21% jump from 33% born illegitimate to 54%. Whitehead refers also to the Pew Research Center study that reported on decline of marriage and middle class income from 1971 to 2011, showing a decline from 61% to 51%. This decline has been slowed by government welfare subsidies

But also households of married couples in the middle class are dropping even faster, from 74% percent to 55%, involving the economic depression of 2008.[94] Thus the decline in marriage and of the number of children also means the increase in the ratio of older people and the lack of care for them. To help people stay in the middle class and achieve "the American dream," Whitehead suggests the need is more education and better jobs. She suggests this must come from more government help by "earned income tax credit," but admits that politicians "remind us there is a limit to what public policies can do."[95]

---

[93]Carolyn May used government data of child trends quoted by *The New York Times*. This was from *The Business Insider*, February 21, 2012 but originally appeared in *The Daily Caller*.

[94] Barbara Dafoe Whitehead, "What's Missing From Our Middle Class Debate?" Propositions 9 (New York: Institute For Family Values, October 2012) 4, 5.

[95] Ibid., 5

Establishing personal worth on material success, and equality based on justice causes elected representatives in a democracy to make benefits available to those with less. The breakdown of marriage and the family causes people to look to government for help in need and for the elderly. Before the feminist movement in 1950 under the Eisenhower administration those dependent were only about 5%. Peter Ferrara's study found in 2011 there are 185 federal means tested welfare programs costing $700 billion yearly.

The decline of marriage and the loss of family support have involved the Federal government in supporting and caring for the elderly. The Social security program with health care is the largest in the world costing more than $1.2 trillion a year and growing with the baby boomers, and now with only about 40% as many young people supporting the program. The sexual revolution has progressively reduced the birth rate for those to support the elderly. Part of this is because there have been about 56 million children aborted that would have been paying into these programs.

Probably the most serious problem from the sexual revolution is the results upon the children. Children born out of wedlock or who lost their parents through divorce are more likely to have psychological problems, addiction problems, difficulties in education and work, or have criminal tendencies. Many mass shootings are committed by angry fatherless youth, and prisons are filled with them. The *Economist* magazine once commented that perhaps one of the greatest economic problems for the United States is the lack of work ethic of millions of youth. Children often resent new parents from multiple marriages.

Jennifer Morse who is an economist, wife, and mother, and writes on family matters has pointed out the major issue.

> Without some basic structure to function in, it becomes every person out for himself. Forget gay marriage: That's a sideshow. *The main show is the deinstitutionalization of marriage.* By making it so we're free of attachments and obligations and responsibilities, we don't have the ability to cooperate with each other *or the structure that allows us to invest together* over a long period of time.

Single motherhood is becoming more and more prevalent, because you can't get men to commit. Why can't you get men to commit? Number one, because they don't have to; number two, it's dangerous for them to, because the obligation level ratchets up but the benefits do not. The irony of the whole feminist movement, which started off being something to liberate women, is that now women feel like the only free thing they can do is have a child completely by themselves because there is no way of attaching a child to a father and to the family. The move towards same-sex marriage and artificial reproductive technology are accelerating that trend, and making it more likely that more women are going to end up spending their lives alone and doing their child-bearing completely alone. [96]

Even worse: The educational institutions founded as Christian schools such as Yale, Princeton and Harvard are now holding "Sex weeks" that promotes individualistic sexual pleasure.[97]

Conclusions

The cycle of modern civilization shows the same pattern of moral decline and conflict after rejecting faith in God as has all previous ones. The change to belief in a determined nature and the worship of creation/mammon has resulted in competition of male and female. While exalting self and trying to promote equality, the conflict between the sexes has resulted in the inability to change the differences, and the efforts to be god or goddess have become irrational with acts of madness. But evidences of the created differences have remained. The influence of the Western and American thinking on the world is now directed toward global materialistic worship and conflict for sexual equality that is preventing the divine purpose of marriage to show God's image. A major world wide crisis is emerging being led by the West.

---

[96]Jennifer Roback Morse , "Minimizing Marriage: An economist looks at a world without husbands and wives." An interview with Marvin Olasky editor of *World* magazine. She is the author of two books: *Love and Economics* (about motherhood) and *Smart Sex: Finding Lifelong Love in a Hookup World.*
[97] Harden, Nathan, *Sex and God at Yale: Porn, Political Correctness and a Good Education Gone Bad,* (New York: Thomas Dunn Books of St. Martins Press, 2012).

Chapter 12
The World's Last Night of Adultery
And Light from the Power of Covenant Love

Introduction

C. S. Lewis wrote *The World's Last Night*, an honest presentation of evil preceding the Christ's coming to reign in glory in the final "Day of the Lord."[98] Lewis warned against predicting a time of Christ's return, since Jesus said not even he knew the day or the hour. The end of the world's night and hope of the future final day calls for obedience and readiness as his servants witness and wait for him. While Jesus, Paul, and Peter described an increase of evil of the last night of the world's darkness before that time (Matthew 24, 2 Timothy 2:1-9; 2 Thessalonians 1, 2; 2 Peter 3), the dawn of that great day of eternal light remains unexpected. We are told of the kinds of things happening just before Christ's return in order for us to be ready as one expecting the sudden coming as a thief in the night. This chapter is not primarily on prophecy, but you will see it is extremely important.

In this chapter it is important to see where we are in the progression toward the evil days before the return of Christ, and the importance of the witness of the Covenant love in marriage. As described by Paul, the pattern of the growth of evil for nations exhibited in Greece and Rome is one that gets increasingly wider with each successive generation, building on the other's brilliance, and covering an increasingly greater geographical area. Alexander the Great expanded Greece from Eastern Europe to Asia, Egypt and North Africa. The Romans conquered all that area, and to the East, including the British Islands. The modern civilization resulted in the European powers conquering and colonizing most of the world, and paving the way for the United States seeking to establish world influence. Never has the whole world been involved in the evil that is leading to the anarchy and judgment of

---

[98]C. S. Lewis, *The World's Last Night*, (New York: Harcourt Brace Jovanovich, 1960).

all nations. That is why this time seems to be the twilight of the end times before the coming of Christ.

If we understand what is happing in the unfolding of evil, it will reaffirm our faith in God's sovereignty, and enable us to be his witnessing elite of the good news to all nations in these days of Great Tribulation. Christ has his elite who are to boldly be his ambassadors to fulfill his Great Commission being his light in these dark times. The actions of the individualistic sin nature of men under demonic influence are called foolish by Jesus and Paul. This is because the long range effects of selfish greed and lust are not seen as mankind's sins bring tragic tribulation in the outworking of the future. This chapter will disclose where America and the Western world are in the steps towards terrible anarchy and judgment.

Sexual Revolution Reaching Its Night in America and World?

Individuals as Sexual Gods Seek to Dominate Other Sex

Success for materialism drives sexual role changes. In the last chapter the evidence revealed that the sexual revolution has destroyed the underlying structure of marriage and family which causes individual anarchy. The United States is the leader for the world! Today the feminists in the U. S. are boasting of the changes whereby they are *replacing men* as a new stage of evolution. Liza Mundy, an award winning reporter for The Washington Post, in her book *The Richer Sex: How the New Majority of Female Breadwinner is Transforming Sex, Love and Family*, boasted as follows.

> Not long ago, in 1970, the percentage of U. S. wives who out earned their husbands was in the low single digits. ... Almost 40 percent of the U. S. working wives now out earn their husbands, a percentage that has risen steeply in this country and many others, as more women have entered the workforce and remained committed to it. Women occupy 51 percent of managerial and professional jobs in the United States, and they

dominate nine of the ten U.S. job categories expected to grow the most in the next decade.[99]

Mundy boasts that "a large part is due to women's own grit and initiative." Others boast of women's success without and over men. In an interview with a women business consultant of Fox News, Patricia Powell of Powell Financial Group boasted that women were now rapidly producing successful businesses, and that four out of ten of such women used their own maiden names – even when married – because they succeeded better as individuals.

Mundy's book and similar feminist books are written with an anti-male attitude and purpose. This gaining of the male role in a superior way is seen by them as achieving *a new condition of human history*. Mundy further says,

> It would be hard to overstate the historic nature of women's economic ascendancy. With few exceptions, the world has been ordered until quite recently so that the bulk of wealth and earnings lay under the control of men. What we are witnessing is the gradual but relentless upending of a global tradition in which women were obliged to rely on men economically and to fashion their behavior accordingly. For centuries, women's dependence was seen as not just a necessary ingredient for marriage *but the foundation of the male-female union.*[100] (Emphasis mine)

Mundy is declaring that there is now a new foundation of individualistic relationships for men and women in society because women are blessed by Baal/mammon as the leaders.

This is a relationship in which the woman not only has the power of women, but more important for her, she also has the power once belonging to men. To gain this power, a woman has to forfeit her feminine abilities to have children and nurture them with her husband. This shift is now obviously not a foundation for union in marriage, but is the relationship that is destroying marriage union. The new condition is *one for individualistic*

---

[99]Liza Mundy, *The Richer Sex*, (New York: Simon & Schuster, 2012), 6.
[100]Ibid. 20.

anarchy. This claim that women have won is now being claimed by others.

A cover article by Hanna Rosin in *The Atlantic* magazine was "The End of Men."[101] Rosin made the following claim.

> Earlier this year, women became the majority of the workforce for the first time in U.S. history. Most managers are now women too. And for every two men who get a college degree this year, three women will do the same. For years, women's progress has been cast as a struggle for equality. But what if equality isn't the end point? What if modern, postindustrial society is simply better suited to women?

While Mundy and Rosin have exaggerated the facts, the main story is clear that the proclamation of the sexual neutral idea at the end of the twentieth century was not true, because in the new third millennium, women's efforts have turned out to be suicidal to the feminine, and at enmity with men to dominate them. This is just as Marynia Farnham had predicted after women gained individual suffrage. This is not peace and health but destruction and judgment.

Misinterpretations about Women as Superior

There are other important factors which Mundy distorts, and she omits other things that were highly important. The bust in the economy in 2008 greatly reduced the male construction industry, reducing jobs for men. Rosin said that over eight million jobs in the housing and financial downturn were men's jobs. Those are not the jobs women like and do best. Also, the aging of the population expanded the retirement of many men, and also created the need for jobs in health care. Men are dying much earlier than women, leaving them single. Another factor allowing more women to work, especially at home, was the production and use of computers and high tech instruments. Also robots enable women to do many jobs that formerly only men could do well.

---

[101]Hanna Rosin, "The End of Men," *The Atlantic* magazine, July/August 2010.

Another highly important thing not fully emphasized by Mundy, Rosin, and others is the fact that the liberal intellectual elite, who control the educational system, have since the modern feminist movement, favored women in education so that about 65% of college students are now women. The bias for having the same roles as males with power to control is now established in favor of women.

Control of college education has rapidly and radically changed. Only 10% of college presidents were women in 1986, while 21% in 2001 were. By 2010, half the board of the American Council on Education (ACE) consisted of women, and ACE had a female president. One half of the Ivy League college presidents are women, and there are estimates that about 25% of other colleges have female presidents.[102] This has been promoted not only by feminists, but by secular men who believe women should be the same as men. Whereas women have in the past falsely accused men of being biased, the feminists who have become leaders really do discriminate and take advantage of men.

This dominance of women has been won at the cost of sacrificing the role of partner to her husband, and the woman's power to bear and nurture children. The power given to Eve to be the mother of all living is being forfeited. This suicide to her womanhood has the implications of killing the whole race.

Sexual Trends Are Causing the Night of World Civilization

The selfish conflict of the sexes for material success and sexual pleasure, while claiming to promote equality, leads to the decline in women's fertility rate, to men's loss of sperm and aggression, and to homosexuality. The trends of pride to make everyone individually equal caused by rejecting God for materialism, and seeking to promote this egalitarianism are now beginning to lead to disaster. The differences of sex and abilities which God created are what make civilization grow and work. The

---

[102] cf. "Helping Women Get to the Top." *The Economist* magazine, July 23-29, 2005, and ACE later reports, and 2010 census.

secular educated elite are seeing the results of rejecting God and trusting in mammon. This is being driven by the neo-communist postmodernists who are simply trying to destroy all past tradition without knowing how to make a society of equals that will work.

Decline of Fertility Rates for Women Destroys Civilization

The new millennium has awakened the educated elite with a new concern about the *rising generation's infertility trends that poses a serious world crisis*. Instead of a peaceful utopian and prosperous global society, secular unbelief as spiritual adultery for the world is now producing a rapid increase of women and some men who don't want to have children. This unexpected rapid decline in fertility promoted by secular leaders threatens to end civilization. About a dozen studies and many surveys by reliable researchers now predict *an accelerating rate of decline in having children* because of rejection of complementary differences in marriage. While professing to want equality and favoring same sexual roles, males have selfishly dominated material wealth and promoted the selfish individual reaction of women to dominate men and not have children. This worship of mammon has created the blind eyes putting mankind in darkness.

The interpretations of this trend are, on the one hand, the death of civilization. On the other hand, secular leaders are afraid this trend may be causing the reemergence of "fundamentalist religious groups" to world dominance, since these groups are producing a higher rate of children. The aim of secular beliefs was to end religious faith. Because these studies have been conducted mostly by those with a secular perspective who know many facts about the groups, they tend to lump very different groups together and interpret them all as "fundamentalist" religions. These faults will be pointed out.

Importance of the Studies of World's Sexual Trends

There are hundreds of pages giving demographical statistical details and information for many groups and nations, especially Western Europe. These trends in Europe preceded those in the

U.S., such as we have just detailed above. Two highly respected secular scholars, David Goldman and Eric Kaufmann, have provided the data used here. These scholars, along with other researchers, have taken into consideration other demographic information as well. What is given here is not by fly-by-night authors seeking to gain attention by scare tactics. David Goldman emphasizes the dangers for world civilization, and Eric Kaufmann focuses on the probable reemergence of "fundamentalist religions" because of their high rates of fertility.[103] Both see the *situation as unprecedented in history*. The effort of this book is to show the importance of the trends, especially for Christians, in how it will affect our sexual relations and marriages, but also the importance of our witness to be the light of the world as disciples of Christ.

Kaufmann, who has done the most statistical research said,

> The world is in the midst of *an unprecedented shift* from population growth to decline. Europe is leading the way, but East Asia is aging more quickly and may overtake it, while other parts of the world – especially India, Southeast Asia and Latin America – are trending the same path. These changes are *driven by rising prosperity*, women's education, urbanization and birth control. Europe's fertility rate – i.e. the number of children the typical woman is expected to bear over her lifetime – has been below the replacement level for four decades. As a result, its native population has begun to fall in absolute terms – a slide which will accelerate over time. *World fertility is predicated to sink below the replacement level by 2035.* Global
> will follow several decades later.[104] (Emphasis mine)

Replacing God with nature and worshiping the created is the main cause. Both Kaufmann and Goldman agree the European

---

[103] David P. Goldman has done research for Wall Street, Bank of America, and Forbes, has been elected to other research teams, and has a million readers a month in his column at *Asia Times Online.* He has just published *How Civilizations Die (and why Islam is dying too),* (New York: Regnery Publishing, Inc. 2011), 306 pages. The other, Eric Kaufmann, is of a third generation of secular thinkers, a Reader in Politic at Birkbeck College, University of London, and a Fellow at the Belfer Center, Harvard and his book is *Shall the Religious Inherit the Earth? Demography and Politics in the Twenty-First Century, London: Profile Books LTD,* 2010), 330 pages.

[104] Eric Kaufmann, *Shall the Religious Inherit the Earth?* ix, x.

decline is because of secularism that is based on the dominant atheism from the European Enlightenment going back to the eighteenth century. This has changed worth of people from those given by God with created differences, to values from nature that threaten individualism, and therefore require sexual roles be changed to be the same.[105] Europe and the United States now have a strong anti-Christian secular bias and are influencing this change in the whole world.[106]

Goldman calls this darkening trend toward death of civilization the "twilight of the world" (or toward the "world's last night"). He attributes it to the influence of the materialism of Hobbs. While Hobbs was a significant thinker, his was a limited influence. I have shown this trust in materialism is mainly derived from the scientific deterministic view of nature. The basis of this for the Western world was the nebular hypothesis of the evolutionary development of all things put together by Kant. Kant's theory and desire was to remove faith in a supernatural God. His theory was intellectually promoted by Kant's view of knowledge that he created excluding knowledge of the supernatural *a priori.*

The theory of evolution has progressively gained ascendency in modern education.[107] The effect is the same that Aristotelian pantheism had on the Greek, Roman, and Holy Roman European empires in causing the people to worship natural creation. Goldman mentions that the effect was the same as previously. "The repudiation of life among advanced countries living in prosperity and peace has no historical precedent, except perhaps in the anomic of Greece in its post Alexandrian decline, and Rome during the first centuries of the common era."[108]

---

[105] My 606 page documentation, *True Enlightenment*, shows the occult beginning of the evolutionary theory by biased men, and not by science, to change the biblical faith of Europe, and now the whole world.

[106] Goldman, *The Death of Civilizations*, xvi; Kaufmann, *Shall the Religious Inherit the Earth*, xiii.

[107] Wilson, *True Enlightenment*, Chapters 4-6.

[108] Goldman, *Why Nations Die*, xiii.

Secular Education Promotes Mammon and Low Fertility

There is an imminent social threat to most developed countries with material success. Two out of three Italians and three of four Japanese will be elderly dependents by 2050. The fertility rate in Germany, the largest European nation was 1.4 in 2010, much less than the 2.1 replacement rate. Also, one of three German children was born out of wedlock, which is twice what this was a generation before. Goldman said,

> Population decline is the elephant in the world's living room. As a matter of arithmetic, we know that the social life of most developed countries will break down within two generations. ...No pension and health care system can support such an inverted population pyramid.[109]

Until recently the reports on fertility of the United States rates were encouraging, as they were more than replacing the population when other developed countries were not. But in December 2012, the census bureau revealed that since 2007 this has suddenly changed. The population is now projected to be 9 % less, those over 65 years old will grow to 22% instead of 14% now, and the working age population will slip from 63% to 57%, which means The Fertility Rate (TFR) has fallen to 1.9 which is below the rate of replacement of 2.1. This means that the care of the elderly in Social Security and Medicare that is causing a rapidly growing debt of $17 trillion (and is fearfully already rapidly rising) will be increased at a more rapid rate with less responsible youth to care for the elderly.

This change has been caused by later marriages, by more people going into early retirement because of fewer jobs, and because of less immigration, especially from Mexico, of women who have more children. These are likely to be continuing factors. Since the depression of 2008 there have been fewer jobs in the U.S. for immigrants to seek. But more importantly, the economy of Mexico is rapidly growing, and more and better jobs are being

---

[109] Goldman, *How Civilizations Die,* ix.

created. The U.S. situation is worsened by a great increase of people on welfare for a longer period of time, and because the children born out of wedlock are often more involved in crime and have a poor work ethic. The drive for materialism and lust can only be changed by a renewal of faith in God, which would also increase fertility of women. This renewal must come from a repentance of the American people stemming from God's grace.

Bias Against God for Mammon, Forces the Undesirable

The most significant aspect of this trend toward world civilization change is entirely driven by man's biased mind to trust material nature instead of God. Jesus said, "No one can serve two masters, for either he will hate the one and love the other, or he will be devoted to the one and despise the other. You cannot serve God and mammon/money" (Matthew 6:24). As Paul said, "For the mind that is set on the flesh is hostile to God, for it does not submit to God's law" (Romans 8:7). That is why every national civilization (about 150 of them) has gone to destruction in this way. Kaufmann, as a third generation liberal, rightly sees change by secular nations as unlikely since it means a change in their whole motivation. He has said,

> Our social environment is unlikely to change any time soon. Liberals are simply too committed to the ideal of presentist individualism for themselves and tolerance for others. In matters of demography, they insist on a politically correct laissez-faire. This redounds to the advantage of fundamentalists. *Yet to do otherwise would be to act against liberal principles, selling one's soul in order to win.* Secular liberalism lies hoist on its own petard.[110] (Emphasis mine)

Therefore, paradoxically the intellectually secular political elite who lead the world and control the United Nations are foolishly and increasingly promoting the world feminist agenda to be equal and like men, and they continue to accelerate promotion of women's infertility to gain leadership rights. In March 2010 a

---

[110] Kaufmann, *Shall the Religious Inherit the Earth?*, xxii.

consortium of major feminist organizations under what they called a Gender Equality Architecture Reform Campaign (GEAR) met with the United Nations Commission on the Status of Women to create one U.N. agency from the present four agencies for women's causes, to form one powerful agency. This would have about a billion dollar beginning budget with a global mandate to restructure relations between the sexes that weaken the bonds of marriage in a change for new independent relationships. This agency was endorsed and promoted by the Obama administration, and will only further accelerate infertility.

Surprise: Muslim Demographic Change to Low Fertility

There has been a shocking change among Muslim nations from what has been reported as a threat to Europe. [111] This is now in process of change; the details for various countries are covered by Kaufmann. [112] For Europe, but also more importantly for the Muslim nations, this portends a serious crisis. There has been a recent quick change of Muslims in having many children (6 or 7) to few (2 or 3) that has been missed by much of the world. Muslim nations have been influenced by rapid acceptance of Western education and American technological advances. While Western efforts to control are resented, Western engineered material products have been desired and distributed for use. To attain these educational advantages and products there has been a large migration to urban centers. Television, cell phones, and modern transportation make these Western material products available and have given independence to individuals as never before.

What is happening to the Muslims is Western secularization that removes faith in God, and puts hope on prosperity now. In recent generations, Muslim women have received secular education to now earn and gain more material prosperity. To do so, Muslim women have turned to birth control to enable them to prosper. This growth of global modernism to increase wealth and pleasure has led women to reduce their number of children. This

---

[111] Mark Styne, *America Alone: the end of the world as we know it,* 2006.
[112] Kaufmann, *Shall the Religious Inherit the Earth,* chapter 4, 118-157.

has occurred in an increasing number of countries to the extent they are now not replenishing their population.

By 1975 to 1980 the younger generations in Muslim countries began promoting the idea of fewer children. Goldman said, "Literacy explains about 60 percent of the fertility differential across the Muslim world."[113] Goldman and Kaufmann both see Western secular education replacing the Creator for worship of creation or mammon caused by evolutionary Enlightenment views of seventeenth century as the main cause.[114]

Along with this, the Muslim Brotherhood had gained strength by promoting education for the Muslims to overthrow Muslim dictators. Their higher education emphasized individualism to promote democracy for power of the Muslim Brotherhood.[115] While they also emphasized the Koran and Sheria law, the Western atheistic education has overridden the strong Islamic emphasis. The emphasis on individualism for democracy motivated Muslim women to desire equality, and to do so reduced the desire for children. This reduction in children also was motivated by the large number of Muslim youth who were already without work. Now these youths have taken low paying jobs with the government[116] and have been influenced by the communist postmodern Service Employees International Union with Muslim Brotherhood.

Several organizations facilitated and motivated this. After the Iraqi war, Zainab Salbi, the daughter of the personal pilot of Saddam Hussein, migrated to America and with her Palestinian husband, Amjad Atallah founded a movement called *Women for Women International* specifically aiming at Muslim women. Not attacking Sharia law, this movement was successful because it aimed at helping abused women, and was a powerful force in communicating women's rights for Muslims. The former UNICEF

---

[113] Goldman , *How Civilizations Die*, 5, 6.
[114] Goldman, How Civilizations Die, xvi, Kaufmann, *Shall the Religious Inherit...*, xiii
[115] Kaufmann, *Shall the Religious Inherit the Earth?*, 136-139.
[116] Ibid. 145, cf. Chapter 4, The Demography of Islamism in the Muslim World, for details about various nations and rates of change.

CEO Afshan Khan now directs this effort which has a multi-million dollar budget.

Muslim Countries' Fertility Falls
Much Faster Than the World Average

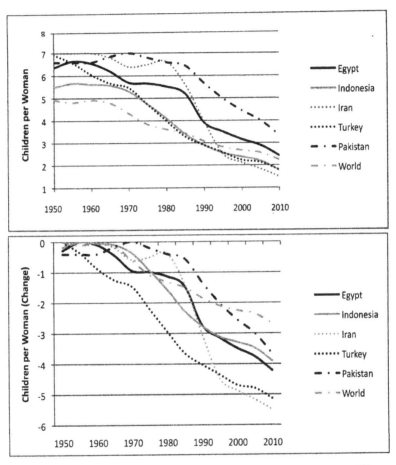

The World CIA Factbook above has graphed the fertility rate in the thirty Muslim nations showing their decline in the fertility rate (TFR) as going from about 6.5 to 1.6.[117] Other graphs of the

---

[117] Goldman, *How Civilizations Die*, graphs above and next page, Chapter 1, the Closing of the Muslim World, p 4,5,12.

U.N. show how the decline has occurred in Muslim countries.[118]

The change in population to reduction of births means that the Muslim populations are being faced with a growing number of older people with fewer young people to provide the pensions or to care for them. The Muslim countries have inoculations and other benefits to allow more youth to live, but have few of the technological instruments and medications to treat the elderly. These countries that have a growing number of older people have little retirement and health benefits, so they are facing a growing demographical problem as shown in this graph.[119]

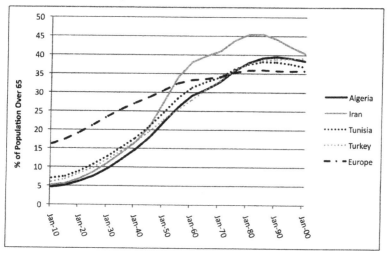

Percentage of Population over 65 Years, Europe vs. Selected Muslim Countries

Motivation by materialism and secularism also promotes change in sexual roles toward immorality and divorce.

Muslim leaders in Iran, Turkey, Tunisia, Algeria, and other nations with a high literacy rate, realize the crisis coming that will bring anarchy to their countries. Other poor Muslim countries with

---

[118] Ibid. 4
[119] Ibid. 5.

high fertility rates are those that are remote tribal nations, and where the people are starving. The nations are between the two extremes. Mahmoud Ahmadinejad in Iran and Tayyip Erdogan in Turkey have tried to persuade their women to marry earlier and have more children, but the opposite has occurred with the TFR going lower. Muslim leaders see this as a Western conspiracy against them.[120]

An additional threat of violence is that Sheria law presents a harsh patriarchy, and this change puts a strain on male control by Sheria law. The Muslim Brotherhood that has promoted education has wanted all the people to study the Quran and Sharia law to form a democracy of their own that rejected Western-style influenced nation states. The women who are educated to be independent offer a reason for strong Muslim males to resent this Western influence, and therefore are a recruiting ground for the terrorists like Al-Qaeda whose leaders have multiple wives and many children. Terrorists make their appeal against wealthy Muslim leaders on the basis of Sharia law.

The clash of young and the elderly in need, and of the Sharia law and western-educated, less committed Muslims, along with resentments from the Western nations offer tremendous tensions for conflict. Goldman discusses this and has said,

> Declining populations do not necessarily portend a peaceful outcome. On the contrary, in the short term they may well motivate aggressive behavior provoked by a belief that the opportunity to fight may never return. ...In the Islamists' own view, the encounter of Islam with the globalized world has had catastrophic effects on a religion so deeply rooted in the habits of traditional society that it cannot survive in the harsh light of modernity. The closing of the Muslim womb is a symptom of a shock to the spiritual condition of the Islamic world, a loss of faith more sudden and more devastating than the past century's trend towards secularism in the West. ...Like Europe, the Muslim world is engaged in the slow-motion suicide of failing to create the next generation. But the flip side of suicide by infertility is jihad."[121]

---

[120] Ibid. cf. statements 7-11.
[121] Ibid., 13.

Millions of people in Western counties, in many developing countries, and now in most of the Muslim countries are caught up in the folly of demonic deception; they are rejecting God and seeing themselves as gods to own creation and make sex a selfish pleasure.

The modern world is seen as a challenge to many Christians, but that is not the case of Muslim leaders. If we view these sweeping changes as they do, the change in women's fertility from Western influence appears differently. Ali A. Allawi who was a former Minister of Finance, Defense and Trade of Iraq and teacher at Oxford and Princeton has said,

> The much heralded Islamic 'awakening' of recent times will not be a prelude to the rebirth of an Islamic civilization; it will be another episode in the decline. The revolt of Islam becomes instead the final end of a civilization.[122]

Perversion of Roles Affecting Sperm Production Worldwide

The worldwide perversion of sexual roles is initiated by male greed, arrogance and lust that affects women. Now the threat of feminism that has reduced fertility has other significant threatening consequences for the male. The role changes are affecting male sexuality, and causing a serious drop in sperm production throughout the world.

Shiva Dindyal MBBS (London) BSc. (Hons) Imperial College School of Medicine London United Kingdom has reported these findings.

> However, according to the ever-increasing literature on sperm counts, these "normal" values are steadily decreasing and only a minute proportion of males will have semen values that satisfy these ideal figures in today's Western industrialized countries. Not only are sperm counts decreasing, but also are the average sperm volumes

---

[122] Ali A. Allawi, The Crisis of Islamic Civilization, (new Haven, CT: Yale University Press, 2009), 273.

which contain a greater proportion of deformed spermatozoa that have reduced motility's. [123]

Professor Niels Skakkeback, a Danish scientist, and his team reviewed 61 international studies involving 14,947 men between 1938 and 1992. They found that the average sperm count had fallen from 113 million per milliliter in 1940 to 66 million in 1990. In addition, the definition of a "normal" sperm count fell from 60 million per milliliter to 20 million in the same period. *This showed more than a 50% decline in about three generations*. This was questioned until further studies confirmed this. A survey of 1,350 sperm donors in Paris found a decline in sperm counts by around 2% each year over the past 23 years, with *younger men having the poorest-quality* semen. In another study at the University of Helsinki led by Jarkko Farjarinen, testicular tissue was examined at post-mortem from 528 middle-aged Finnish men who died suddenly in either 1981 or 1991. Among the men who died in 1981, 56.4% had normal, healthy sperm production. By 1991, however, this figure had dropped dramatically to 26.9%. Adamopoulos et al in Athens examined 23,850 men between 1977 to 1993 (17 years) and found similar results to Farjarinen. In Edinburgh a recent study by Irwin saw a 25% decrease in sperm count over 20 years; the results are shown in table 1 below. The worrying thing about this downward trend is that a sperm count less than 20 million sperms per ml is *interpreted as being infertile*, if this downward trend of counts were to continue then values less than this will be the average in the next millennium. [124] (Emphasis mine)

YEAR	AVERAGE SPERM COUNT (SPERMS PER ml)
1950	100 million
1970	75 million
1990	50 million

The health of male genitals and sperm involve testosterone and man's ability to perform. The world's increase in use of modern drugs to promote erections reflects this sexual change in male normal ability. The Department of Veteran's Affairs says that

[123] Shiva Dindyal MBBS *The Internet Journal of Urology*. 2004 Volume 2 Number 1 DOI: 10.5580/118d.
[124] Ibid.

purchases for veterans of Viagra, Levitra, Alprostacil and Cialis gradually increased from $27.3 million in 2006 to $71.7 million in 2012. Our military men are thought of as being most manly.[125]

There is no clear explanation for this statistical change in sperm count which was recorded in the Western nations, but there are two areas for possible cause being searched: *the lifestyle* of men, or the *environmental influences* of modern society. The latter relates to estrogen in plastics, therapeutic drugs, food sources, and insecticides. These amounts are small, but could over time be found to be detrimental, even though they are not yet known. The rise in temperature is also suggested but not apparently yet significant. There is resistance to blaming lifestyle, but it seems this may be the main source of the problem.

The greatest change in lifestyle is in younger men, and it is in them the change seems to be growing. In the summary of this study this statement is given. "However if the general fall in sperm counts are a consequence of *altered estrogen exposure in utero*, then they are preventable"[126] (emphasis mine). The major birth control pills now being produced contain estrogen, and are regularly used throughout the world. Estrogen reduces sperm count. This suggestion will be rejected by the goddess model of absolute in standards to do what gives the woman power.

This loss of sperm suggests that the adoption of the world of the change of sexual roles is catapulting the male into a loss of ability to reproduce the race, with women who want fewer children. Since sperm count is related to the amount of testosterone that affects male aggressiveness and muscle, the loss of maleness is not just a philosophical issue but a physical one affecting creative work and other male qualities. More importantly, male and female in their individualism and rebellion against the good of God in creation are destroying the purpose of God to show his

---

[125] Kathleen Miller, "VA's Viagra Spending Soars…" *Bloomberg News, Orlando Sentinel,* January 20, 2013, A6.
[126]. Shiva Dindyal MBBS *The Internet Journal of Urology.* 2004 Volume 2 Number 1 DOI: 10.5580/118d.

image in the union of male and female in marriage. These conflicts for sexual superiority are creating a basis for world anarchy.

Homosexual Wave, the Extreme Individualism is Anti-God

The end of individualism and the effort for making all to be the same is homosexuality. All other sexual perversions tend toward that destination. God's judgment of Sodom and Gomorrah was for the materialistic greed that distorted all sex, and produced the violent demands of homosexuals. The individualism in the West and America is leading the world down the road of conflict over material worth that likewise ends at homosexuality, claiming each person is right as god.

Europe has led protests for homosexual normalization, and in the United States homosexuals came out the closest at the Stonewall riots in 1978. Legalization of homosexual unions have begun in Europe, and now are being accepted in the United States: the Netherlands led the way in 2001, and since, Iceland, Norway, Sweden, Belgium, Denmark, Spain, Portugal, Argentina, and Mexico City have followed suit. Currently 22 of the 51 countries in Europe recognize some type of same-sex unions, among them a majority of members of the European Union. Eight European countries legally recognize same-sex marriage. Now Canada and nine of the United States (in the Northeast and Washington in the West) as well as Washington D.C. have legal approval for same-sex marriage, supported by the Obama Administration and The Democratic Party. Now the United States National Cathedral in Washington, D. C. is holding homosexual weddings.

An article in *The Economist* said,

> Just a dozen years after the Netherlands became the world's first country to legalize gay nuptials, the global trend toward giving homosexuals full marriage rights seems to have gained unstoppable momentum.

> Fifty years ago homosexuality itself was still a crime throughout most of the world. Britain decriminalized it only in 1967 and it was not until 2003 that America's Supreme Court struck down the remaining sodomy laws in 14 states. Now across most of the West, polls show a

majority of public opinion in favor of equality for gays, including allowing them to marry and adopt children. [127]

The whole world is now following suit for approving homosexuality. This rapid change is already politically acceptable *except for some Muslim nations and most of Africa.* But Western education is now impacting these countries. Unless there is God's grace for repentance and a return to faith the majority of the world will soon count this extreme of individualistic sexuality to be normal.

In my book, *Man Is Not Enough* [128] there is a comprehensive review of the claims to normalcy and the deceptive way homosexuals gained approval of the psychological and sociological sciences. I have shown there are five possible causes of homosexual preference that are given documentation from studies, but the most basic reason is a childhood experience *of conflict between male and females, especially in the parents.* This affects hormones, and a rejection of the other sex. The claims of necessity from physiological differences as cause for homosexual preference are shown to be perversions. Homosexuals are driven by a strong sexual passion. They are extremely driven and promiscuous, and even when "married" are seldom faithful. But about 25% can change to heterosexual lifestyle with help and trust in God, and then have a satisfying marriage. [129] Obviously the homosexuals who want approval for normalcy vigorously deny all of these facts.

Homosexuality is the extreme of the individualistic sin nature, and is a potential for all of us humans who are in demonic control and have not experienced the cross and resurrection power of Christ. Sinful men put self above God for one's own pleasure, but also react to the difference of male and female as in Genesis 3. Because homosexuality is the most extreme rejection of the

---

[127] "Gay marriage: to have and to hold," *The Economist*, November 17-23, 2012, 57, 58, and cf. "Homosexuality" *Wikipedia free encyclopedia.*
[128] Wilson, *Man Is Not Enough*, Chapter 18, 375-391.
[129] Ibid. 384,385

purpose of the image of God designed to show his love in a complementary marriage, the homosexual is the most hostile to the man of faith.

As indicated, at the end of a civilization the leaders usually also practice homosexuality. This practice is the defiant end of the sexual revolution, the road to world anarchy, tribulation, and judgment. God's destruction of the city of Sodom and Gomorra is used in Scriptures and by Jesus as a warning of the end times (Genesis 19:4, Amos 4:11; Luke 10:12; 17:29, et al.) These cities were an example by God in early human history of judgment for materialistic greed and the individualism of sex it promotes.

Jeffery Satinover is one of the most extensively trained and experienced scientists regarding the subject of homosexuality. He has said,

> Because it is not really a battle over mere sexuality, but rather over which spirit shall claim our allegiance, the cultural and political battle over homosexuality has become in many respects the defining moment of our society: It has implications that go far beyond the surface matter of "gay rights." And so the most important dimension of this battle is not the political one, it is the one for the individual human soul.[130]

The most important issue is that God's plan for creating male and female to unite in showing his image of love to the world is reaching an end. It is therefore now becoming *the defining moment for the world* and the last light for all civilization as night is coming. Never has Christian Covenant love in marriage been so vital as perhaps we face the final generations of mankind.

---

[130] Jeffery Satinover, *Homosexuality and the Politics of Truth* (Grand Rapids: Baker Books, 1996), 250. He is an Orthodox Jew. He earned his Bachelor of Science degree at the Massachusetts Institute of Technology in 1971. He obtained a Master of Education degree in Clinical Psychology and Public Practice from Harvard University, a medical degree at the University of Texas, and a Master of Science in Physics at Yale University. He received a diploma in analytical psychology from the C. G. Jung Institute of Zürich, becoming their youngest graduate. He trained there and became an accredited Jungian analyst.

Conclusions: The Power of New Covenant Love: Revealing God's image in Sexual Union in the World's Last Night

Blind Confusion of Religion as Salvation by Higher TFR

Eric Kaufmann as a liberal has faced the question in his book, *Shall the Religious Inherit the Earth?* He suggests that fertile families are going to happen through religious groups. While admitting that religion accepting belief in God is the answer, he does not see the basic issue for sorting out the answer. He and David Goldman have recognized that accepting the European Enlightenment views from the Eighteenth century is the poison that affects the change of the sexes in religion, but they do not face the real issue of human sin and selfish individualism for the power, ownership of wealth, and personal pleasure through lust that drives the change.

They acknowledge that in the 1960s the old-line liberal religious denominations began to promote the sexes as equal, ordaining women, and since then ordaining homosexuals. These denominations all declined numerically as a result, but without repentance. This also is seen as the problem for the whole Muslim world now. Moreover, they both admit that the secular leadership of the world cannot reverse this trend, because that would be a denial of their secular claim for power.

The issue is not just religion and secularism, but also the issue of religious power and control through legalism for earthly power of men, and control by God's supernatural grace of suffering love. Kaufmann sees the groups that believe in a God as the hope to save the decline in population. He especially shows how separatist groups such as the Anabaptist, the Amish and the Hutterites, as well as the other orthodox remnants like the Laestadian Lutherans in Finland, and the Dutch Orthodox Calvinists are multiplying by reproduction of children as do the conservatives of the old line denominations. He commends the Mormons for continuing to replenish their congregations. He also shows that for every child Mormons baptize, they evangelize 2.4 converts.

He refers also to emerging evangelical Christian couples who identify with the Quiverfull movement in the United States, Canada, Australia, New Zealand, Britain, and elsewhere who promote increased procreation. Many eschew birth control, family planning, and sterilization. While all of these do show promise of population growth, they are in the millions, which is still small compared to the 7.5 billion people in the world.

Moreover, Kaufmann fails to distinguish the groups that accept the message of Christ and his lordship and control of the churches by his power of suffering love motivated by hope of eternal rewards. Some groups have ambitious leaders who control the people by a legal system to build a big earthly kingdom for themselves. The failure of liberal Protestantism, of Islam, of some branches of Roman Catholicism, and of Mormons is they want to multiply fertility to build their organization for worldly power. The groups seek legal obedience to a religious system controlled by men. The Bible shows that this has been the failure of all the nations of the world, including Israel under the Law of Moses. Men who trust in their own legal abilities have and will always fail and end up bringing Baal or mammon into the Holy Place. A whole other book would be required to sort out the groups that have vitality in marriage and why.

But the issue of Christian marriage and fertility is to replace law by grace in Christ, who is the Son of God. Christ alone has dealt with sin, and by New Covenant sacrificial love he has made a way to an eternal kingdom, not one that follows the devil for individual selfishness in this world.

World Syncretistic Religion Ends Divine Reproduction

This supernatural Christian Covenant of grace and love is precisely the thing that the world of sinful men is now seeking to reject. The conclusion of secular elite scholars is that *all religions were naturalistic and created by man for his good*, but have been the source of conflict and wars. So they are putting *together a global syncretistic religion where all religions can be treated as equal* and each contribute to the good of man, and not worship a nonexistent, mythical, supernatural God[131]

Because religious conflict and war has destroyed many people, the current educated elite want this one syncretistic religion to be controlled by a one world government, now probably by the United Nations. Each religion should admit its wrong in competition, especially Christians who have sought to evangelize the world. This would be the ultimate political legalistic control. This effort at one religion has been launched by the Archbishop of Canterbury, Dr. Rowan Williams (who resigned in 2012) and by American leaders. Meetings have been held in Christian sacred cathedrals and prestigious universities. All the various religions have participated, reading from their sacred books and praying to their god.[132]

The world's intellectual elite who are now neo-Marxist/communists are promoting this together. They are working to promote a world pantheism involving liberation theology churches, secularized Muslims, liberal Protestants, and Jesuit Roman Catholic Liberation Theologians. The aim is to equalize all people under their control, taking from the rich and giving to the poor, and making male and female equal. The enforcement of this one world religion will persecute any who refuse to comply in perhaps the worst world holocaust. Those persecuted will be the Christians and the Orthodox Jews who believe in a Messiah of grace to come. This will prepare for the biblical Antichrist and the final darkness of the Great Tribulation.

Challenge to Witness by Evangelism and Covenant Marriages

In dying civilizations God's covenant people have been the remnant to witness his love to the nations. Goldman and Kaufmann have indicated the importance of Orthodox Jewish and Christian

---

[131] Wilson, *Man Is Not Enough*, see Chapter 27, 471-485 as developed from naturalistic reasoning traced in 435-570.

[132] Melanie Phillips, *The World Turned Upside Down: The Global Battle Over God, Truth, and Power*, (New York: Encounter Books, 2010), 360-363.

believers increasing the population as a religious witness in the world's collapsing culture. Jesus said a major event before he returns is for the Great Commission to be the fulfillment of making disciples in all nations (Matthew 24:14; cf. 2 Peter 3:1-9). The true churches that trust in Christ's love are called to be witnesses in these dark times. If the churches are to be a light in the coming anarchy and darkness, the power of New Covenant love in marriage is the most fundamental element. Christ said, "My kingdom is not of this world" (John 18:36-38; 19:9-11). Therefore, as his disciples, we do not increase our number of disciples to compete for worldly political power; but rather, we increase disciples in order to call men and women to trust Christ's love. The increase of children is therefore to increase Christ's children for heavenly citizenship. Our rewards will be at the *day of the Lord* after the resurrection and Christ's second coming.

Moreover, these Christians of the end time require a way of maintaining their distinction without being separatists, and requiring women who are highly educated to be partners to help train our children. The change of the church method to use the power of New Covenant love in marriage and the family will require a whole other book to define and explain.

Conclusion

For now Covenant love is the important light in the darkness of what appears to be the world's last night of Great Tribulation. Christian men and women are now citizens of heaven called to be foreign ambassadors to show Christ's love to sinners. Christians are to call sinners to be part of Christ's kingdom now, and participate in his eternal kingdom when he returns in power and glory soon. In a world of individualistic competition, we invite sinners to voluntarily submit to obey our sovereign, loving, glorified Christ. This requires true faith in Christ who showed us his love, and became the author and finisher of our faith. God's Covenant suffering love to unite in marriage union is an amazing power to change. Paul's offer of salvation by faith is still the light for our world as it was in that of Rome. God is call his people

"Hear and give ear; be not proud, for the Lord has spoken. Give glory to the Lord your God before he brings darkness" (Jeremiah 13:15, 16).

Only those who trust the sovereign power and love of God in Christ's death and resurrection can be apostles who go into and love the evil world. Only men and women who die to self with Christ to love as he loved can unite their different images of God in marriage union. In doing so, they can show God's love by their marriage, to their children, and to their surrounding community. As never before, we must lose our life here to find it again in the resurrection and a new heaven and earth. Christ's powerful love that is beyond understanding can by his Holy Spirit in us "do exceedingly abundantly beyond all we ask or think" (Ephesians 3: 17-20).

Chapter 13
From Rejected Wife to Eternal Bride

Introduction: Story of God's Goodness in Justice and Love

The story of the Bible is about God as the center of the picture of his creation, which was completed by man, male and female. It is about their union in marriage to show the glory of God's goodness where he was to reign through them. God is the infinite, eternal, Trinitarian Spirit in his being, wisdom, power, unique perfection and holiness, goodness, and truth. The heavens and the earth are made by him, and the earth and all in it was prepared for man to see the Creator in all things he made. Man completed the picture by reflecting the image of the invisible God's goodness and wisdom and to visibly reflect these qualities to God's heavenly creatures and to all things in the earth.

The story of this beginning that climaxed in the union of male and female had a direct meaning for the union of God with man and his whole created order. This chapter is written to give the story of the *escatos* or the meaningful end of God's great wisdom and that of marriage. The purpose of God in creation and man's marriage to rule goes far beyond what man can see and know, to God's revelation of himself to the unseen creation in the heavens.

God himself is the higher heavenly context in which man and woman were made to reveal him below. Chapter 1 of this book discussed how in the beginning, in just six days, God spoke into being the entire awesome world and its creatures that reveal his eternal power and deity. And then in his greater deliberative wisdom, God made man as his son to rule over all in the earth. That act of God required not just the male, but the female to unite as mankind in joyful pleasure the manifestation of his Fatherhood. But the whole was not complete to reveal God himself in his goodness until Adam's bride was created from his very essence, but with a complementary difference in image. The climax of creation was when male and female were joined in the awesome wedding as king and queen in the midst of the Garden. Both male and female and their union to multiply were required to fulfill God's wise purpose to show his glory.

God's purposes of the union of male and female and his union with them on earth involved a detour to reveal that goodness, and is discussed in this chapter on the *tellos* or completion in the eschatological ending. The first adulterous relationship that caused divorce was because man (male and female) responded to the devil, and chose to love the created tree of knowledge over the Creator. Man's divorce by worship of the creation has been turned to reveal the goodness of God to man and all creation in heaven and on earth, far beyond our imagination.

The breaking of the union of God and man came because the male and female were deceived into thinking their idea of good surpassed that of God. Thinking they could be wise as God and know good and evil, man in pride rejected the created good and chose the evil world, which was beautiful to his eyes and pleasing to his flesh (Genesis 3). By choosing to have the knowledge to claim creation as his own as an individual, god or goddess, man was divorced from God's presence. That was the beginning of the worship of Baal or mammon. Chapter 10 of this booked showed that mankind's choice of Baal/mammon — which God allowed to be repeated over and over in civilization after civilization — cost the loss of the brilliant cultures, which only God in his grace enabled man to build. The demonic idolatry led to the adultery of male and female requiring God to put man and his civilizations away time and again. Man's wisdom was folly in his individualistic, adulterous worship of the world. This folly made man aware of differences, bringing offense and shame, and ultimately destroyed the union between male and female.

In the previous chapter of this book, the facts revealed that the United States and the Western world, now as never before, are leading *the whole world to prostitution with materialistic Babylon*. This seems to indicate the coming ending of all man-made civilization and man's sin. That story of the nations shows the inability of any man or men in civilization to reveal God's goodness. This evil of all men revealed the justice of God in his righteousness of what is good. But also it has also been shown that God has revealed the power of New Covenant love in Christ, the goodness of God in a new way in which he forgives and accepts man, male and female, when man changes his mind or repents from thinking he is wise as God and turns to trust in his Son's great love. After man repeatedly acted in adulterous folly toward God, which led to adulterous relationships destroying marriage, God revealed justice on the cross, and then love to unite exceeding all imagination of man. In God's wisdom, the failure of all nations revealed the folly and sin of all men. "For God has consigned all to disobedience, that he may have mercy on all" (cf. Romans 11:11-36, esp. 32). This chapter of this book is to show the hope of New Covenant love, and how that love in marriage of man and wife is now important for showing God's love in these evil end times.

Terrible Effect of Idolatry of Church as Adultery Against God

The terrible social consequence for women, men, and children is not the major tragedy of broken human sexual marriage. The change of God's plan of union of man and woman to reflect his image to all creation is *the major loss in adultery with idols that dishonors God.* The relationship of God and his people is integrally related to the marriage of man and women in uniting his image, and therefore the importance of union through New Covenant love is powerfully joined to God's plan and redemption.

The beginning of the darkness and night of sin began when Adam's bride Eve listened and followed demonic wisdom rather than God's word through Adam. This led them both to foolishly eat the fruit of the knowledge of good and evil. This act of adultery, resulting in divorce from God, began the spiritual darkness of Adam and Eve and their children. This disobedience in Eden was the initiating wave of culture that broke in evil.

Both male and female then focused on their differences, threatening their authority as gods and goddesses, calling God's good in creation, evil. As shown, the change of offensive sexual roles toward being competitively equal in wealth drives men and women apart and separates humans in marriage, reflecting the separation of God from his people in sin.

This shame from their differences in the flesh indicated symbolically that as selfish individuals, man and woman would be offended at any other created difference of abilities of race or class. The drive of man's sin nature was to remove the basic sexual difference particularly, but also any and all differences of abilities God created that allowed some persons to excel over others. God created some men to be rich and others to be poor (Proverbs 22:2), all to be stewards, some with ten talents to invest, other five, and others only one (Luke 19:11-27). Any difference threatens man and woman as individualistic god and goddess. The love for the world is enmity against God, and endorses the anti-Christ principle that was evident of the first child, Cain. Cain's murder of Abel who humbly offered a lamb as his sin offering was the first antichrist act.

Throughout the history of God's people of Israel, in turning from God to worship creation, they esteemed nature as the god who provided wealth. The idols that pervert are Baal, nature as "provider" of wealth, and Ashtoreth, the goddess meaning "to be rich." The worship of gods and goddesses was not to be produced in images. Such worship for material prosperity was the **worship of the devil** as the god of this world (Deuteronomy 32:17; Psalm 106:37; 1 Corinthians 10:20; Exodus 20:4, 5, 23; Romans 1:23, et al.). Such images were made and then stories were told and repeated about the power and the prosperity these gods or goddesses gave. Some of goddesses such as Seti also hated and destroyed men.

It was previously pointed out that Jesus used the Aramaic name, mammon (or wealth) for these adulterous partners. He warned that the love of money is enmity against God, and will lead to love of the world, and the rejection and hatred of God (Matthew 6:19-34). God's people were illustrated as his bride or wife. Mankind's perversions of roles for self-esteem, wealth, and sexual pleasure that destroy man's marriage were symbolically related in Scripture with adultery against God.

In all of Scripture, from Genesis to Revelation, there is an intertwining involvement with the idea against worshiping wealth attributed to nature as pagan gods and goddesses, and the intermarriage of God's people with the women of pagan cultures, which was idolatrous and strongly prohibited. Abraham and Sarah wanted Isaac to marry a girl from their own family rather than from the Canaanite daughters and because of this, they sent to Haran to bring Rebecca as a bride for their son (Genesis 24:4 ff.). Rebecca and Isaac again sent Jacob to his family to find a bride (Genesis 28:2 ff.). After the conquest of the land, the children of Israel were forbidden to intermarry with the women of the land lest they turn and worship their gods of Baal, Ashtoreth, or Asherah. When the children of Israel retuned from Babylonian captivity, the major crisis that painfully had to be dealt with was the intermarriage with those of other people who worshiped gods and goddesses (Ezra 9, 10).

When the nation of Israel turned to these pagan gods and goddesses, the prophets identified the *people as God's wife who had played the harlot* (Jeremiah 3:20; Hosea 3:1 et al.). The tragic story is of God's heart being broken when his wife whom he had saved, raised, married, and bestowed with wealth committed harlotry using the beauty which he had enabled her to attain (Ezekiel 16). The prophet Hosea was asked to marry a harlot to portray the terrible unfaithfulness of God's people to him and how God still loved Israel as his wife. The nations of Israel and Judah were judged and destroyed because of forsaking the covenant of marriage. Jerusalem, or Zion, as the capital represented the nation of God's people. All nations and Judah, and the capital of Jerusalem, were judged for their adultery.

But God had a greater plan for his church to remove her shame and know his love. Isaiah said,

> Your Maker is your husband, the LORD of hosts is his name; and the Holy One of Israel is your Redeemer, the God of the whole earth he is called. For the LORD has called you like a wife deserted and grieved in spirit, like a wife of youth when she is cast off, says your God. "For a brief moment I deserted you, but with great compassion I will

gather you. In overflowing anger for a moment, I hid my face from you, but with everlasting love I will have compassion on you," says the LORD, your Redeemer. "This is like the days of Noah to me: as I swore that the waters of Noah should no more go over the earth, so I have sworn that I will not be angry with you, and will not rebuke you. For the mountains may depart and the hills be removed, but my steadfast love shall not depart from you, and my covenant of peace shall not be removed," says the LORD, who has compassion on you (Isaiah 54:5-10).

These sentiments of God's covenant love are repeated by Isaiah and by other prophets.

The New Covenant Church is Christ's Beloved Bride

Christ's disciples were seen as his bride. The New Covenant Church is called to be the bride of Christ to show his suffering love to the world. From the beginning of Jesus' ministry his followers that began to make up the church were identified as his bride. John the Baptist called for repentance to trust the Messiah, and he saw himself as best man to wed the new followers to Jesus as the groom for the wedding (John 3:27-30). Jesus taught that he was the bridegroom celebrating his wedding of joining his bride, and therefore it was not a time to fast (Matthew 9:15; Mark 2:19, 20). Jesus took his followers to the wedding in Cana. There he did his first miracle and disclosed he was the bridegroom who traditionally provided the wine for the wedding. By that miracle they *first believed on and were joined to him* as his disciples (John 2:11).

The statements of Paul about Christ as the head of the church as his wife was shown in Chapter 3 of this book to be the example for the husband in leading his wife. By sacrificial suffering love the husband should follow the example of Christ, giving himself for his bride, the church. This is tied to the example of Adam giving from his side for the creation of Eve so that they would be of one essence. "The two shall become one flesh" is like the church being "members of his (Christ's) body" (cf. Ephesians 5:29-33). Thus the history of male and female from the beginning is linked to God's ultimate plan for his people whom he loves.

Christ's Glorious Union with His Bride after His Coming

At the end of history (the *escatos*) God will have reached the perfection (the *telos*) of his plan for man, both male and female. By understanding his great love, the members of his body will be filled with all the fullness of God. And by the power of his Holy Spirit in those who believe Christ, God will do mighty things through his bride, the church, "for his glory throughout all generations forever and ever" (Ephesians 3:16-21). The picture of this is so large, meaningful, and amazing that all about the final *"escatos"* would take many books to describe.[133] Only the aspects of the end times that relate to understanding marriage and its relationship to God can be briefly referred to here.

Adulterous Mammon Worship of Nations Will End

When mankind turned away from God's grace to follow the demonic pattern of sin at the Tower of
, God divided the nations that successively have repeated building a prosperous civilization to then follow sin to judgment, revealing the wisdom and greatness of God's justice and love (Genesis 11:1-9; Acts 17:26-28). God had demonstrated his worldwide power to judge after the perversion of Cain's followers in their greed and sexual desires in hate (Genesis 4:17-24). Then, all men had turned to the indiscriminate worship of heroes or supermen, and fulfilled their evil thoughts in perversion of sex (Genesis 6). God sent the judgment of the flood of Noah. He then began again with the believers in the family of Noah. Then Babylon continued as the example of spiritual adultery.

Babel became the symbol of people worshiping Creation instead of the Creator. It is the symbolic product of male dominance where Nimrod as king exerted himself as God, and people united in urban cities for a rich culture, and claimed to be the "gate of God" in their own name. But Babylon the Great is the symbol of man's worship of the world, the mother of all prostitutes, leading to forsaking God and therefore being antichrist.

---

[133] I have an unpublished book of over 400 pages, *A Quest to Understand the End of History.*

Nebuchadnezzar called this city he rebuilt Babylon the Great. The kings of other cities claimed powers like God as the devil, and their cities were identified by the prophets as being *prostitutes:* cf. Tyre (Isaiah 23:15-17), Nineveh (Nahum 3:4), and Jerusalem (Isaiah 1:21; Jeremiah 2:20). Rome may be another city symbolized as a prostitute, but certainly not the only one.

Before Christ returns for his people as his bride, he will end the prostitution for mammon worship symbolized by Babylon. She rides on the beast, the demonic world dictatorial power, and she is loved by all the people of the world. She is the center of affection for wealth of luxuries, and pleasures that motivate sexual perversion of marriage. She is the mother of adulterous spiritual prostitution, and the source of blasphemies against God. Since she is the source of world evils, she must first be destroyed to end demonic prostitution before the marriage of the Lamb and his bride (Revelation 14:8; 17:3-18). John had the revelation of the destruction of Babylon.

> After this I heard what seemed to be the loud voice of a great multitude in heaven, crying out, "Hallelujah! Salvation and glory and power belong to our God, for his judgments are true and just for he has *judged the great prostitute* **who corrupted the earth with her immorality**, and has avenged on her the blood of his servants."

> Once more they cried out, "Hallelujah! The smoke from her goes up forever and ever." And the twenty-four elders and the four living creatures fell down and worshiped God who was seated on the throne, saying, "Amen. Hallelujah!" And from the throne came a voice saying, "Praise our God, all you his servants, you who fear him, small and great." Then I heard what seemed to be the voice of a great multitude, like the roar of many waters and like the sound of mighty peals of thunder, crying out, "Hallelujah! For the Lord our God the Almighty reigns. Let us rejoice and exult and give him the glory, for *the marriage of the Lamb has come*, and *his Bride* has made herself ready; it was granted her to clothe herself with fine linen, bright and pure" — for the fine linen is the righteous deeds of the saints.

> And the angel said to me, "Write this: Blessed are those who are invited to *the marriage supper of the Lamb*." And he said to me, "These are the true words of God" (Revelation 19:1-9).

Union by Suffering Love Invites to Lamb's Marriage Supper

In this hour of the end times of judgment of the world prostitute, the angel or messenger of heaven offers the blessing of God to all "who *are invited to the marriage supper* of the Lamb." The witness of the church is still vitally needed, especially as modeled in marriage. The world is divided by those who are elect believers in the kingdom of Christ, and those who are blinded by the devil in their worship of mammon and love of the world. Jesus warned that the great division is love for God or the carnal mind who loves mammon (Matthew 6:22-24; Corinthians 4:3-12).

The blindness of worshiping mammon or creation is bringing darkness, and perhaps the world's last night may be approaching before the wonderful day of the Lord. Jesus warned that in our witness in the last days, the hate of the elect would be great and some would be put to death (Matthew 24:9-12). John was told, "I saw the woman, drunk with the blood of the saints, the blood of the martyrs and witnesses of Jesus" (Revelation 17:6; cf. 18:24). The saints as his bride will have victory while Babylon will be destroyed (Revelation 19:1-8). In the last night of darkness by the blindness of the devil, it has been shown that marriage will be disdained, and the sexual differences are diminished in that male and female may be equal as individual gods or goddesses to possess the wealth of Babylon. In such a world, the individual selfishness will destroy social union. In this darkness, the union of man and wife in the power of Covenant love may be the brightest light to reveal the cross.

Even though disciples, both men and women, in his kingdom are now sons of God to reign with him, Jesus had taught the importance of suffering love now for union in marriage to his disciples (Matthew 19:4-9). Paul and Peter both taught that while Christians are sons of God now, as they are heirs to receive their inheritance in the resurrection, they are still suffering servants in the world until Christ comes.

> For in Christ Jesus you are all sons of God, through faith. For as many of you as were baptized into Christ have put on Christ. There is neither Jew nor Greek, there is neither slave nor free, *there is neither*

male nor female, for you are all one in Christ Jesus. And if you are Christ's, then you are Abraham's offspring, *heirs* according to promise (Galatians 3:26-29).

Paul is talking of our future state to which we are now heirs. He continues to illustrate this by saying we are free from the law, and by Christ's redemption we have received the Holy Spirit and adoption as sons who recognize God as Father. "So you are no longer a slave, but a son, and if a son, then *an heir* through God" (Gen 4:1-7, verse 7). An heir now continues in submission under the Father's instructions as an obedient son with a hope for the future. Peter exhorts husbands to have understanding, and show honor to their wives as the weaker vessel, "since they are *heirs* with you of the grace of life" (1 Peter 3:7).

Until the resurrection at the day of the Lord, submission and suffering love is needed to show God's love by man and wife, by children and parents, and by servants and masters (Ephesians 5:18-6:9; Colossians 3:18-25). This is based on the submissive love of Christ which enables us to show trust in God's sovereign love to work in us, and to reward us for the life we have given for him here (Philippians 2:5-13).

Suffering Love Still the Needed Witness to Selfish World

In John's revelation a voice from heaven described to John the Christian brothers accused by the devil,

And they have *conquered him by the blood of the Lamb and by the word of their testimony,* for they loved not their lives even unto death. Therefore, rejoice, O heavens and you who dwell in them! But woe to you, O earth and sea, for the devil has come down to you in great wrath, because he knows that his time is short! (Revelation 12:11, 12).

In his earthly ministry, Jesus had said, "And this Gospel of the kingdom will be proclaimed throughout the whole world as *a testimony* to the nations, and then the end will come" (Matthew 24:14). After his resurrection, Jesus had commissioned his followers, "Go therefore and make disciples to all nations,

...teaching them to observe all things that I [as king] command you, and behold I am with you always, to the end of the age" (Matthew 28:19, 20).

The meaning of victory by their witness and the blood is in the words of the voice to John, "They loved not their lives even unto death." Jesus had made it clear, "*If anyone* will come after me, let him deny himself and take up his cross daily and follow me. For whoever would save his life will lose it, but whoever loses his life for my sake, will save it" (Luke 9:23, 24; cf. Matthew 16:24, 25).

Paul explains this acceptance of our death with Christ as the way of victorious transformation to witness.

> For the love of Christ controls us, because we have concluded this: that one has died for all, therefore all have died; and he died for all, that those who live might *no longer live for themselves but for him who for their sake died and was raised.*

> From now on, therefore, we regard no one according to the flesh. Even though we once regarded Christ according to the flesh, we regard him thus no longer. Therefore, if anyone is in Christ, he is a new creation. The old has passed away; behold, the new has come. All this is from God, who through Christ reconciled us to himself and gave us the ministry of reconciliation; that is, in Christ God was reconciling the world to himself, not counting their trespasses against them, and entrusting to us the message of reconciliation.

> *Therefore, we are ambassadors for Christ*, God making his appeal through us. We implore you on behalf of Christ, be reconciled to God. For our sake he made him to be sin who knew no sin, so that in him we might become the righteousness of God. Working together with him, then, we appeal to you not to receive the grace of God in vain (2 Corinthians 5:14-6:1).

In the Old Testament, a man put his hands on the lamb of the sin offering and confessed his sins before it was slain. The lamb symbolically was he himself dying for his sins. So Paul says Jesus was the sin offering for the entire world and "that those who live might no longer live for themselves but for him who for their sake died and was raised" (cf. Romans 7:14- 8:6).

This transformation by repentance for our sin from Adam and Eve gives the believer the power to be free from the devil that has existed for man, and drives him by the world's appeal symbolized and reigning in Babylon. It is the undoing of the bondage of Genesis 3 whereby we are freed from demonic power to be seated as citizens of heaven with Christ (Eph. 1:18- 2:10).

The eating of the created fruit, and the worship of the created, or mammon, produced men and women who saw themselves as gods. That resulted in seeing the difference in the other sex (their nakedness) as a threat to their own sovereignty. But the flaming sword that closed the gate to God's presence was experienced for us by Christ's death for sin, freeing us from the fear of death and the devil's power, and granting us access to the throne of God again. Repentance and heart confession of faith in Christ is what saves (Romans 10:9-11; Acts 20; 21).

Saying that the saints overcame the devil "by the word of their testimony because *they loved not their lives even unto death*" does not mean they all were put to death by the world. It means they have given up their lives to be in Christ, and now are unashamed to witness and invite men from the kingdom of the world to be disciples of the kingdom of Christ. The victory of the saints by the blood of Christ, and witness to God's love and power will certainly lead to persecution by the selfish individuals under the deception of the devil. But it may also lead to the actual physical death for Christ by some (Matthew 24:9-14). It always means death with Christ to this world, and to the beast of Satan's power that controls the world through Babylon. The disciple's love for God and for each other is a rebuke to the self-righteous and sinful. That is why the Gospel of the cross and resurrection is an invitation to be saved.

The third millennium postmodern world has changed the roles of sex to deny showing love by union in marriage. Instead, it makes it convenient to be free to gain wealth of mammon, and to seek individualistic lust in sex. The 2010 census revealed the majority of men and women are living out of wedlock, and children are being avoided, aborted, and brought into the world without seeing the love of Christ in the union of marriage. America is leading the world in this prostitution and the entire world is now moving toward an end by women who restrict the fertility rate for mammon. David P. Goldman has seen this as the coming death to world civilization as prostitution of Babylon in his book, *How Civilizations Die*. Eric Kaufmann has, on the other hand, asked the question through his book, *Shall the Religious Inherit the Earth?* He sees women and men who in faith have and nurture children as pointing the only way to salvation of the race. But the destruction of civilization can only be saved by God's love seen in Christian union by that suffering love. The Covenant love in marriage is the most powerful witness in these end times.

Christian Marriage is Based on Faith, Hope, and Love

Christian union in marriage showing we are now heirs as sons of God has to do with our faith, hope, and love for our happiness, and for the glory of God. In serving Christ **our faith is fixed** on Jesus Christ who is the author and finisher of our faith, who has endured the cross to pay the price for our redemption, and now as king-priest is set down at the right hand of God. While we are already children of God and raised with Christ, "we are his workmanship created in Christ Jesus for the good works which God prepared beforehand that we should walk in them" (Ephesians 2:5-10). Previously, we discussed the good work of marriage (Ephesians 5:18 ff.). Our calling as his bride is to complete the work of witnessing to make disciples until the end of this age. Then Christ will come for our wedding to him and we will see him in all his glory.

The hope of all men and women who are the bride of Christ is hope for the unseen, unshakable eternal kingdom of God. When a Hebrew married the bridegroom, he would come and take his bride to the home he had prepared for her. The hope in the old and new covenants of Abraham, and all who died in faith, was a heavenly city of Jerusalem whose builder and maker is God (Hebrews 11:10, 13-16, 39; 12:22-28). Jesus said, "I go to the Father to prepare a place for you with many mansions," and he promised he will come

243

again to receive us (John 14:1-3). Much is said about this in all of Scripture.

Love in Sexual Union Will Be Superseded by God's Love

When God's *escatos* of the marriage supper of the Lamb with his bride the church is accomplished, there will be no longer a need for our suffering love to witness to a sinful world. Our prayer now is to *know the love of Christ that passes knowledge* that we may be filled with all the fullness of God (Ephesians 3:19). The more perfect and exhilarating love of God will be reached. Paul said the members of the body of Christ share in union of ministry with each other to grow toward the more perfect love. He said,

> [Leaders are] to equip the saints for the work of ministry, for building up the body of Christ, until we all attain to the unity of the faith and of the knowledge of the Son of God, to mature manhood, to the measure of the stature of the fullness of Christ, so that we may no longer be children, tossed to and fro by the waves and carried about by every wind of doctrine, by human cunning, by craftiness in deceitful schemes. Rather, speaking the truth in love, we are to grow up in every way into him who is the head, into Christ, from whom the whole body, joined and held together by every joint with which it is equipped, when each part is working properly, makes the body grow so that it builds itself up in love (Ephesians 4:12-16).

> For we know in part and we prophesy in part, but when the perfect comes, the partial will pass away. When I was a child, I spoke like a child, I thought like a child, I reasoned like a child. When I became a man, I gave up childish ways. For now we see in a mirror dimly, but then face to face. *Now I know in part; then I shall know fully, even as I have been fully known.*

> So now faith, hope, and love abide, these three; but the greatest of these is love (1 Corinthians 13:9-13).

> Love bears all things, believes all things, hopes all things, endures all things. Love never ends (1 Corinthians 13:7-8).

Adam *knew* his wife Eve and she had a son. We *know* God's love in Christ now, and we are called to show that love *by knowing* each other in suffering love for union with one another and for the world. But that Covenant love that unites man and wife in marriage will end. At the *escatos* of the union of Christ and his bride, our male and female bodies will be raised into a spiritual body and no longer be fleshly. The devil and all evil men and angels will be forever separated. Nothing evil will affect our relationships or tarnish our heavenly city. We will all have and glory in our sexual differences and in our specific God-given identities and abilities as heirs in Christ. But these will be of no offense, and we will be equal as sons having received our inheritance.

Jesus made it clear that Scriptures teach after the resurrection God's power will change the marriage union. "For in the resurrection they neither marry nor are given in marriage, but are like the angels in heaven" (Matthew 22:30). God's perfect love will be realized in us. As Jesus always knew the Father's perfect love, and did not need marriage to show God's image, so we will be sons of God experiencing that love. Jesus' prayer will be fulfilled. He had prayed:

> The glory that you have given me I have given to them, that they may be one even as we are one, I in them and you in me, that they may become perfectly one, so that the world may know that you sent me and loved them even as you loved me. Father, I desire that they also, whom you have given me, may be with me where I am, to see my glory that you have given me because you loved me before the foundation of the world. O righteous Father, even though the world does not know you, I know you, and these know that you have sent me. I made known to them your name, and I will continue to make it known, that *the love with which you have loved me may be in them, and I in them*" (John 17:22-26).

What a wonderful marriage this will be, in which there will exist no more loneliness, no more suffering, pain or tears. Our fullness will reign with Christ in his kingdom when we rule over the world and over angels with him (1 Corinthians 6:2, 3).

False religions like Islam and Mormonism look for marriages for sexual pleasure in heaven, and they know not the perfect love of God in Christ.

God's Justice and Love are Disclosed in the Two Destinies

The end of mammon worship that produced hatred of God and sin of sexual abuse that causes evil harm in the entire world will be removed by judgment and will reveal God's justice. After the judgment and end of Babylon, the mother of prostitutes, John spoke of the coming marriage of the Lamb. He reported this future return of Christ in glory to conquer all evil and judge the world. And then the salvation will be accomplished (Revelation 19:10-20), completing the wonderful marriage between God and his people in the eternal city in a new heaven and new earth. The final words about this end the Scriptures.

> Then I saw a new heaven and a new earth, for the first heaven and the first earth had passed away, and the sea was no more. And I saw the holy city, new Jerusalem, coming down out of heaven from God, prepared *as a bride adorned for her husband*. And I heard a loud voice from the throne saying, *"Behold, the dwelling place of God is with man. He will dwell with them, and they will be his people, and God himself will be with them as their God.* He will wipe away every tear from their eyes, and death shall be no more, neither shall there be mourning, nor crying, nor pain anymore, for the former things have passed away."

> And he who was seated on the throne said, "Behold, I am making all things new." Also he said, "Write this down, for these words are trustworthy and true." And he said to me, "It is done! I am the Alpha and the Omega, the beginning and the end. To the thirsty I will give from the spring of the water of life without payment. The one who conquers will have this heritage, and I will be his God and he will be my son. (Revelation 21:1-7).

> Then came one of the seven angels who had the seven bowls full of the seven last plagues and spoke to me, saying, "Come, I will show you *the Bride, the wife of the Lamb."* And he carried me away in the Spirit to a great, high mountain, and showed me the holy city Jerusalem coming down out of heaven from God (Revelation 21:9-10).

The vision of our heavenly Jerusalem is presented in terms of all the wealth the world now wants of white gold, precious jewels, pearls greater than any known, and the river of life with every imaginable fruit to satisfy. The very presence of God himself is the light with no night, and wall that eternally protects from every evil. These things of present earthly wealth are given to show how our eternal home will supersede all that the devil promises to individual selfish men and women. Every man and woman will, by God's grace, have power to rule over even angels, and perhaps the cherubim that kept men from entering to know God. This eternal city will be ours by grace alone, and eternally so for God's children.

Isaiah foresaw the New Jerusalem born without pain in a moment by God's power and grace (Isaiah 66:7-14). He said,

> For as the new heavens and the new earth that I make shall remain before me, says the LORD, so shall your offspring and your name remain. From new moon to new moon, and from Sabbath to Sabbath, all flesh shall come to worship before me, declares the LORD. And they shall go out and look on the dead bodies of the men who have rebelled against me. For their worm shall not die, their fire shall not be quenched, and they shall be an abhorrence to all flesh (Isaiah 66:22-24).

Those in the blessings of the New Jerusalem are those who had humble and contrite hearts and responded to God's invitation of mercy (Isaiah 66:1, 2). Those that are visible in the sufferings of hell are those who in pride rejected God for self satisfaction.

> These have chosen their own ways, and their soul delights in their abominations; I also will choose harsh treatment for them and bring their fears upon them, because when I called, no one answered, when I spoke, they did not listen; but they did what was evil in my eyes and chose that in which I did not delight" (Isaiah 66:4).

The devil and men who follow him in their final judgment in hell will be an eternal witness to God's righteousness and justice. We are living which appears to be the last night. Our rejection of God's purpose of union in marriage to show his goodness is evident as individualism is destroying the fertility rate and children throughout the world, and greed is bankrupting the world's nations. Therefore there is blasphemy against God and his Christ, and pain and death. The terrible pain of the entire world seems near, and God will soon have to end it.

Toward the end of every civilization, when God has been rejected for selfish individualism, men have believed in the value and worth of man, and reject justice and the idea of suffering pain. After Socrates warned the Greeks of their worldly preoccupation, Plato said he would like to delete all references to future pain from Homer. When Rome had rejected Jupiter as the one God, the Republic was in confusion, and Marcus Tullius Cicero said not even old women believed in future suffering for wrongs. Our postmodern world has become like all previous civilizations who believe man is so wise, good, and valuable that no pain will or should come to him. But we may be in the twilight of the Great Tribulation.

The Economist magazine is one of the most widely read publications and a leading voice in world ideas. They repeatedly warn of the devastation of world debt from greed of all the people that continue to demand that the government supply what they want. As the United States and the West are facing going over the fiscal cliff, *The Economist* published an article on the teaching of hell, and refer to ancients like Plato, Cicero, and Seneca. They said, "For hundreds of years, Hell has been the most fearful place in the human imagination. It is also the most absurd. ...to man in the West, Hell is just a medieval relic. It went out with ducking stools and witchcraft. It should have disappeared...".[134]

While the article deliberately misrepresents the biblical idea, it is really a very trivial article. It misses the whole point. It avoids *the question of what standard of justice can be applied* to a world where men and women as gods and goddesses inflict such pain by their selfishness. The real issue is that each man or woman foolishly sees self as all important, and *ignores the great worth and wisdom of the infinite eternal God and Creator.* Man's

---

[134] *The Economist*, "Hell: Into everlasting fire," December 22, 2012, 25-28.

esteem of God is always reflected in how he treats other men in need who are made in the image of God and are his representatives (Matthew 25:41-43).

But Hell is precisely a place for those little men and women, each who see themselves as wise as God and blaspheme him, and in pride and greed destroy others. In a world economy with world communication and transportation, there are those who reject God and are planning an antichrist world government, but they can't maintain families or control themselves. The evils of Columbine, or Newtown, or the hundreds of shootings in Chicago or the other millions of painful situations are answered by man's wisdom with ideas such as gun control, better psychological treatment, or government acts. The problem is never the guilt of man and his evil, especially the anger between man and wife in the home, and the answer for them is not to go back to God and his love.

The prophet Isaiah reminds his sinful nation that is about to be judged,

> All flesh is like grass and the flower of the field that withers and fades, but the word of our God will stand forever. ... The nations are like a drop from a bucket and are accounted as dust on the scales. ... They are accounted as nothing before him ... as less than nothing and emptiness. ...The earth's inhabitants are like grasshoppers. ... [God] brings princes and rulers to nothing and makes the rulers of the earth as emptiness. ... Scarcely has their stem taken root in the earth, when he blows on them, and they wither, and the tempest carries them off like stubble (Isaiah 40:7-8, 15, 17, 22-24).

Isaiah then writes, "'To who then will you compare me that I should be like him [man]?' says the Holy One of Israel. 'Lift up your eyes on high and see who created these.'" (40:25, 26). God has allowed man to repeatedly build a prosperous civilization in all the nations, and then destroy it in order that his *justice may be eternally revealed* in heaven and earth in painful punishment in hell.

But also in his awesome, infinite wisdom, "God has consigned all to disobedience, that he may have mercy on all" (Romans 11:32). By God's wisdom the bride of Christ, the church, has *revealed his love* to the all nations and to those in the greater heavens above. Paul said he led the saints in this mission of mercy.

> This grace was given, to preach to the Gentiles and nations the unsearchable riches of Christ, and to bring to light for everyone what is the plan of the mystery hidden for ages in God who created all things, so that *through the church the manifold wisdom of God might now be made known* to the rulers and authorities in the heavenly places. This was according to the eternal purpose that he has realized in Christ Jesus our Lord (Ephesians 3:8-11).

Conclusion

In the final heaven and earth, God will unite his church family who will rule with his Son, Jesus Christ. The purpose of creating male and female to witness to his image of justice and love and have dominion in the earth has reached its purpose and is over. Now male and female as individuals who experience his perfect love will rule with Christ over the nations of the earth, and over the angels of heaven (2 Corinthians 6:2). Christ, as the seed of the woman, the descendent of Abraham to bless the world, and the son of David born from Mary, is victorious in risen glory to rule as the second Adam, male and female, as God planned in Genesis 1:28.

> Then comes the end, when he delivers the kingdom to God the Father after destroying every rule and every authority and power. For he must reign until he has put all his enemies under his feet. The last enemy to be destroyed is death. For "God has put all things in subjection under his feet." But when it says, "all things are put in subjection," it is plain that he is excepted who put all things in subjection under him. When all things are subjected to him, then the Son himself will also be subjected to him who put all things in subjection under him, that God may be all in all (1 Corinthians 15:24-28).

Chapter 14
Epilogue: Practical Ways to Experience
The Power of Covenant Love in Marriage

Suggestions for Practical Progress

The experience of the power of covenant love comes from experiencing God's love for you and in you toward your neighbor, the nearest being your spouse in marriage. Each of us must humble ourselves unto death as did Christ, and receive new resurrection power from God by his Spirit. Stop grumbling and complaining, and yield to God's power so that he can work out your salvation from the evil world by "working in you, both to will and to do *His* good pleasure" (Philippians 2:5-13). Christ's will for you has power, it is extremely good, and is filled with the most pleasure. This is accomplished by walking in faith in his grace, and not by trying to work to gain approval.

Your faith must be a practical faith! The word *practical* involves *practice*. As mentioned before, one must go beyond head knowledge (expressed in the Greek by *oida*) to experience by trust in that knowledge (expressed by the Greek, *ginosko*). *Belief about* Christ does not save from the demonic forces that defeat and keep us from love. In that sense, as James says, "Even the devils believe and shudder" (James 2:19). Actual *trust in* Christ releases us and gives us freedom from the power of our sin nature and our sinning (cf. John 8, verses 32, 36). Jesus here emphasizes practice — "if you *abide in* my word, you are truly my disciples, and you will know (experience) the truth and the truth will *set you free.*" Trusting in his covenant love is the simple and practical issue. This chapter gives some helpful suggestions to grow and know the love of Christ that passes knowledge (Ephesians 3:19, 20).

Each Person Needs Daily Time Alone with God in the Bible

Each of the two individuals, husband and wife, must grow in this love to merge as one. The first practical step to love your spouse is to have a private time with God daily to know his love for you. The book of Psalms recording the devotional experiences of King David and others began by what we now label as Psalm 1. In the Hebrew Bible this was actually an introduction to all the Psalms and Psalm 2 was the first. Psalm 1 tells us how to act in a life of obedience and the results.

> Blessed is the man who walks not in the counsel of the wicked, nor stands in the way of sinners, nor sits in the seat of scoffers; but his delight is in the law of the LORD, and on his law he meditates day and night. He is like a tree planted by streams of water that yields its fruit in its season, and its leaf does not wither. In all that he does, he prospers. The wicked are not so, but are like chaff that the wind drives away. Therefore the wicked will not stand in the judgment, nor sinners in the congregation of the righteous; for the LORD knows the way of the righteous, but the way of the wicked will perish (Psalms 1:1-6).

Meditating on the Scriptures day and night that reveals Christ to us will, with certainty, produce the fruitful life now. That fruit will endure forever and **whatsoever** we do will prosper (Psalm 1:3; John 15: 15-17). By beginning each day in his word we will abide in him.

As David, Paul, and all who experience God's presence, we must have a definite time or times alone in a certain place to meet with God. Jesus said, "Go into your closet and pray to God alone" (Matthew 6:6-13). Jesus himself would regularly rise a great while before daybreak so that he could go alone to meet with and receive directions and power from God (Mark 1:35 ff.).

Such a time alone with God daily is not an option — it is our life breath. We have died with Christ, and now only by the power of his Spirit can we let his love be expressed through us. Communion with him reminds us that by grace we are constantly forgiven when we fail, but also that we should constantly forgive our spouse and children. We cannot regularly draw upon the heavenly breath of the Holy Spirit without beginning our day with Christ.

When I used to fly in small airplanes we used a gyrocompass that we had to set before we took off to constantly have the proper direction. That is what beginning our day with Christ and his word does for our daily life. While we are exhorted to "pray without ceasing" (1 Thessalonians 5:17), we will not do that unless we have a time alone. Pray for him to meet with you and guide you.

We desperately need this for our daily walk in the Spirit, so that we don't lose our way, or fail to have the armor of God to fight the devil (Ephesians 6:10). The devil will do everything to keep us from looking to and trusting in Christ. Without God's light to guide us, we will light our own torches to find our way in the darkness, and be lost, hurt, and tormented (Isaiah 50:10, 11). Having a time to meet with him gives light for the day, helps us see the traps of the devil before us, and delivers us from the evil one. Moreover, because of our love for God, we should desire to be with him as young lovers want to be together. No one will always faithfully seek him as he should, but Christ is with us at all times. But without faith we will not experience that power.

What do you do to meet with God in this quiet time? You can approach this in many ways, but you always need exposure to the Scriptures that are the inspired word of God to enable us to know wrong and good, and grow toward perfection (2 Timothy 3:16). Personally, I change what I do from time to time. One suggestion is to read a chapter in an Old Testament book and another in the New Testament, and prayerfully think about it. I now read only one chapter a day. If you read three chapters a day you will read through the whole Bible in a year. Sometimes God leads me to learn more about a subject and I read Scripture that I know relates.

Read thought my commentary on a Unique Harmony of the Gospels entitled, *Fulfillment: The Life and Ministry of Jesus the Christ*. If you have a small group, you can discuss the questions for each section with them. This book will help you get a picture of how all the Bible leads to Jesus and his saving work, and will give you a greater appreciation and understanding of how to interpret the whole Bible. Read biographies of great Christian men and women along with the Bible. Pray over the things you learn and ask God to help you apply them to what you are doing. As Christ's love becomes central in your life and that of your spouse, you can begin to share that love with each other for unity.

Secondly, Have a Time Nightly Before God with Your Spouse

It is highly important that the centrality of Christ's love be transferred into the marriage relationship to become one. For most of nearly sixty years, my wife Sara Jo and I have ended our day before we go to sleep in a time together before Christ. We read one passage of Scripture together, have prayer, and kiss good night. I read one night and she prays; she reads the next night and I pray. Sometimes we will discuss something from those Scriptures, but avoid ideas that might be controversial until another later time. If there is something in our relationship that is troubling, or maybe a misunderstanding, we ask for forgiveness of each other and the Lord. Then a kiss is very meaningful. Getting to bed early enough so you aren't too tired is important. Television can be a major enemy to this important time.

This nightly time together should focus on Christ. If you are fatigued at night, find another time. Do not try to preach to each other, or use Scripture to imply guilt. Do not use this time as a way of trying to tie your spouse to yourself, but to individually both worship Christ together.

Dennis and Barbara Rainey of Christian have found this nightly time so meaningful that Dennis has recommended it in conferences and teaching all over the world. They have expanded on the idea in a little book, *Two Hearts Praying as One* which they dedicated to Sara Jo and me.

Sara Jo and I do other things to center our relationship on Christ. For example, on Sunday afternoons she reads for us a Psalm or part of a Psalm (if it is long) out of Charles H. Spurgeon's commentary, the *Treasury of David*. We have also enjoyed reading Randy Alcorn's books on special Bible themes, but we don't read his long fictional books together. We also read the history of the writing of one of the many Christian hymns, she plays it on the piano, and we sing it together. These hymns traditionally sung in the churches come from almost every century of the church's history, and this blesses us to see Christ's working in the life of believers throughout the ages.

There are many other ways to make Christ more central in your marriage, such as prayer of thanks at every meal, and other traditional opportunities to pray together. Thank God for new things such as new cars, new clothes, etc. Pray for God to bless your time together in bed. Sometimes he will make your time exciting; while others he might show you hindrances that need to be dealt to help unite you spiritually.

Participate in a Meaningful Small Group Together

Being in any kind of Christian small group together with other couples is helpful, but some can be much better than others. Until the fourth century, the early Christian churches were mostly small house churches. For a really good small group there should be a mature qualified leader who has a good marriage (1 Timothy 3). The failure of most house church groups is that the leader is not given the responsibility to be the pastor of the group. The leader should have a pastoral interest in the members, and lovingly hold the members accountable. The group should be able to pray together, discuss the Scriptures together, and share things God is doing in their lives. All the members in the group should pray for each other, their marriages, and their families. There should be a sense of accountability to each other. Having one good Christian couple as special friends is also very helpful. More about leaders and small groups can be learned from my books, *With Christ in the School of Disciple Building* or *Biblical Principles for Training Discipleship Leaders.*[135]

Congregational Worship Together

Find a church congregation that promotes small groups and encourages their leaders to equip each person to use his gifts to minister to others. Then each person who attends and participates in the larger congregation will feel he is a vital part of the whole

---

[135] You can view them and order from the web page, bravegoodmen.org.

255

and in a sense he is a vital member of Christ's body (Ephesians 4:4-15). A man and wife and children can greatly profit from worshiping together with the whole church congregation. If the pastor is a good teacher, you and your children can discuss these things learned together.

While congregational worship does not make Christ as relevant to unite a couple as do the above suggestions, congregational worship also has a unique contribution. One of the great values is that you realize the importance of marriage and family for the experiencing of the broader family of God, and through God's people for the broader community. This also offers opportunity to serve with God's people. Attendance together at Christian conferences and retreats offers similar opportunities to unite your thoughts and worship.

Do Thoughtful and Surprising Things for Each Other

Surprises in a marriage always add a spark of interest. Christ's love often surprises us. When either spouse can come up with an idea to surprise the other, it is a good thing. These "surprises" can be at a no or low cost. Perhaps the wife (or husband if he likes to cook) could make a surprise dessert for the two of them that would only be made for special company. Or knowing the husband is tired and dreading coming home to mow the lawn, maybe the wife could do it. Changing roles around as surprises keeps interest in a marriage. Even a simple thing such as stopping and picking up a rose at the store for no reason at all will show such appreciation of the other.

Weekends and Vacations Together

Every couple needs to get away for a weekend alone if possible. The change of environment and away from jobs, house chores, and children helps a couple focus on each other and play together. This should be a time of discussion about how both work to contribute to the marriage and family together. If these contributions need to be expanded for better cooperation or diminished for less stress, they need to be considered and revised together. Be careful not to do this as complaints, but as a way of mutually helping each other. These should be times to prayerfully plan objectives together, plan finances, and discuss additional education for husband or wife, job changes, new friends, the future of having children, children's education, and the like. Find ways of having fun together.

This can be especially rewarding if one of the spouses makes plans to surprise the other with a special getaway. This can take a lot of planning, as our lives are very busy, and issues such as children, pets, etc. have to be considered. It can be a glamorous time at an expensive resort or a simple time borrowing a friend's cabin or condo. It isn't the place but the time spent alone that is important.[136] Christ took his disciples away to rest.

Money and Finances

Almost all idolatry (Baal and Ashtoreth worship, etc.) and subsequent evils grow out of material concerns. The devil will try to use this area to divide if there is not prayerful agreement. Money is his great deception, and he is a liar and murderer (John 8:44-47). Mammon worship produces a sick eye that can put the marriage and all of life in darkness (Matthew 6:22-34). Recognize together that the tithe belongs to God and by giving that and other gifts beyond that, together you are investing in eternity.

Prayerfully agree on the amount of work each does and on schedules, and make some boundaries. Pray for each other that you may be enabled to keep these, but be forgiving when there is failure. At times violations may be for the glory of God and the good of the family if there is agreement on this. John Adams and his wife Abigail willingly suffered much time apart, both working incredibly hard — she in running the plantation and caring for the family, while he sacrificed to help form the government of the United States. In this God was glorified and we can be thankful for them. The abilities of every wife should be used, as often she will be not only a supplemental provider but a good manager.

---

[136] Watch for getaway packages in the local newspaper or on the Internet.

Everything belongs to Christ and there should be no jealousy over funds. God is able to provide more by prayer. Pray for specific things and thank him together for the answers. "You do not have, because you do not ask. You ask and do not receive, because you ask wrongly, to spend it on your passions" (James 4:2, 3).

Consider How to Avoid Temptations

In order to keep the unselfish love of Christ and the blessing of your spouse more important than your own pleasure, in your daily times in devotion with the Lord, pray for God to enable you to put your spouse first in every way, including in your physical relationships. Express your love and show affection daily when no sexual intimacy is involved. Pray, "Lead us not into temptation but deliver us from evil" (Matthew 6:13). God is able to deliver from every one of them (1 Corinthians 10:13). Discuss your temptations with each other and pray for each other.

When in public, a husband that sees a beautiful woman to be admired should turn his attention to her eyes. If the devil offers a tempting thought, the husband should ask the Spirit to help him think about his wife and the pleasure she gives him. If a wife sees a man she admires for his brilliance, or his apparent ability to provide, or his manly attractiveness, she should resist the temptation by thinking of her husband and all he has done for her. Thank God for your spouse daily. Each of you needs to tell your spouse you love them and give them hugs and a kiss. Both women and men appreciate this affection. Remember that Christ in his love has given you to each other.

Seek to be kind to each other at all times, and be spontaneous in your sensual suggestions or touching, and if passion is aroused, be available to be stimulated. Be prayerful that you may hear and feel the desires of your spouse. But be aware of inappropriate times of tiredness or other obligations that are at hand. Since the husband is stimulated by visual suggestions, the wife can wear a provocative dress at times, which can be an invitation that she want to show him love. Patience and "listening" or waiting for a wife to be moved in foreplay is important. Let your wife or husband be comfortable about the timing and implications of others (children, etc.) being aware of your times of intimacy. Christ in his love is always ready to let you know his love and give you comfort in trials.

Openness and Cooperation About Medical Problems

Both men and women have medical problems that can have a strong influence on being one in marriage. This has been discussed in chapter 8 about physical union. Women probably have more physical problems than men, but men are the ones with the greatest demand to perform. Jesus said, "The sick need a doctor...' (Matthew 9:12).

I once had a prominent, capable woman drive over a hundred miles to seek my counsel. Her marriage was about to end. I soon suspected that she needed the help of an obstetrician and gynecologist to help her with her hormone adjustment. I also saw that her bad attitude toward her father communicated from her mother was amplifying the difficulties. She went to a doctor and prayed through her attitude toward her good husband. Soon afterwards she contacted me and said these things had saved her marriage and added, "Maybe my life." She was on the verge of suicide. They have since been happy for many years.

Today there are many infertility problems from both husband and wife because of the results of greed and lust in the culture. These can be confronted as opportunities from God. Men, as they get older, but even in middle age, may have problems with impotency. If these problems are physiological, they may be helped by discussing and praying over them together. Special counsel from a qualified Christian is sometimes needed. These matters should be handled with open, loving concern in prayer, assistance, and with patience.

Bad mental images can be ingrained in the minds of people from the past that also cause difficulties. Many men and women have been drawn as youths into sexual experimentation, pornography, and naked and drunken orgies. This is happening widely in many colleges, and now is reaching even high school students. These kind of tragic practices are increasing and can leave mental images that are hard to erase. But with suffering love, forgiveness, and tender love with your partner, these may be removed. These sins may always leave some scars and difficulties that hinder oneness, but all sin is forgiven by true faith in Christ's death. Such great sin requires greater suffering love to become one.

Seek One Mind about Children

Agree ahead of time on having children for the glory of God, or otherwise know together why this is not God's will. The father should lead in discussion and agreement on how to teach children. This should be done in practical daily situations (sitting, rising, walking, and lying down, Deuteronomy 6:6-8). Decide whether you can home school, send your children to private school, or if they will go to public school. Prayerfully agree on discipline and be consistent together, always showing the grace of Christ toward each other and them. Before God you are together responsible. Remember, the mother's evident respect and obedience to her husband is highly important as an example for the children. In adolescence parents should move children from legalism toward freedom in responsibility by encouraging their children to pray about whether what they want to do is right. At first ask them to share their decisions with you and why they made that decision. When they are mature enough let them decide. You will be surprised that the children will not like you shifting the responsibility to them, but they need to begin to learn from Christ. This freedom should be complete when they are adults at twenty years of age, according to the Scriptures.

Twenty years of age was the time of conscription in the army, and when new adults were fully accountable to God (cf. Numbers 16 and elsewhere). This is the time when marriage can be intelligently decided, and the new adults can "leave father and mother" and be married. They, too, should then begin to become "one flesh." Marriage should be made when income is adequate to live a simple life, and not until the husband or wife are fully successful in a career. Materialism is not the issue for decisions.

260

Family Devotions with and Teaching of Children

The importance of multiplying children for extending the kingdom of God must have practical implementation. Keep this objective in your prayers, because it is important to God (Psalm 78:5-7). These devotional times together need to be varied so that the children can have fun. Especially allow participation of the children in asking questions and sharing. Bible games, memory competition, sharing of experiences with God, and sharing answers to prayer are important. Discussions with the children on how God would have the family give to him, to the church, to missions, and to the poor are helpful. Explain that this is laying up treasures in heaven. Do not force children to let you read to them without interaction, for it can build a reaction to the word of God.

There are whole books on the important subject of family devotions, and these are only some practical guidelines. Repeating the same things every day, or failing to include the children in participation will make this time boring and counter-productive. Both the mother and father should lead these devotions, and find agreement on how to involve the children. Traditionally, Christian families read the Bible and pray together either at an evening meal or at bed time. Often this is done in a boring way. Reading and explaining the word of God is preferable, but devotional readings from books by great believers are useful at times. A list of some can be found in Addendum A to this book.

Devotional times should not be the only learning times for children. Mothers can especially relate Bible stories and information, and apply these to the children and draw them out to share their experiences with God. The father should teach about theology or who God is, give vision, and moral control to honor God, teach obedience to authorities, and teach the children to care for each other. Mother and father should support each other in answering questions.

Remember that being "one flesh" in marriage should be by your growing sacrificial love for each other. Your excitement about each other in the Lord and your love for him and each other is the greatest motivation for children to love the Lord and want to know Him. Working toward this end will be the greatest witness for Christ, joining many with the eternal family of God in the New Jerusalem of the new heaven and new earth. This will eternally glorify our God and be an eternal blessing to you.

The most basic factor in uniting sinful men and women is God's compelling power of his love in us. We cannot by argument, good works for them, or anything else we do can *make them accept us* and unite to know and reflect his love to a sinful world. *God must do the work of grace in our spouse's life* and in our own to humble our individual sin natures to unite as one. Prayer, our willingness to show suffering love and patience to let God work in each other by grace is the only way. The fruit of the *Spirit* is love.

Addendum A

Devotion with God Together

Some Specific Devotionals

1. *Night by Night : A Devotional for Couples*, James C. Dobson, Shirley Dobson, Multnomah Publishers

2. *Jesus Calling: 365 Devotional for Kids*, by Sarah Young, Thomas Nelson, Inc.

3. *Grace for the Moment: 365 Devotions for Kids*, by Max Lucado, adapted by Tama Fortner, Thomas Nelson, Inc.

General Devotional books

4. *Unto the Hills: A Daily Devotional*, 2000, Billy Graham, $15.99 (4 ½ stars).

5. *Walking With God Day by Day: 365 Dailey Devotional Selections,* Martin Lloyd-Jones and Robert Backhouse, 2003, (5 stars).

6. *Morning by Morning, Charles Spurgeon, revised by Whitaker House.*

7. *Grace for the Moment Daily: Spend 365 Days Reading the Bible With Max Lucado, (for adults)* (5 stars), Thomas Nelson, Inc.

8. *My Utmost For His Highest,* Oswald Chambers., updated by James Reumann, editor, Discovery House.

9. *A New Testament Walk with Oswald Chambers,* compiled by James R. Adair, and Harry Verploegh, Fleming H. Revell of Baker Book House.

10. *Streams in the Desert, Volume I, 2,* MVS Charles E. Cowman. Zondervan Publishing House.

11. *Living Light: Daily Light in today's language (from the Living Bible),* morning and evening. Compiled by Edythe Draper. Tyndale House Publishers.

By Reformers and a Biblical Arrangement

12. *Faith Alone: A Daily Devotional,* 2005, by Martin Luther, updated by James C. Galvin, Zondervan Publishing Company.

13. *Golden Booklet of the True Christian Life,* John Calvin, modern translation by Henry Van Andel, Baker Books.

14. *God's Wisdom for Daily Living: Every verse in Proverbs topically arranged. Thomas Nelson Publishers.*

* There are many others, but these are some well known ones. But keep priority on Scripture.

Addendum B

(Introductory note by Carl Wilson about this addendum which is explicit, and for you to choose whether or not to read it. It is given because it shows how the surrender or death to self with Christ is so important to both the husband and wife in their relationship.)

The Power of Sexual Surrender,
Chapter 2, THE NORMAL ORGASM
Marie Robinson, M. D.
Noted Psychiatrist, member of National Academy of Science

The first thing I am going to do on this chapter, so to speak, is journey with you to give you a view of your destination. I am going to describe an orgasm to you. I am going to describe it in detail. We occasionally do this in psychiatry when dealing with a frigidity problem, and sometimes it has astonishing results. I have seen women who, after hearing for the first time a complete description from an authoritative and objective person of what to expect of themselves in the act of love, almost immediately win through to the sensual goal they had been deprived of.

On one occasion a patient of mine, who over a period of months had worked through a rather severe frigidity problem, detailed to her younger sister the wonderful sexual experience she was now able to have. The younger sister had been married only two months and had not once reached sexual climax. She had seriously contemplated consulting a psychiatrist about her "problem." The very night her older sister described true orgasm to her she was able to achieve her own first complete satisfaction with her husband.

My chief motive in approaching the subject of frigidity by describing the normal orgasm is not to try to bring about a sudden or miraculous cure. In cases where such a sudden release of mature sexuality is achieved and thaw comes like a sudden spring, the frigidity problem is generally, even though it may appear to be deep-seated, a superficial one, lightly rooted in the personality.

The real reason I start with the orgasm is that a picture of the normal is an absolute necessity if you are to understand deviations from it with any real clarity. It is a truism that in order to understand illness in the body it is first necessary to understand health. Every doctor knows this and so do his teachers, for in medical school he first learns, through classes in anatomy and physiology, the structure and functions of the healthy body.

I think you will understand frigidity more thoroughly if we pursue the same technique here, first describing the genital anatomy of woman and from there proceeding to a description of the normal orgasm, what it is, where it is located, its function in the healthy man and woman, and other pertinent material.

everywhere; this is followed by sexual excitation in her genitals, and this is an important fact for both men and women to understand. Ignorance of this fact has given rise to many misunderstandings between the sexes, for of course it makes the woman somewhat slower in reaching the moment when she is ready for intercourse than the man is. It must be taken into consideration by both parties to an act of love.

A woman's genital apparatus is both internal and external. The external genitalia are called the vulva when they are referred to all together. The most obvious part of the vulva is the part we called the major (or sometimes outer) lips, which enfold the rest of the genitalia. If these lips are parted we see two smaller lips; these are called the minor lips and have a very high degree of sexual responsiveness. Even in books for laymen the Latin words are often used for these two organs: labia majoris and labia minoris, which mean, simply enough, the major lips and the minor lips.

The labia majoris also contain within their folds the rest of the external genital structure of woman. Here we find the clitoris, the vestibule, and the urethra, or opening to the bladder.

The clitoris is by far the most important and most widely misunderstood part of the external genitalia. It lies immediately above the top fold of the labia minoris and is a little piece of tissue slightly less thick than a pencil. This organ is enormously important to the whole psychological and sexual development of the individual woman. It is often called the "homologue of the male penis" and this simply means that in the embryo the cells which form the penis in the male are the same cells which form the clitoris in the female. Thus the two organs have the same cellular derivation.

The clitoris, like the male penis, is made up of erectile tissue, and when a woman is sexually excited it becomes erect in the same manner that the penis does. It also has a head and a foreskin covering it, and the head of the clitoris, at least in children and adolescents, is generally extremely sensitive to stimulation. In the fully mature female this sensitivity often diminishes, giving way to the vagina as the primary source of the greatest sexual pleasure. However, many women who become fully mature sexually maintain much of the original sexual responsiveness of the clitoris. The remainder of the external genitalia is contained within the vestibule. This is the entrance proper to the vagina and is very susceptible to sexual excitation. The vestibule lies between the minor lips and is directly beneath the clitoris. It contains the hymen, the urethral opening, and the openings of the glands of Bartholin.

The hymen is generally referred to as the maidenhead. It is a thin membrane which partly covers the entrance to the vagina. There is no direct sexual sensation on the hymen, and sometimes pain is experienced when it is perforated, usually during the first intercourse, although the hymen can be broken by an accident in childhood, through the insertion of surgical instruments, etc. Because of the pain associated with its perforation and the stories that a young girl often hears about this pain, it can be a source of much anxiety to her and condition her attitude toward sex in general.

The glands of Bartholin are of great importance to the act of love. These glands discharge a thin colorless mucus in sexual excitation, and this lubricates the vaginal opening and canal during intercourse. The amount of secretion varies greatly with each individual. Sexual frigidity often affects these glands adversely, causing the secretions to be inadequate or nonexistent. However, the amount of secretion will also vary rather dramatically at times in the individual who has no basic sexual blocking, and therefore the glands of Bartholin cannot be taken as a final criterion of sexual adequacy or inadequacy.

And now we come to the most important part of a woman's anatomical sexual equipment: the vagina. This is a passageway of some three to three and a half inches which extends from the vestibule on the outside of the cervix, which is the bottom end of the uterus. The vagina is, of course, the canal which accepts the penis, and it may interest you to know that in Latin the word literally means "a sheath for a sword." The sexual act in its purest form expresses the essential passivity associated with women and the aggressiveness of the male, the actor and the acted upon. The Romans understood this basic difference at least linguistically.

It may have surprised you to learn of the relatively short length of the vagina. The tissue of its walls are extremely elastic, however, and not only can it contain a penis of virtually any thickness or length, but it can stretch enough to allow the newborn infant to pass through it. The penis presses against the cervical end of the uterus, which may be forced upward until the penis gains full entrance. Contact with the soft tissue of the cervix is a source of great pleasure for the male, and the pressure can be an equal pleasure for the woman.

The vaginal walls are lined with a soft skin, not unlike mucous membrane, but it does not secrete as mucous tissue will. A secretion is, however, released from the cervix, and this also helps to lubricate the vaginal canal during intercourse.

I have said that the vagina is the most important part of a woman's sexual equipment. This is so because it is within the vagina that the orgasm of the truly mature woman takes place. Upon it and within it she receives the greatest sensual pleasure that it is possible for a woman to experience.

And this brings us to the subject of orgasm. I think you will understand it more fully if I describe it in the context of the sexual experience as a whole.

The sexual instinct in both men and women is marvelously complex. When it is unencumbered by neurosis it gives color, shape, brightness, charm, vividness, and direction to the entire personality, and the mechanisms by which it operates encompass both body and mind.

Desire can be set off in a woman either in response to a touch or by some act, sight, or thought which she has been exposed to. One of the chief things to which a woman responds is a cumulative tenderness expressed in words or in acts.

Whatever the stimulus, however, the brain receives the signal and, through the nervous system, sends out preparatory reactions throughout the body. The response of men to stimuli perceived by the brain as sexual is amazingly fast; some men arrive at full sexual preparedness for intercourse within three seconds—that is, their penis becomes fully erect and ready to enter the vagina within that time. Women react, on the whole, somewhat more slowly, though full preparation for intercourse, under the best of conditions, is often only a matter of a few more seconds than the man's.

As the sexual excitement increases, tremendous changes go on throughout the body, changes that might frighten you if they occurred under other circumstances.

The pulse rate goes up astonishingly. There are records of its reaching 150 and more as the individual approaches and then reaches the sexual climax. Such pulse rates generally occur, in health, only in athletes who are performing prodigious tasks of speed or endurance.

The blood pressure, too, goes up precipitately. In a matter of a few seconds it can rise well over 100 points. Breathing also becomes much deeper and swifter. With the approach of orgasm the breathing becomes interrupted; inspiration comes in forced gasps and expiration occurs with a heavy collapse of the lungs. It is as though the sexually excited person had been in a race.

As the sexual act continues there is a general shortage of oxygen throughout the body, which accounts for the unusual breathing. This gives rise to a tortured expression on the face, as if the person were undergoing severe pain. This fact has been observed by Kinsey in his famous study of female sexuality, and I quote here an interesting paragraph on the phenomenon:

". . . Prostitutes who attempt to deceive (jive) their patrons, or unresponsive wives who similarly attempt to make their husbands believe that they are enjoying coitus, fall into an error because they assume that an erotically aroused person should look happy and pleased and should smile and become increasingly alert as he or she approaches the culmination of the act. On the contrary, an individual who is really responding is as incapable of looking happy as the individual who is being tortured."

Within seconds after sexual arousal the blood supply in the veins and arteries lying close to the skin increases, causing the body to become flushed and the temperature to rise slightly. Certain areas of the body are engorged with this blood, become swollen and erect, notably the penis of the man, which swells, often to twice its size. In women, this also happens to the clitoris, which becomes firm, and to the nipples of both sexes. The firmness of these organs increases as the sexual climax approaches.

Muscles throughout the body begin to tense at the onset of sexual excitement, and this tension increases as the excitement grows. Certain glands and tissues also increase their secretions as the sexual act commences and moves closer to completion. The salivary glands and the nasal mucosa flow freely, and it is this latter fact which causes, in conjunction with the engorgement of the surface blood vessels, the characteristic nasal stuffiness so many people notice after inter course. In some women the secretions of the glands of Bartholin and the mucus from the cervix of the uterus become amazingly copious as sexual excitement rises, and particularly during orgasm itself. This profuse flow may have given rise to the widely held and entirely mistaken idea I have mentioned—that in orgasm women have an

270

ejaculation similar to the male's. There is no such ejaculation—nor indeed any female organ that could make one possible.

One of the most amazing aspects of sexual intercourse is the fact that all five senses become extremely dulled as the act increases in intensity. The ability to feel hot and cold, to feel pain, or to hear sounds becomes almost nonexistent. The eyes take on a characteristic trance-like stare, and vision becomes constricted. The entire mind and body are concentrated fully on the mounting sexual feeling and exclude all else. In orgasm itself the anesthesia of the senses is almost total. Indeed many people experience a temporary loss of consciousness for a matter of seconds. Some, according to Kinsey's findings, remain unconscious for two or more minutes.

This last fact brings us to our examination of the experience of orgasm itself. If you are to understand frigidity in women it is of tremendous importance to grasp the nature of orgasm and what it means physically and psychologically. The importance of such understanding is due, of course, to the fact that orgasm, of the type described here, is the very thing the frigid woman is unable to have. In fact, its absence from her experience is the usual definition of frigidity. Certain kinds of frigid women may experience one, two, or all of the physical and psychological reactions described above, which normally would terminate with orgasm. But the final experience eludes them; at the vital juncture the body, despite an agonizing need to come to a climax, refuses to respond; it draws back, goes dead.

Orgasm is the physiological response which brings sexual intercourse to its natural and beautiful termination. It is preceded by a very dramatic increase in all of the phenomena noted above. In the moment just preceding orgasm, muscular tension suddenly rises to the point where, if the sexual instinct were not in operation, it would become physically unendurable. The pelvic motions of the man and the movement of the penis back and forth within the vagina increase in speed and in intensity of thrust The woman's pelvic movements also increase, and her whole body attempts with every move to heighten the exquisite sensations she

271

is experiencing within her vagina. According to many women with whom I have discussed this experience, the greatest pleasure is caused by the sensation of fullness within the vagina and the pressure and friction upon its posterior surface.

At the moment of greatest muscular tension all sensations seem to take one further rise upward. The woman tenses beyond the point where, it seems, it would be possible to maintain such tension for a moment longer. And indeed it is not possible, and now her whole body suddenly plunges into a series of muscular spasms. These spasms take place within the vagina itself, shaking the body with waves of pleasure. They are felt simultaneously throughout the body: in the torso, face, arms, and legs-down to the very soles of the feet.

These spasms, which shake the entire body and converge upon the vagina, represent and define true orgasm. At this moment the woman's head is thrown back and her pelvis tips upward in an attempt to obtain as much penetration from the penis as is possible. The spasms continue for several seconds in most women, though the time varies with every individual, and in some women they may continue though with decreasing intensity, for a minute or even more. Many women can repeat this performance two or more times before their partner has his orgasm. The pathway neurologically and psychologically, has been set for orgasm, and if her partner continues she can respond. I have had women report that the last orgasm is sometimes more in tense and satisfying than the first.

If the woman is satisfied by her orgasmic experience she will discharge the neurological and muscular tension developed in the sexual build-up. When satisfaction has been achieved, her strenuous movements cease and within a short period blood pressure, pulse, glandular secretion, muscular tension, and all the other gross physical changes which characterize sexual excitement return to normal, or even to subnormal, limits.

There have been detailed studies made of the physical reactions of both men and women during intercourse I think it is important to realize that in almost every detail including orgasm, these reactions and the subjective experience of pleasure parallel each other in the sexes. The major differences are that the woman is slightly slower to respond at the outset than the man, and the orgasm of the man is characterized by the ejaculation of sperm into the vagina.

Full sexual satisfaction is followed by a state of utter calm. The body feels absolutely quiescent. Psychologically the person feels completely satisfied, at peace with the world and all things in it. The woman in particular feels extremely loving toward the partner who has given her so much joy, such a transport of ecstasy. Often she wishes to hold him close for a while, to linger tenderly in the now subdued glow of their passion.

As you can see from this description, orgasm is a tremendous experience. There is no physiological or psychological experience that parallels its sweeping intensity or its excruciating pleasure. It is unique.

There are many who take a mystical view of this ecstatic coupling of man and woman in love. They think of it as a symbol of a lost unity between the sexes that strives to reassert itself in the act of love. Others see in it a foretaste of heaven, the carnal representation of endless spiritual delights for mankind. Many who are able to experience orgasm in intercourse find it difficult not to ascribe some purposive intent on the part of the Creator; the experience is that profound.

The individual perceives orgasm as a reward equal to none. It puts the sacrifices and compromises necessary to an enduring marriage into their proper perspectives, makes the constant giving done by the woman seem not only worth wile but highly desirable. It is the strongest link in the unbreakable bond between two who love.

Physical difficulties often disappear. I have known women who had been plagued with intense pre-menstrual and menstrual pains all their lives to lose such symptoms in a matter of weeks. I have known women whose irregular periods have become regularized. And I have also know women with one or two desperately difficult pregnancies behind them who, becoming pregnant again, went through the entire nine months not only without discomfort but with a highly accelerated feeling of pleasure and well-being.

These, then, are the results, or some of them, that a woman who is willing to give up the things of childhood and yield to her true self may expect. The return on such an investment of self is enormous. It is paid in the coinage of love returned for love given; love from one's husband and children, love from friends, new and old, attracted by the endless largesse of the woman who has surrendered all to find all.

The ability to achieve normal orgasm can be called the physical counterpart of psychological surrender. In most cases of true frigidity it follows on a woman's surrender of her rebellious and infantile attitudes as the day the night. It is the sign that she has given up the last vestige of resistance to her nature and has embraced womanhood with soul *and* body.

The achievement of orgasm, usually, is the *last* step in the process of growing up. If one reviews in one's mind the actual orgasmic experience it is not difficult to see why this is so.

For a woman orgasm requires a trust in one's partner that is absolute. Recall for a moment that the physical experience is often so profound that it entails the loss of consciousness for a period of time. As we know, in sexual intercourse, as in life, man is the actor, woman the passive one, the receiver, the acted upon. Giving oneself up in this passive manner to another human being, making oneself his willing partner to such seismic physical experiences, means one must have complete faith in the other person. In the sexual embrace any trace of buried hostility, fear of one's role, will show clearly and unmistakably.

But there is even more to the psychic state necessary for orgasm than faith in one's partner and readiness to surrender. There must be a sensual eagerness to surrender; in the woman's orgasm *the excitement comes from the act of surrender.*

SELECTIVE INDEX

Abel, 29, 34, 37, 77, 127, 167, 234

abortion, 81, 84, 86, 195, 196

Abraham, Abram, 35, 39, 40, 41, 42, 44, 57, 60, 68, 74, 78, 82, 83, 85, 89, 148, 150, 151, 235, 240, 243, 250

Abzug, Bella, 191

Adam, vii, 1, 5, 10-15, 18, 19, 21-29, 31-36, 39, 47, 53, 61, 65, 70, 75, 77, 84, 94-97, 116, 125-127, 132, 140, 143, 147, 154, 155, 171, 172, 194, 231, 233, 236, 242, 244, 250

Ahmadinejad, Mahmoud, 219

Akhenaton, 43

Allawi, Ali A., 220

alone, 1, 3, 5, 11, 57, 76, 92, 105, 118, 125, 126, 133, 145, 146, 204, 227, 247, 252, 253, 256, 257

Al-Qaeda, 219

Amenhotep, II, 43

Amoritic, 41, 178

animal, animals, 4, 6, 7, 9, 10, 12, 18, 21, 22, 31, 35, 80, 82, 106, 116, 125, 127, 148, 166

Antichrist, 34, 186, 228

Aquila, 153

Ashtoreth, 24, 109, 234, 235, 257

Babel, Babylon, 19, 21, 35, 37, 232, 237-239, 242, 243, 246

mother of prostitutes, 246

Beauvoir, Simone de, 190, 193, 196, 200

Bell, Daniel, 80, 187

birth control, 82, 83, 195, 196, 211, 215, 222, 227

bisexuals, 201

body, v, 26, 46, 56, 58, 60-63, 65, 72, 94, 97, 112, 272

bone of my bone, 5, 12

boundaries, 118, 119, 257

bread, 28, 32, 46, 59, 160

bride of Christ, 12, 95, 156, 236, 243, 249

Brizendine, Louann, 106, 108

C. S. Lewis, 193, 205

Cacioppo, John, T., 126

Caesar Augustus, 151

Cain, 29, 34, 35, 39, 77, 234, 237

Calhoun, Arthur, 180

Canaan, Canaanite, 224, 41, 43, 44, 109, 235

Cato, 151

children, v, 1, 2, 6, 10, 14, 16, 26, 28, 30-32, 36, 42, 46, 55, 57, 60-63, 65, 67, 70, 94 102, 104, 105, 107, 109, 112, 117, 121, 122, 126, 127, 134, 136, 137, 141, 142, 145-151, 153, 154, 157-161, 164, 168,

169, 173, 175, 177, 181, 189,
191, 195, 196, 199-203, 207,
216, 219, 222, 224, 229,
234,240, 242, 244, 247, 252,
255, 256, 259, 261, 267, 274
church, vii, 40, 47, 50, 52,
    56, 59, 61, 63-65, 67, 69,
    78, 79, 82, 90, 91, 95, 96,
    105, 109, 123, 131, 134,
    140, 148-150, 152-158,
    161, 162, 165, 229, 235-
    237, 239, 244, 249, 250,
    255, 261
circumcision, 41, 52, 54, 102
civilization, vii, viii, 2, 8, 23,
    39, 58, 73, 79, 81, 82, 88,
    106, 107, 127, 128, 163,
    164, 166-168, 170, 172,
    173, 175-178, 181, 195,
    204, 205, 209-211, 212,
    214, 220, 225, 232, 237,
    243, 248, 249
Columbus,Christopher, viii,
    179
communication, 2, 12, 15, 22,
    75, 81, 82, 90, 103, 105,
    108, 110, 111, 113, 114,
    118-120, 123, 124, 132,
    141, 162, 249
compete, competition, 26, 36,
    45, 82, 87, 108, 110, 112,
    138, 163, 169, 172, 173,
    193, 194, 196, 201, 204,
    228, 229, 261
complement
complementation, 15, 106

conclusions,
    chapters 1:15,16; 2:37, 38;
    3:56; 4:71; 5:91, 92; 5:112;
    7:124; 8:145, 146; 9:161,
    162; 10:178; 11:204; 12:229;
    13:280
Condorcet, Marqui de, 188
conflict, 11, 19, 29, 35, 86,
    89, 93, 94, 96, 98, 107-
    110, 122, 155, 163, 165,
    175, 192, 194, 204, 209,
    219, 223, 224, 227, 228
contraception, 81
creation, 2, 4-15, 17, 24, 25,
    27, 31, 32, 36, 39, 40, 43,
    53, 54, 57, 58, 65, 74, 75,
    104, 125, 127, 138, 152,
    161, 163, 166-168, 170,
    178, 181, 185, 204, 212,
    216, 220, 222, 231-234,
    236, 239, 241
Creator, 3, 17, 24, 27, 51, 76,
    154, 164, 166, 170, 172,
    179 181, 182, 231, 233,
    237, 248, 273
culture, viii, 2, 19, 34, 41, 43,
    13, 74, 79-81, 94, 103,
    109, 114, 126, 153, 156,
    168, 171, 172, 175, 177,
    178, 183, 229, 233, 237,
    259
curse, 31, 32, 34, 41, 65
cursed, curses, 22
Darwin, Charles, 185
death, viii, 2, 3, 19, 25, 26,
    30, 32, 35, 37, 39, 40, 44,

46-49, 53, 55-57, 60, 62, 63, 70, 77, 80-82, 93, 95-99, 101, 107, 113, 114, 127, 129, 130, 140, 147, 164, 173, 187, 194, 210, 212, 230, 239, 240-243, 246, 248, 250, 251, 260, 265

deceive, viii, 19, 22, 25, 28, 77, 154, 155, 232

Declaration of Independence, 184

The Declaration of the Rights of Man and the Citizen, 184

Declaration of Sentiments and Resolutions, 189, 199

decline of marriage, 202, 203

demographical, 210, 218

demonic deception, 220

Derrida, 81, 192

design

God's design, viii

devil

Satan, demonic, god of this world, prince of the power of the air, angel of light, 2-4, 18, 19, 21-25, 29, 37, 45, 46, 48, 55, 56,77, 79, 94-99, 102, 103, 107, 113, 114, 119, 121-123, 139, 155, 159, 165, 166, 194, 227, 232, 234, 238-240, 242, 245, 247, 253, 257, 258

Dewey, John, 186

dictator, 172, 175, 176

Dindyal, Shiva, 220-222

disciple, 48, 49, 54, 55, 58, 64, 79, 98, 113, 122, 124, 148, 160, 242

divine purpose, 2, 204

dominion

rule, ii, 1, 3, 4, 6, 10, 13, 14, 18, 19, 55, 63, 66, 77, 107, 147, 148, 250

Douglas, Fredrick, 200

Edersheim, Alfred, 46

edification, 119

Egypt

Egyptian, 43, 44, 46, 62, 178, 205

Elijah, 49

Eller, Cynthia, 199

End of Men, 208

Enoch, 35

equal

equality, egalitarinian, 16 193

Equal Rights Amendment, 191

equality for women,

be same, 188, 189

Erdogan, Tayyip, 219

estrogen, 222

European Enlightenment,

eighteenth century, 188, 212, 226

evangelism

evangelization, 149, 161

Eve, vii, 1, 11-15, 18-29, 31-34, 36, 39, 47, 61, 65, 70, 75-78, 84, 94, 106, 116,

125, 127, 140, 143, 147, 154, 155, 169, 171, 172, 194, 209, 233, 236, 242, 244

evil age, 164

excellent wife, 159, 160

exodus, 43, 49

extension

reproduction, offspring, 6, 10, 71, 106, 177

Family Life Today, 254

Farjarinen, Jakko, 221

Farnham, Marynia,112, 132, 133, 189, 208

Farrell, William, 198

father, 5, 6, 13, 35, 41, 59, 67, 75, 79, 85-87, 91, 105, 109, 126, 132, 192, 204, 259, 260, 261

feminine qualities, 104

fertility

The Fertility Rate, TFR, 81, 197, 209-211, 213, 214, 216, 217, 219, 220, 227, 243, 247

fill the earth, ii, 4, 35, 36, 77, 147

Fisher, Seymour, 135

five words for love, 128

flesh, 5, 9, 12, 24, 26, 50, 52, 54, 59, 65, 67, 74-76, 93-100, 102, 103, 105-107, 112-114, 120, 125, 130-134, 141, 143-157, 161, 183, 187, 214, 232, 234, 236, 241, 247, 249, 260, 261

flesh of my flesh, 5, 12

foot washing, 47, 48

freedom, 15, 23, 24, 36, 40, 80, 82, 83, 100, 101, 105, 107, 111, 113, 118, 119, 122, 123, 136, 143, 146, 151, 152, 158, 168, 170, 177, 179, 181, 183, 191, 193, 195, 251, 260

Freidan, Betty, 190, 191, 198, 200

French Revolution, 184, 188

Freud, Sigmund, 81, 200

Garden

Eden, paradise, 1, 3, 22, 33, 34, 46, 61, 75, 77, 84, 94, 96, 127, 231

gender, 12, 68, 91, 155, 196, 197

Gender Equality Architecture Reform Campaign (GEAR), 215

generation, 16, 36, 43, 56, 125, 170, 175, 178, 187, 194, 196, 220, 234, 235, 240, 242, 249

gentleman, 145

glass ceiling, 109, 198

god, gods, 36, 43, 56, 125, 170, 175, 178, 187, 194, 196, 220, 234, 235 240, 242, 249

God's goodness, 6, 8, 10, 11, 14, 16, 23, 35, 36, 70, 94, 125, 231, 232

280

God's image,
image of God, ii, vii, 4, 6,
7, 9-11, 14, 15, 29, 50, 57,
62, 63, 66, 67, 75, 76, 84,
86, 90, 91, 124, 138, 150,
158, 161, 204, 226, 245
Goldman, David P., 80, 211-
213, 216, 217, 219, 226,
228, 243
Great Commission, 45, 79,
147-149, 206, 229
Greek Minoan Empire, 43
Haran, 41, 235
Harley, Willard F. Jr., 110
health care, 203, 208, 213
heaven, v, 3, 19, 29, 33, 35,
50, 53, 66, 70, 71, 76, 79,
95, 97, 101, 113, 118, 124,
127, 140, 146, 149, 164,
166, 176, 229, 230, 232,
238-240, 242, 245, 246,
249, 250, 261, 262, 273
hell, 33, 164, 172, 247, 248,
249
helper, 5, 12, 13, 93, 108, 111
Herod the Great, 29
Herschel, William, 184, 185
homosexual, 176, 223-225
Horus, 43, 74
house church
home church, 255
How Civilizations Die, 80,
211, 213, 216, 217, 243
humble

humility, 47, 52, 54, 56, 60,
61, 69, 70, 98, 113, 117,
148, 161, 247, 251
husband, 13, 14, 18, 24, 28,
30, 55, 58, 59, 61-65, 67-
69, 70, 76, 79, 84-88, 91,
92, 104-111, 115, 116,
118, 119, 130, 131, 133-
148, 150, 153-161, 199,
200, 207, 209, 216, 235,
236, 246, 251, 256-260,
265, 274
Hutton, James, 185
illegitimate
marriageless births, 202
impotency
Viagra, 259
in the beginning, 3, 67, 231
individualism, 26, 51, 88, 223
infanticide, 81, 195
Institute For Family Values,
202
instrument, 76, 95, 99-101,
112, 186, 208, 218, 267
Jones, Amelia, 201, 263
Joseph, 61, 134
Kahun Gynaecological
Papyrus, 82
Kant, Immanuel, 183, 184,
193, 200, 212
Karsen, Carol, 180
Kaufmann, Eric, 211, 212,
214-216, 226-228, 243
Keller, Rosemary Skinner,
180
Kenosis in Crete, 43

Khan, Afshan, 217
Kiefer, Otto, 151
Kierkegaard, Sorin, 81
kingdom
nation, empire, 1, 6, 14, 30,
    45, 49, 51, 57, 58, 71,
    78, 79, 95, 101, 102,
    113, 118, 147, 149, 151,
    161, 164, 165, 178, 227,
    229, 239, 240, 242, 243,
    245, 250, 261
Kingma, Daphne Rose, 110-
    112
knowledge of good and evil,
    5
Laplace, Pierre-Simon, 184
law, 17, 32, 42, 46-49, 58,
    78, 90, 93, 94, 99, 101-
    103, 167, 171, 179, 180,
    189, 214, 216, 219, 227,
    240, 252
leader
head, 14, 19, 31, 35, 66, 79,
    93, 102, 103, 108, 109,
    140, 141, 144, 150, 156,
    160, 172, 206, 255
lesbian, 201
Lever, Jan, 31
live by faith, 165
Logical Process
progression, 167
loneliness, vii, viii, 56, 125,
    126, 136, 143, 196, 245
Lydia, 153
Lyell, Charles, 185

Mansfield, Harvey C., 184,
    196, 200
marriage supper of the Lamb,
    45, 67, 238, 239, 244
Marxist, 187, 189, 191, 228
Mary, mother of Jesus, 47,
    61, 62, 78, 250
masculine qualities, 103
Massey, Marilyn Chapin,
    192-196, 200
masturbation, 133, 144, 201
materialism
mammon, Baal, 107, 151,
    169, 170, 173, 177, 178,
    182, 188, 206, 209, 212,
    214, 218
May, Carolyn, v, 201, 202
mental
intellectual, 52, 94, 134, 259,
    260
Messiah
Christ, 29, 78, 228, 236
Millett, Kate, 191, 200
mind of Christ, 53, 96, 98,
    100, 113
Morse, Jennifer Roback, 203,
    204
Moses, 5, 42, 49, 227
mother, 5, 6, 28, 33, 47, 59,
    61, 67, 68, 85, 87, 91, 122,
    126, 132, 155, 173, 189,
    195, 203, 209, 237, 238,
    246, 259-261
Mott, Lucretia, 189, 199
Mount Sinai, 46
Ms. Magazine, 191, 199, 200

multiplication, 77, 144
Mundy, Liza, 206-209
Muslim Brotherhood, 197, 216, 219
naked
nakedness, vii, 5, 11, 18, 21, 25, 39, 119, 143, 259
Napoleon, 184, 188
National Organization for Women (NOW), 190, 198
natural role, 170
nebular hypothesis
evolution, 183, 212
New Covenant, New Covenant Love, iii, 2, 34, 37, 39, 40, 41, 44-51, 53, 55-61, 63, 64, 66, 67, 69-71, 89, 93, 107, 112-114, 120, 121, 127-129, 131, 134, 138, 144, 147-149, 154, 157, 160, 166, 226, 227, 229, 233, 236
new Jerusalem, 246
Newton, Sir Isaac, 183
Nicodemus, 51
Nietzsche, Friedrich, 81, 186, 194, 200
Nimrod, 19, 35, 237
Noah, 35, 37, 57, 77, 148, 236, 237
Old Covenant, 40, 61
orgasm, 136, 265, 266, 268-275
Pangaea, 10
parent, 73, 74, 86, 88, 90, 109, 173, 203

parenthood, 74
Passover, 42-47, 53, 55
Phoebe, 153
Pinker, Steven, 197
Powell, Patricia, 207
priority, 15, 76, 83, 264
Prisca
Priscilla, 153
Promised Land, 42
prostitute
prostitution, 238, 239
quiet time
daily time with God, 253
Rainey, Dennis and Barbara, 110, 254
Re, 43, 74
Reagan, Ronald, 191
reconcile, reconciled, reconciliation, 50, 54, 56, 161, 241
redemption
plan of redemption, 233
Reese, 7, 8
Reformation
reformers, 179, 182, 195
regional nations, 178
relationship, vii, 1, 3, 5, 9, 11-15, 25, 30, 39, 41, 48, 64, 73-75, 104, 105, 108, 115, 123, 136-138, 142, 144-146, 148, 201, 207, 232, 233, 237, 254, 265
repentance, 51-53, 95, 99, 167, 214, 224, 226, 236, 242

reproduction, 9, 10, 14, 15, 42, 106, 226, 227,

resurrection, 33, 40, 44, 45, 49, 53, 56, 68, 70, 75, 90, 97, 101, 113, 179, 224, 229, 230, 239, 240, 242, 245, 241

Reuther, Rosemary Radford, 180

revelation,
   general revelation, 6, 8, 9, 16, 35, 42, 57, 58, 60, 73-76, 94, 95, 131, 167, 231, 234, 238

Rich, Adrienne, 195

Rights Amendment, 191

Robinson, Marie, 112, 132, 133, 135-139, 265, 274

Roman, 60, 82, 101, 151-153, 158, 163, 166, 178, 183, 212, 227, 228

Rosin, Hanna, 208, 209

sacrifice, 34, 35, 46, 50, 77, 95, 98, 127, 140

sacrificial suffering, 236

Salbi, Zainab, 216

Sarai

Sarah, 39, 41, 83, 151

Satinover, Jeffery, 225

science, 126, 135, 199, 225, 265

Scopes monkey trial

John Scopes, 187

self-righteous, 17, 27, 28, 102, 171, 188, 242

self-righteous, 109

serpent
   dragon, 8, 12, 14, 18-23, 25, 28, 29, 35-37, 39, 77, 78, 147, 165, 166, 169

Seth, 34, 39

sex, vii, 1, 2, 27, 36, 86, 94, 104, 106, 108, 114, 119, 126, 127, 129, 130, 132, 144, 145, 171-173, 177, 182, 190, 192, 196, 200, 201, 204, 209, 220, 223-225, 237, 242, 267

sexual differences

sexuality, vii, viii, 6, 10, 11, 26, 36, 47, 114, 152, 183, 193, 239, 245

shall the religious inherit the earth, religious TFR, 211, 212, 214-216, 226, 243

Sharia law, 219

sin

Skakkeback, Niels, 221

Sommers, Christina Hoff, 197, 198

Sorokin, Pitirim, 176-178

sovereign

sovereignty, control, dominion, 2, 3, 6, 8, 40, 43, 51, 64, 81, 96, 127, 152, 163, 164, 167, 175, 176, 229, 230, 240

sperm, 76, 104, 209, 220-222, 273

Stanton, Elizabeth Cady, 189, 199, 200

Steinem, Gloria Marie, 191,
    200
steps of decline, 182
Strauss, D. F., 186
submission, 7, 13, 15, 16, 23,
    52, 55, 58-64, 66, 67, 69,
    85, 93, 130, 134, 135, 139,
    140, 173, 181, 193, 195,
    200, 240
Sumerian, 41, 176, 178
superman, supermen, vii,
    171, 172, 185-188, 194,
    196, 237
superwoman
goddess, 172
Supreme Court, 86, 179, 223
tabernacle, 46, 78
teaching, 4, 14, 48, 50, 59,
    70, 84, 98, 121, 123, 150,
    152, 155, 157-159, 161,
    241, 248, 254
Tell el-Amarna Tablets, 43
temple, 24, 46, 52, 78
temptation, 8, 18, 21-24, 34,
    79, 97, 103, 120-122, 156,
    171, 258
TFR, 213, 217, 219, 226
The Vindication of the Rights
    of Women, 188
Theophrastus, 82
Thutmose III, 42, 43
Tocqueville, Alexis de, 171,
    184
Tournier, Paul, 111
training, 90, 186, 202

transformed, transformation,
    17, 49, 55, 56, 95, 97, 99,
    101, 110, 112, 114, 130, 135,
    136, 141, 142, 187, 193, 206,
    241, 242
Trinity
trinitarian, 74
Tyre, 19, 238
union
joined together, know
    intimately, i, iii, iv, 7,
    39, 51, 57, 114, 124,
    138, 144, 160, 163, 188,
    191, 216, 223, 226, 237,
    239, 244
United Nations, 214, 228
United Nations Commission
    on the Status of Women,
    215
Unwin, J. D., 176, 177
Ur, 20, 41
values changes, 175
Warren, Earl,
Chief Justice of the Supreme
    Court, 179, 180
welfare
    U. S., 87, 109, 137, 191,
    202, 214
Wheat, Ed and Gaye, 132,
    143
Whitehead, Barbara Defoe,
    202
wife, v, viii, 5, 11, 12, 13, 24,
Wilcox, W. Bradford, 202
wine, 45, 46, 58, 59, 143,
    159, 160, 236

Winthrop, John, 180, 184
wise, wisdom, 2, 18, 24, 25,
    27, 39, 47, 58, 70, 77, 97,
    99, 102, 125, 126, 166,
    169, 183, 232, 233, 248,
    249
Wollstonecraft, Mary, 188,
    200
women in education,
    college presidents, 209
World Syncretistic Religion,
world pantheism, 227
world's last night, 212, 229,
    239

CPSIA information can be obtained at www.ICGtesting.com
Printed in the USA
LVOW01s0412240915

455536LV00014B/138/P